The TV Scriptwriter's Handbook

Alfred Brenner

Writer's
Digest
Books

Cincinnati, Ohio

Grateful acknowledgment is made for permission to reprint the following:

"Blues for Sally M." *McMillan and Wife* episode. Copyright by Universal Studios, Inc. All rights reserved. Courtesy of MCA Publishing, a divsion of MCA, Inc. Thanks also to Oliver Hailey.

"Courage at 3:00 A.M." *Ben Casey* episode. By permission of Bing Crosby Productions.

"A Material Difference." *The Rockford Files* episode. Copyright by Universal Studios, Inc. All rights reserved. Courtesy of MCA Publishing, a division of MCA, Inc. Thanks also to Cherokee Productions and Rogers Turrentine.

First paperback printing, 1985

Library of Congress Cataloging in Publication Data
Brenner, Alfred, 1916-
    The tv scriptwriter's handbook.
    Includes index.
    1. Television authorship. I. Title.
PN1992.7.B69   808'.066791021   80-23700
ISBN 0-89879-178-2

Book design by Barron Krody.

To my students,
from whom I've learned so much

Contents

Chapter 10: Character 71

How to develop a character. Character is action. Which comes first, plot or character? Character development in terms of goals. In terms of conflict. The use of contrast. The protagonist. The blind spot. Heroes and heavies—how to make them real.

Chapter 11: Progression 79

Action—dramatic and nondramatic. Unity. Select, eliminate, condense. Using exposition. Preparing the scene. Suspense and surprise. Your basic story line. Time in television writing. The time lock. Arranging the incidents. The three units of a script and what goes into each one.

Chapter 12: The Scene 92

The basic structural unit. Beginning, middle, and resolution. How the scene advances the plot. How it reveals character. How long it should be—in a play, a teleplay, a film. The sequence and how it is used.

Chapter 13: The Climax 99

Finding the right one means success or failure. How the theme emerges. A good climax is satisfying. Making sure it's right.

Chapter 14: The Treatment 105

What it is. What it should contain. Using 3x5 cards to build a treatment. Gathering your materials. Putting them in the proper order. The treatment format. Checking the structure. The historical importance of treatments.

Chapter 15: Story Conference (2) 110

The waiting game. Confusion at the network. Cutoff! A new beginning.

Chapter 22: The Marketplace 153

How to sell your script. How the Writers Guild can help. How to register your script. Agents, good and bad, large and small. Approaching production companies. Going it alone.

Chapter 23: Epilogue—
To the New Writer 158

Will you make it? The importance of determination and persistence. Writing discipline and what it means to success. Do you want it badly enough? What this book can do for you and what you have to do yourself.

Preface

This book is a complete guide to the craft of dramatic writing for television.

Dramatic writing, in the sense I am using it here, means creating stories intended to be acted before an audience in a theater.

Dramatic writing *for television* means playwriting for the most popular theater ever invented.

Dramatic writing is the heart of prime-time network television, the means by which most television writers earn their daily bread. Dramatic writing is the basis of all episodic series; drama and comedy; movies for television, plays for television; limited, or mini, series; serials, or soaps; dramatic specials; and animated programs.

The writers who create, develop, and write scripts for this incredibly demanding and varied medium must be skilled in the special art of dramatic writing *for television,* in all the techniques and conventions peculiar to the tube. Any new writer who wishes to join the ranks of this privileged and highly paid group must learn that craft. In fact, the *only* way a new writer can break into television is to prove that he has command of his craft by writing a professional script.

This book will help the new writer do exactly that.

It developed out of the specific needs of beginning writers: my students. What they want, and what this book will provide, is a simple, step-by-step approach to the construction of their own teleplays, from idea to finished script. In the process they must explore basic dramatic principles; the successful plays of any age reveal the essentials of drama throughout time. In that sense, the construction of Sophocles' *Oedipus Rex*, Ibsen's *A Doll's House*, and episodes of *Remington Steele* or *Hardcastle and McCormick* or *Dallas* have much in common, even though the theaters in which these dramas were first produced bear little resemblance to each other. In this book I will discuss those common essentials and show you how they relate to the specific problems of writing a television script.

The playwright of the past did not write in a vacuum. Neither does the television writer today. Dramatic writing is both a *lonely creative act* by an individual working alone in his own room or office and a *collaborative effort,* first among writer, editor, and producer, and then among writer, director, and actors during production, and finally between the writer and his audience. What one writes, as well as how one writes it, is determined, especially in television, by the needs of a multifaceted, rapidly changing medium, a very large and powerful industry. The new writer must understand how that industry functions. Indeed, the close connection between the writer and the industry is one of the themes of this book.

Today, after little more than three decades of existence, television is changing faster than ever. Like an adolescent just emerging from childhood, it is bursting out in all directions. As Melville Shavelson, the president of the Writers Guild of America (WGA), West, informed his membership, what is happening in our industry, and what is about to happen—a technological revolution in communications—will soon make *Star Wars* seem as outdated as *The Birth of a Nation.* Pay TV, cable TV, theater-size home screens, a multiplicity of additional high-frequency channels, communication satellites making possible immediate transmission and reception of broadcasts from any part of the world, cassettes, videodiscs, and other new inventions must end the near-monopoly of the air-waves by the networks that now exists.

Viewers are already having a greater choice in the kinds of programs available to them. Various "minority" audiences whose numbers can be counted in millions are beginning to have their entertainment and/or educational needs met. Sports fans, theater buffs, ballet lovers, people interested in news, art, science—now have their own channels. Like periodicals today, television will soon offer education and entertainment for specific groups of viewers: men, women, children, highbrows, low-brows, music lovers, senior citizens, people of all occupations and inter-ests. Scriptwriters now have new and additional markets. Indeed, for any writer who can understand and apply his craft, the future is nothing less than fantastic.

Can television writing be learned? Indeed, if one is to become a professional television dramatist, it must be learned—by one means or another.

"It is possible," says theatrical director and critic Harold Clur-man, "to become an effective playwright [for television] without classes or lessons—all by oneself—but study shortens the process. Indeed it may be convincingly demonstrated that *no one has learned dramatic technique without one form or another of study*" (italics mine).

This book gives the beginning writer—or the writer experienced in other fields but new to television—a concrete grounding in the craft of dramatic writing, but also presents a real-life look at the world of television from the writer's point of view. I have included a brief history of the medium by one who has actually lived through it and an inside view of how the television writer in Hollywood func-tions today—where he gets his ideas, to whom and how he sells his scripts. I will show you what a script, a treatment, an outline, a presentation, a concept look like. I will explain the role in the writer's life of the producer, editor, network executive, and agent; types of programs on the air, pilots, the Writers Guild of America, contracts, collaboration, credits, fee structures, residuals, work habits, and the future. I will try to answer all your questions about how a new writer breaks into this field—and what he can expect after he gets there.

One final note: Television at the present time is largely an adver-tising, merchandising medium—one of the most nakedly commer-cial institutions in a country dominated by selling and by com-merce. I believe this book reflects that fact openly and realistically. My underlying focus takes for granted an opposite point of view, however: that television drama is an art form, possibly one of the most varied, complex, and vital that ever existed, and that we have only scratched the surface of its vast potential. The tension between these two points of view—commerce and art—affects everyone seriously involved in the medium and permeates every page of this book.

Introduction

The Medium: From Live Theater to Filmed Motion Pictures

> It may seem foolish to say, but television, the scorned step-child of drama, may well be the basic theater of our century.
> —Paddy Chayevsky

When Chayevsky wrote this, TV *was* theater. That was a long time ago, during a period that has since been widely referred to as television's Golden Age. In those days, during the 1950s, plays were written, produced, and performed live on TV very much as they were on the stage. They were rehearsed fully before performance. The actors were able to develop and build their roles exactly as they would in the theater, in sequence from beginning to end. The author was usually on the set to cut, revise, or rewrite. The audience saw the play as it was being performed. There was the same sense of immediacy as in the theater.

Of course there were differences. One was the time factor. Scripts had to be written to a rigid time slot, often hurriedly, to meet a production schedule. There was not enough time for preparation, not enough time for anything. Budgets, compared to today's, were minuscule.

Electronic television cameras and microphones moved noise-lessly about the set during performance, photographing, recording, and transmitting the action to millions of TV sets throughout the country, in accordance with the director's instructions. By cutting from one camera to another, from one monitor to another in a control room, in much the same way as a conductor leads an orchestra, the director was able to determine not only what the viewer saw but how he saw it (this is still done in the broadcast of sports events). Good directors could thus intensify the meaning as well as the emotional content of both script and performance. The audience, scattered all over the nation, sometimes thousands of miles away, was brought much closer to the actors than an audience in a theater ever gets. Each subtle gesture—the blink of an eyelash, the trembling of a hand, a fleeting half-formed frown or smile—could have great dramatic significance. In this respect TV resembled motion pictures. But there were differences from motion pictures, also—mainly in the method of production, which we will discuss. But also in the audience.

There was no audience in the theatrical sense, no large group of people seated together, responding to a common experience. The TV audience, though numbered in millions, actually consisted of one or several individuals sitting before each little ten- or twelve-inch set isolated in their own living rooms, subject to all kinds of distractions.

In that one respect, watching television was almost like reading a novel. The new medium had the same kind of intimacy. In fact, during those years the best television plays dealt with revealing moments in the lives of ordinary people—in Chayevsky's words, with the "needlelike perception of human relationships."

To us who were there—despite fluffs and faux pas (once, in a television play of mine, *Survival,* produced by the Theatre Guild on *The U.S. Steel Hour,* the leading actress vomited *on camera*), despite pressure and censorship from sponsors and advertising agencies (after all, it was the political and social ice age of the 1950s)—those were exciting times. The new medium was not only fascinating, but its possibilities for dramatic expression seemed limitless.

The End of the Golden Age

But the law of life is change, and in our world, where science fiction fantasy is constantly being overtaken by everyday reality, change comes swiftly and radically. This is especially true in television. The Golden Age was largely over by the end of the 1950s. By the early 1960s most television production had moved from New York (the heart of the theater) to the West Coast (the heart of motion pictures). By then TV drama, with very few exceptions, was no longer live. Now it was filmed by motion picture companies, ground out in series formula on an assembly-line basis.

The main reason for this change was economic. Filmed programs could be sent to local stations throughout the country and the world and played over and over again on a rental basis. These rentals, rather than the original production, provided the main source of the production company's income. Furthermore, videotape had not yet been perfected. Light, portable recorders—which now can be purchased anywhere for home use—had not been invented. Videotape looks very much like audiotape—the kind you use in your tape recorder or your home music system. Images are recorded on the tape electronically as video cameras photograph their subjects. The overall effect is similar to live. Production methods of tape are also similar to live. In those days, however, the tape was difficult to edit; it often broke; nor were devices yet available to transmit videotape over the air as readily as film.

But whatever the causes, the consequences of this change in production were profound. Motion pictures, from their beginnings, had also gone through many changes: from silent to sound, from black and white to color. Later technical innovations added to the size of the screen, the depth and realism of the picture, the quality of the sound. As the 1920s began, motion pictures were well on their way to becoming the popular theater of the world. At their best they had achieved, and in many cases surpassed, artistic standards long associated with the theater.

But producing *motion pictures to be shown on television* was another matter.

Why?

In the first place, making a motion picture involves photographing the action of a story *on film.* Thus the audience sees the play *after* it is completed, not while it is being performed, as in live. The element of immediacy is lost.

Second, motion pictures are shot *out of sequence,* mainly for reasons of economy. All the scenes at a particular location are filmed at the same time—or as close to the same time as possible—regardless of their position in the script. If, for instance, scenes 6, 19, 37, and 81 of a motion picture scenario take place in the Cafe Deux Magots in Paris, they will all be filmed there on the same day, or the days following. Then cast and crew will pack up and move to another location.

When the filming is complete, the various sections, the shots, scenes, and sequences, are assembled and spliced in their proper order, then cut and edited.

Afterwards, music, opticals, titles, background scenery, and other postproduction elements are added.

When the picture is completed it is viewed by the producer, his assistants, company executives, and network representatives. Sometimes further changes are made.

Finally, weeks or months later, at the appointed time, the film is projected on a screen at a television studio and transmitted over the air or through a cable to an audience.

But the film as seen on the big theater-size screen in the projection room is vastly different from what it will look like on the small screen at home. The millions of dollars put into visual effects, location shots, and background material are largely lost. The small screen diminishes the total impact of the film.

From this very sketchy and distilled description of how motion pictures are made for television, several other points should be made:

One, many more skilled technicians and craftsmen are necessary in film than in live television. In live, for instance, the director, using the three or four electronic cameras described earlier, edits the play while it is being performed. This makes film editors and cutters unnecessary. This is true also for the expensive and time-consuming film developing process.

Two, film requires a different type of acting from live. On film, the actor cannot build his role over the course of a play's performance. He acts in bits and pieces, in individual shots and scenes. Actually his performance is—just as the entire picture—put together in the editing room by the editor and/or director. The actor is thus diminished creatively. What is important is how he looks, his type, personality, and so on. Nonactors have sometimes given brilliant performances, as have animals—impossible in the theater or on live television.

Three, filmed production is much more expensive. This means that individual sponsors can no longer pay for (and control) programs as they did in the past. Now multisponsorship is necessary. Nor can advertising agencies and small New York theatrical organizations such as the Theatre Guild produce television dramas. The new TV films are, as previously stated, produced by motion picture companies for the networks—NBC, ABC, CBS—who, as the ultimate buyers, are now in the saddle. And though the networks are in competition with each other, their authority over ideas and personnel—what is eventually shown on the tube—has become absolute.

The Assembly Line

The change from live to film production also affected the writer. Those who came to Hollywood in the late 1950s or early 1960s (only a few could remain in New York and survive; some wrote novels or plays or feature films; some drifted into other lines of work; some became writers of soaps, the last bastion of live on the air) were subjected to a major transformation. Formerly they had been individual craftsmen, television dramatists. They wrote plays for the new medium, leasing them for one performance only, plus a rerun (for which they were paid). Like a playwright's work in the theater, the work that the television writer created was his. He was the author and was treated as such. His script was almost never rewritten by another writer. He made all the necessary changes himself, usually willingly. On the air he received full and proper credit. As the play faded in, the credits read: "*Marty* by Paddy Chayevsky," or "*Twelve Angry Men* by Reginald Rose," or "*Visit to a Small Planet* by Gore Vidal." And after each commercial break, as Act II or III began, the announcer usually repeated the title of the play and the author's name. The writer owned his script. He might have it produced on the stage later, or sell it as a feature motion picture, or have it published. Like a novelist or short story writer or a playwright, he not only had a certain status, but the work he produced had his own personal stamp or style. Audiences looked for plays by certain favorite authors. Sometimes, if the writer was talented and/or lucky enough to work with a creative and dedicated producer and/or director (there were quite a few in those days), he might lift his script to the level of art.

In Hollywood the television dramatist became part of the motion picture industry. In the process he was transformed from individual craftsman to assembly-line worker. He no longer leased his script for one performance only (plus a rerun). The work no longer belonged to him. Even though he wrote it, the company who hired and paid him owned the script and could do with it what it wished. The filmed teleplay had become a "property." The company that had contracted for it or purchased it could, and often did, hire other individuals to rewrite it. Producers, network personnel, actors—as well as other writers—could change the script to such an extent that it no longer resembled what the original writer had written.

The writer was now a kind of skilled industrial worker, a hired hand like a toolmaker or a punch press operator or a draftsman, and what he produced was an industrialized product. It no longer had a personal stamp. After awhile—at least in series television (it has always been true on daytime serials)—one writer's scripts would begin to resemble those of any other writer's, much as one automobile coming off an assembly line resembles all the others of that year and model. No longer did the writer write out of his own imagination and experience, out of his own vision of life; he wrote out of someone else's head, on order. Those who hired him told him what was wanted and he supplied the product. Not only did his script become a property, but he himself became a property—and was treated as such. He became categorized as an expert in suspense, or comedy, or melodrama, etc.

Even when he attempted to write an original script on speculation now, his eye was on the marketplace. Now he began to self-censor his own most cherished ideas as noncommercial. Though he was paid well, sometimes lavishly, while working, both his prestige and his individual self-worth nevertheless began to diminish. Those writers most committed to the Hollywood system, those with their eyes on the main chance, those who knew their limitations from the beginning, or could see what was happening to their creative juices, those least committed to their lonely craft and art, attempted to graduate to the status of producer or executive and stop writing altogether. Writing required talent, dedication, and hard work. It was easier to talk than write, easier to read than write, easier to tell others what to do rather than do it yourself—and a production job or executive position was safer, steadier, and in most cases more financially rewarding than the tough, lonely existence of the freelancer.

The Dark Side—and the Light

The freelance television writer—like the freelance writer in other media—lives by his craft and imagination. He must not only create acceptable/producible scripts quickly week after week and rewrite on the spot, but must be able to withstand the rejections, cutoffs, and changes in his work made by other writers, by leading actors, editors, producers, agents, lawyers, as well as network vice-presidents, computers, etc. (Some of these individuals and machines even receive writing credit for their contributions, in arbitration, and as a result become "writers" themselves, members of the Writers Guild of America, West. The Guild, a trade union for writers in TV, motion pictures, and radio, is more powerful and militant on the West Coast than in the East because in Hollywood industrialization has reached a higher level of concentration. For the same reason it has many more of these nonwriting writers on its membership rolls.) The Guild and the vital role it plays to a writer are discussed in Chapter 22.

Due to the journeyman writer's vulnerable position in relation to the production process, due to the fact that the script over which he labored so hard and with such dedication is chewed up and digested by that process and finally emerges on the tube as something other than what he wrote, the deal, the contract, the package, the money (this is especially true in motion pictures) not infrequently become more important to him than the work itself. After a time this condition produces a certain hardnosed cynicism in almost everyone involved. Often it corrupts talent; sometimes it destroys it. But not always, and not inevitably.

For there is another side, a positive side, to all this. Fine, even outstanding, television dramas are being produced, as well as many, many ordinary ones. And more people are watching them. For the writer this means a steady and continuing market for his scripts. For the new writer, especially, this means great opportunity. Producers need him—they are in constant search for fresh ideas and fresh talent. And as the industry expands into new areas—and expand it will—there will be many more outlets for his work. New channels will allow for more varied audiences, the chance for writers to express themselves in whatever area their talent and interest lie. Videotape production of dramatic programs (which is similar to live) is one of the new methods on the horizon (it has already been in use for some time on most situation comedy series). Cassettes and pay TV are already flourishing new industries and growing markets for writers. In fact, there are unmistakable signs that the wheel has turned, that the medium is returning, but on a higher, more exciting level, to a new Golden Age.

1

The New Writer

Let's begin as every writer does when he starts a new project, with nothing but a blank sheet of paper before him. Let's take nothing for granted. Let's assume that all you know about television (except for what you've read so far in this book) is what you see on the tube.

You live in a large city or small town many miles from Hollywood, the production center of the television industry, or even New York. "Hollywood" is an idea, a concept, a mystery, not a reality. If you've visited there, taken a studio tour, seen some of the landmarks, or heard famous stars or producers or even writers discuss their lives and careers on talk shows, you may have some sense of what it's like. But how the industry really functions—and how the writer functions in it—is still vague.

You may have taken a course in writing for television or attended a workshop, if such exist in your area, or looked through books purporting to teach you how to do it. You've probably picked up some information, but unless the course was taught by, or the book written by, someone who has actually been involved as a writer in the field, it is unlikely that you profited very much.

You may have written poetry or stories or articles, perhaps a novel. You may even be widely published. Or perhaps writing has only been some vague but persistent itch. In school you got A's in your English composition courses. You write interesting, even moving letters.

But what intrigues, what excites the writer within you is that flickering screen in your living room or den.

Everybody watches it.

You don't have to be a statistician to know that most of what you see on the tube is fiction—motion pictures, old or new, dramatic or comedy series, serials (called soaps) shown during weekday after-noons, children's shows, cartoons—that there is a great deal of it, that television uses much more material than all the short stories published in all the magazines put together.

Obviously television writers are in demand. You've heard that they make lots of money. They marry or live with beautiful or handsome movie stars and lead a glamorous life of swimming pools and parties with Beautiful People.

Besides, writing for TV can't be that difficult. What you've watched on your set doesn't seem very good. In your opinion, some of the stories are downright bad, unbelievable. You don't understand how a lot of that mindless junk ever gets produced. You feel that if you really put your mind to it you surely could do better. Right?

Why not?

Why couldn't you write a script and sell it to television and be-come rich and famous?

Well . . . no reason, except . . . somehow, though you have a lot of ideas and think you have talent, you've never quite been able to get it all together. Something is missing.

Exactly how do you go about writing for television? You don't even know what a script actually is, what it looks like.

You do know that at the beginning or at the end of every pro-gram you watch—especially a drama or a comedy, no matter the length—there are *credits*. These include the names of all the creative personnel involved in a particular show: the actors, the director, the producer, the cameraman, the scene designer, sound and lighting personnel—and also the words "written by . . ." or "teleplay by . . ." and sometimes "story by . . ." followed by the names of one or more individuals.

These individuals are the writers.

The "written by" credit means that the writer or writers whose names appear wrote the entire original script, including the "story," from their own idea or concept.

"Teleplay by" means the same thing, except if there's also a "story by" credit listed, the teleplay was based upon someone else's story.

But what, you may ask, is a teleplay? What is a television story? What is a script? What does it include? Dialogue? Camera directions? Physical action? What exactly is a camera direction? Does a writer have to know about such things?

And if you should happen to somehow write a script, what do you do—just put it in an envelope and send it to MGM? Or Twentieth Century-Fox? But whom do you send it to *at* MGM or Twentieth Century-Fox or wherever? Is it like sending a short story you've written to a magazine editor? Or like sending a book manuscript to the editor of a publishing house?

Does a writer need an agent? Where do you find one? Which ones are good and which ones are not worth bothering with? What does an agent actually do? How much does he get paid? Does he charge reading fees?

What does the Writers Guild do? Do you have to join it?

How can a new writer be sure that some of those Hollywood sharks aren't going to steal his precious ideas? How do you protect your material? Can you copyright an idea, a script?

There are a lot of things you don't know or aren't sure of.

The main thing is you have ideas, energy. You're willing to work and learn. You feel you have talent.

How do you, the new writer, break in?

Prove Yourself

The first thing you do is write a good script, a professionally viable, producible teleplay . . . because a script *is* a teleplay.

Is there no other way?

Unfortunately, no—not if you want to become a professional television writer.

But, you protest, you've heard of people who broke into writing by getting a job with a studio as a secretary, or in the script department, or as a messenger, or in the mail room.

True. It's a good idea to get any of those jobs if you can; but, except for secretary, they're hard to come by.

Nevertheless, no one ever became a writer simply by being a secretary or a script reader or a messenger or a mail room clerk.

They were close to where things happened. They knew whom to give their script to. They had personal contact, a receptive reader in a buying position.

But first they had to write the script.

Why?

Because only by writing a good script can you show a producer or agent that you're a writer who understands the medium, who has control of his craft, and who has enough talent to keep producing filmable scripts week after week.

This book, as mentioned earlier, is going to help you do exactly that.

But first there is one important fact you must be made aware of.

Most television scripts which are produced—something like 95 percent—are written by *professional writers, on assignment.*

A professional writer, as defined by the Writers Guild of America Basic Agreement of March 2, 1977, is one who

1. has received employment for a total of 13 weeks as a motion picture and/or television writer, or radio writer for dramatic programs; or

2. has received credit on the screen as a writer for a television or theatrical motion picture; or

3. has received credit for three original stories or one teleplay for a program one-half hour or more in length in the field of live television; or

4. has received credit for three radio scripts for dramatic radio programs one-half hour or more in length; or

5. has received credit for one professionally produced play on the legitimate stage, or one published novel.

Well, if you're not a professional writer according to the above definition, how do you get an assignment?

You don't. You write your script *on speculation.* That means without an assignment, on your own.

But what do you write? Do you aim your script for a particular program or market? For a series now on the air? Or do you write anything you feel like, anything that interests, that moves you? And what about length? Do you have to write to a rigid time slot?

For instance, what does the professional writer do? How does writing on assignment work? How does the pro get an assignment? Who gives it to him? Is he told the idea or concept? Is he given a story, or does he have to dream it up himself, or what? What is a story? An idea or concept? In television terms?

To answer these questions—how to write and sell a script, how to break into this fascinating, exciting, but often heartbreaking industry—let me introduce you to John Bright, a mythical but perhaps typical working journeyman television writer, a composite of many who actually exist. Let's see how he functions, what his actual working life is like. Through his eyes, from his point of view, we'll follow the step-by-step procedure he goes through in the course of *writing* and *selling* one episodic script from idea to production.

Meanwhile, you, the new writer, will go through the same steps in the construction of an outline and the writing of a script—the only difference will be that you will be writing your script on *speculation* rather than on *assignment.* Nor will you, as a new writer, be writing for a series, or consulting with an editor or producer, as John will be doing.

You will be writing this first script by yourself, using this book as a reference and as a guide.

The completed script will be your calling card, a sample of your work which will introduce you to people who can, and hopefully will, eventually hire you. Thus it will be the best script that you can write. It will come out of your own feelings and experience. Into it will go all your talent, your creative energy, and the craft you have learned. This script will be not merely as good as what you've seen on the tube; it will be better! It *must* be better if it's to make an impression on whoever reads it.

Let me repeat: You are going to approach your first script with all the seriousness and dedication that it would take to write *The Great American Novel,* be it comedy or tragedy.

2
The Episodic Series

Of the more than five thousand members of the Writers Guild of America, West, John Bright is one of the select 20 percent or so who consistently write much of what you see in prime time (7:30-11 p.m.) network television. (The majority of these writers are white and male, although the number of women and minorities is increasing rapidly.)

Most of John's output consists of hour-length *teleplays*.

A teleplay is a story written to be performed on television. It can be either comedy or drama. There are various kinds and lengths of teleplays that we'll discuss throughout this book, but the particular kind that John writes is *episodic drama*, that is, scripts for *episodic series*.

Episodic series contain one or more continuing characters—leads—whose various adventures or emotional entanglements we follow on the tube each week at the same time slot.

The idea for this kind of program can be traced back to enduring classic stories such as *Robin Hood* or the *Arthurian Legends*. However, in the 1930s and 1940s there were also a few successful motion picture series, such as the *Andy Hardy* series, starring Mickey Rooney. Early in television's history the powers that be in the industry, many of whom had come from radio where series drama was already a mainstay, discovered that this kind of programming was immensely popular in television as well. Audiences seemed to enjoy returning each week to familiar characters—like tuning in to old friends. Series such as *Bonanza,* with a family group consisting of a strong, wise, loving father-figure and his three very different sons, loyal to each other in every crisis, ran for many years. *Family, The Waltons,* and the comedy series *All in the Family* and *M*A*S*H* were updated and somewhat more sophisticated versions of the same thing.

Filmed series are and have been the staple of commercial television broadcasting almost since its inception, at least on the West Coast. In addition to family drama, there have always been various kinds of melodrama dealing with life-and-death situations. They fall into the following general categories: police and detective series like *Kojak* or *Harry O;* medical series like *Marcus Welby* or *Trapper John, M.D.;* legal series; westerns; adventure; science fiction; and situation comedies (sitcoms) like *Sanford and Son* or *One Day at a Time.*

Episodic drama is the area in which not only John Bright but most television writers work most of the time. This is the big steady market where they make their bread.

Bright can write for almost any dramatic (melodramatic) series now on the air because most of them, no matter what the subject matter or leading characters, resemble each other. He can even use the same ideas, premises, and stories from one series to another, almost interchangeably, like the spare parts of a car. All he may need to do is a little research into the subject at hand: medicine, law, the West, police procedures.

This does not mean that episodes are easy to do, especially for the new writer. In many ways episodic drama is more difficult to write than a straight, ordinary script. Series drama requires a high degree of technical know-how and familiarity with the craft. Many otherwise competent and talented writers have never been able to overcome the pitfalls of this form.

The Season

As we meet John on this particular morning in March, he is eating breakfast in his home in the San Fernando Valley (or Brentwood, or Beverly Hills, or Malibu). Most television writers live somewhere in the western part of the Los Angeles area because it is necessary for them to be near the centers of television production. As we shall see, they need to be in constant contact with producers, agents, and others in the industry, for television writing includes developing and selling ideas, rewriting, and an intimate and personal knowledge of a constantly shifting market. Nevertheless, some successful and well-known writers are based in New York and in various other cities and towns throughout the country. Few of these, however, write weekly series. Instead, they write movies for television, specials, daytime serials, and/or pilots. Often they are active in other areas as well: feature films, plays, novels.

As John sips his coffee, he scans the *Los Angeles Times* and the "trades" (daily Hollywood publications for the television and motion picture industries), *Variety,* and the *Hollywood Reporter.* There might be a news article in the *Times* that interests him—probably one dealing with some aspect of crime or law or medicine on which he might base a future script. If it's sufficiently relevant, he might cut it out and file it away in one of his bulging folders. But today it's a big story (page one of the "trades," or page one of the entertainment section of the *Times)* that immediately attracts his attention. It states that NBC has just announced its lineup of series for the new season and that there are at least half a dozen new ones. (The other two networks—ABC and CBS—will follow with announcements of their own schedules before the week is out.)

Weekly television is a seasonal business. Until recently there was only one new season each year. It began in the fall—September or October. But preparations got under way long before that, from the moment new schedules were announced, usually in March. By then the network executives had officially renewed the previous year's successful series and had selected pilot shows (discussed in the next chapter) from among the many made by the various competing production companies. On these choices they gambled their reputations, their careers, and millions of dollars of network money.

Within the last few years, however, two seasons have developed, the second usually beginning early in the new year. Its purpose is to replace quickly any series that falls behind in the autumn—or first season—ratings. Thus, back-up pilots for possible series are always being developed, and scripts may be bought at any time. For the writer this means that scripts are bought throughout the year. Nevertheless, the fall season is still the main one, and the early spring buying time is when most television writers scramble for assignments.

First Steps

John studies NBC's lineup carefully, noting the names of the production companies and the producers of each series (if they've been selected yet), most of whom he knows and several of whom he's worked for. Two of the series listed especially catch his attention. One, entitled *Naked Stars* (produced by one of the major companies), isn't about Hollywood actors and actresses cavorting about in the buff but deals rather with "the adventures of a couple of space detectives living in the year 1999." The other, called *Mary and Mark* (produced by one of the smaller independents), is about "the relationship between a black woman brain surgeon who supported herself through medical school as a high-fashion model and a white gay male nurse named Mark who used to be a professional football player, in a contemporary hospital setting." These two series interest John not because of their subject matter but because the producers are individuals he's worked with successfully before.

John has had a rather good year. He wrote three hour-length scripts; one ninety-minute job; was rewritten twice; was cut off at story once; but also had a rewrite job himself. His total income, with residuals, amounts to something over $75,000—which is more than the income of most members of the WGA, but less than the top group (actual figures relating to fees for scripts, residuals, etc., will be provided in Appendix E).

Nevertheless, he hasn't worked for almost two months, has been collecting unemployment insurance—and standing in that line has made him a bit edgy. He can't forget a period some five years ago when he didn't have an assignment in almost sixteen months and was forced to borrow money on his house. Although John knows that such periods are occupational hazards, he doesn't want to have to suffer through one again. Moreover, he knows that the longer a writer goes without an assignment the harder it is to get one. The memories of most producers and network personnel are extremely short simply because some of these people are so new they don't know what happened in the industry only last year.

So he calls his agent to find out what the ten-percenter knows about *Naked Stars* and *Mary and Mark.* Are they showing the pilots to writers? Have any assignments been given out? How many scripts do they need? He also asks if there's anything else available or coming up soon.

The agent says he'll check on the two series and get back to John—there are a couple of things on CBS and ABC due to be announced at any minute that may also interest his client. Don't worry, he's on the ball. But meanwhile if John wants to call his producer friends on *Naked Stars* and *Mary and Mark,* he should feel free. John knows this, but at present he'd rather have his agent contact them.

The moment he hangs up, the phone rings. It's the secretary of Walter Hyer, producer of *Naked Stars.* Could Mr. Bright come to projection room three at the studio Thursday afternoon at four to view the pilot? John happily says yes, even though it conflicts with his appointment at the unemployment office.

He arrives at the studio on Thursday at about five minutes before four. There is a pass at the gate in his name. The guard directs him to projection room three and shows him where to park.

Three other writers are seated in the projection room waiting silently as he enters. One is reading the trades. He doesn't recognize any of them and takes a seat in the rear. In the next couple of minutes two more writers enter and, exactly at four, the projectionist switches off the lights and starts to run the film.

3
The Pilot

As John Bright and his fellow writers watch the pilot in the hushed darkness of the projection room, let's step back for a moment and see where that pilot came from. Who made it? How? Why? Let's trace its evolution from the original concept or idea.

First, what is a pilot?

A pilot is a sample episode of a proposed series. It presents the leading continuing characters, the kind of situations and plot they will typically be involved in, and the show's general nature—what the viewer may expect each week.

For instance: is it a family show? The members of the family who will appear from week to week on the series will be included in the pilot. We will be introduced to them in a typical dramatic or comic situation and learn their traits and how they interact. Is the story about a father-son conflict? That of a husband about to divorce his wife? Will the series deal with contemporary problems? Then perhaps the pilot might relate to a father and/or mother's reaction to, and relationship with, their unmarried daughter who decides to have her child, and her difficulties in bringing it up alone. Or a son who has an emotional relationship with a male friend. Or problems of drugs, or social class in America today, or race relations, or the difficulties of senior citizens.

Does the series deal with the law? The leading continuing character or characters will be portrayed and delineated in the pilot. Is the lead a veteran defense attorney with a younger assistant as in *The*

Defenders, a successful and critically acclaimed series produced in New York a few years ago? Each of the cases dramatized was to some degree controversial. Thus, the pilot of such a series might deal with a subject like mercy killing or abortion, or any exciting and important case out of this morning's headlines. It will tell the story not as propaganda but in human emotional terms. In the process it will show how our leading continuing characters are drawn into the plot and how they affect its outcome.

Is the lead a detective, a doctor, a newspaper editor? What kind of person is the detective? What kinds of crimes will he be called upon to solve? The pilot will dramatize one. If a doctor, what is his specialty? Is the typical setting of the series a hospital? Or his office? The pilot will show a typical case, our doctor hero's involvement emotionally as well as professionally, and how he cures—or fails to cure—the patient (the guest star). Does the series take place at a newspaper, as in *Lou Grant?* Is the editor, like Lou, an older, wise, understanding father-figure? (Shades of *Bonanza.*) But at the same time modern and not too sentimental? Is the typical story controversial? Does the publishing of the newspaper article affect or alter the conditions that the reporter uncovered? What's the emotional relationship between the lead (or leads) and the other continuing characters? Between the lead and the guest star? The pilot will try to show the viewer what he's in for week after week.

But before the television audience sees it, the buyer—the network—will scrutinize it closely.

Hard Sell

For the production company that made it (MGM, Fox, Warner Brothers, Universal, Viacom, Filmways, Lorimar, Spelling-Goldberg, QM, Paramount, MTM, Tandem, TAT, etc.), the object of a pilot is to sell the series to the network for presentation over the air.

A successful series—one that is on the air for several years—can make a fortune—millions—for the creators, and even more for the company that makes it. Thus every production company and every producer, director, and writer in television wants to sell and produce a series.

But only a comparatively few new series are sold and go on the air each year.

Thus only a few companies, producers, directors, and writers are involved in their production.

How are these fortunate individuals and organizations selected? Who selects them?

The networks: NBC, CBS, ABC. Directly or indirectly.

The networks and their affiliate stations throughout the country, in effect, own and control most commercial air time in US television. They sell or rent the air time to sponsors—mostly large corporations—who use it to advertise—sell—their products (or their own image or point of view about politics, economics, society, anything).

The price to the sponsor/advertiser of any minute of air time is based upon the number of people watching. This figure is determined by one or more statistical rating systems, which may or may not be accurate. But it doesn't matter, because everyone involved in television believes and trusts the ratings. Thus, the higher the rating, presumably the larger the number of people watching, the higher the cost to the sponsor, and the greater the profit to the network. Since profits are the ultimate and overriding goal, there is a tremendous rivalry among the networks for the highest rating. The conflict is relentless, all-consuming. It involves millions of dollars, the careers of many individuals, and the fate of corporations.

Therefore, what each network is constantly seeking in a new series is a hit—one that attracts the largest number of viewers.

Where do they find such a series?

The Pilot Sweepstakes

Each year the networks put up a certain amount of seed money to production companies for the creation of pilots. From these they select those they think will be the new successes.

But before the pilot is made, a long and arduous process takes place.

It starts with an idea, or a concept, or premise (see Chapter 5 for a full discussion of this subject).

The premise may originate anywhere—sometimes with an executive in the network itself, sometimes with a producer at the production company, often with a writer, either freelance or employed by the production company.

No matter where it comes from, the premise is sooner or later made concrete in a *presentation*. This presentation—a narrative description of what the series will be about, including the leading/continuing characters and several typical plots—may run anywhere from one page to eighty or more, double-spaced. Five to twelve pages is the norm, depending upon the subject matter. The presentation is written by a writer on assignment or on speculation. (See Appendix D for an example of a presentation.)

If on a freelance, speculative basis, the presentation is usually submitted first by the writer or his agent to a production company. If the company likes it, it may take an option on the material and then submit it to a network. If the network likes it, it will make a deal with the production company which in turn assigns a writer—either the one who created the original presentation or another—to *develop* the series.

Writers hired to develop a series—that is, to write a pilot, either their own or the company's creation—are paid well for their work. In addition to fees three times or more the going rate of pay for an ordinary series episode, the writer of the pilot receives royalties for each episode aired if the series is sold, plus a percentage of the profits. Furthermore, he has a chance to become either a producer, executive producer, or story consultant at additional high fees. A total of $5,000 per week is not unusual for the successful writer of a pilot who also participates in the series in a production or editorial capacity.

Clearly this is not an area in which there are many opportunities for a beginner. Only after he has piled up some good credits and achieved a reputation can the writer even think about competing in this sweepstakes. The writers who are hired to create or develop pilots are the most successful in the industry, the ones most in demand. Normally they must be approved by the network, even though they're actually under contract with the production company.

Also, most series development contracts are *step-deals*, in which the writer must first write a treatment or outline of the pilot script for approval by the network before he can go ahead with work on the teleplay, and few pilot deals ever come to fruition. But even if the script is written, the pilot is not necessarily made. Furthermore, even if the pilot is made, the odds are still high against the series actually going on the air because—as noted above—many more pilots are contracted for than the networks ever intend to use.

The pilot, then, is a big gamble.

For the writer, winning that gamble, creating a *successful* series, means winning the biggest jackpot in the business.

Watching the Pilot

Watching the pilot in the projection room, John Bright does not think of all the complications, the revisions and rewrites, the heartaches and backbreaking, numbing hours of work that went into the film flickering on the screen. All he's concerned with is writing an episode (or more than one) for the series. He carefully notes the nature of the two leading continuing characters, Lewis Finn and Ed Ginigen, the space-age detectives, and how they are being played by the actors. Are the characters being played straight or tongue-in-cheek? Is this a serious detective show, or a spin-off a la *Superman* or *Buck Rogers?* He follows the convolutions of the plot, checking the amount of violence, whether there's a love interest, and in the back of his mind is wondering about the kind of world the writer, producer, and others involved want to project in the series. Is society in the year 1999 like ours? What is the relationship between men and women? What is the general attitude toward the family? Casual violence? General morality? Perhaps there are many shortages. People are forced to live in tents. Cars are half the size they are now. The government is a dictatorship. But still the basic story falls right into the detective genre. There is a crime. The detectives must solve it. There's tension, danger, red herrings—and at the end our heroes come through a little wiser and perhaps sadder and maybe a bit more cynical, even. But all in all, John feels, as the final credits flash and the lights come up, that it was well constructed, well acted, and well produced. Moreover, except for the space-age trappings, it would fit into any good detective series.

Even though he knows that pilots always cost more than ordinary episodes, that more time and care are taken in their production than the normal series fare, John feels that this ought to be a good series and he'd like to write for it.

4

The Producer and the Editor

As the lights come up in the projection room and John Bright looks around blinking his eyes, the door opens and Walter Hyer, producer of *Naked Stars,* and his editor, Bill Picker, enter. They step to the front of the room and nod at the assembled writers, half of whom they've never met but have invited here on the basis of previous credits, agents' recommendations, and word-of-mouth reputation.

The Producer

Hyer is a writer as well as a producer (often called a *writer-producer* and known in the business as a *hyphenate*), as are most producers in series television. Although he hasn't had time to take on very many writing assignments in the last three or four years (he wrote two pilots that never got on the air), he used to be one of the top freelancers in the field. Four seasons ago he was asked to be a script editor on a series. The series was a hit, consistently in the first ten on the rating charts; so, when the producer left for a better job, Hyer moved up. He's been producing ever since.

Last year when the network decided to go ahead with *Naked Stars,* the company making it called him in and asked him to produce it. He took the assignment because it offered more money and more opportunity, as well as a challenge.

Producers of television series come mainly from the ranks of the writers because, as has been stated, scripts are of prime importance in the success of a series. The producer's first responsibility is to make his series a success. Since he cannot change the nature of what the series is about to any great extent, since star actors or actresses don't necessarily have much to do with ratings, and since television directors in episodic work do not have the kind of creative freedom their colleagues have in features, the producer must first and foremost get the best scripts he possibly can. Thus he must approach writers in whom he has confidence. He must talk to them in their own terms, in their own language, as writer to writer. He must excite them to write for his series rather than another. Then after they've agreed, he must encourage them to write their very best.

The producer must not only be a master of script construction, able to spot problems quickly and explain to the writer clearly and concisely where they are and how to fix them; he must also be a good idea man, capable of rewriting scripts himself under pressure. He must know immediately whether any premise he hears will work dramatically or not. In addition, he must have a good story mind, contribute creatively in a story conference, and make his own ideas and point of view not only felt but clear. The producer has other functions as well—casting, selecting the proper director and most of the key personnel, keeping the budget within certain parameters, and overall administration. It's not necessary to go into these here. But none are as vital to a series' success (and the advancement of his own career) as strong, exciting, and well-crafted scripts.

In series television the producer is the controlling force. His ideas and point of view dominate.

The Editor

Bill Picker, the editor—in some cases called the *executive story consultant*—is Hyer's assistant (there may be several on any series, depending upon the subject matter, the budget, etc.). Bill is also a writer. He created *Naked Stars* and wrote the pilot. He will participate in the acquisition of scripts, suggest writers, rewrite himself when necessary, and create several teleplays on his own. He will also have "created by" credit on every episode that is broadcast. His interest in the series is, if anything, even greater than Hyer's, for he has a piece of it and will share in its profits as well as collect a royalty as long as the show is on the air.

The Bad News

Although in the past the producer and his editor or editors were almost totally responsible for the direction a series would take, the kind of scripts bought, and the selection of writers—with merely a nod to the network for approval—recently the networks have assumed much of that control for themselves, often leaving the producer out on a limb. This is true especially for a new show. (After a series becomes a success, the network may back off a bit, but never at its inception.)

Every decision the producer makes, every script the producer buys must now be approved by the network. Moreover, the network will often contradict the producer's actions. It will reject a script that the producer loved. It will ask for major revisions in a script the producer had scheduled to shoot. Not only do these decisions place a bureaucratic stranglehold on the producer and drive him up a wall, but think of their effect upon the poor writer. He presented an idea, an outline, a teleplay that the producer said was great. He went home elated. He took spouse or lover or friends out to celebrate. The next morning the producer—or his secretary—called with the bad news: the network turned down the writer's material . . . and his balloon burst. Who was right? What was he to believe? Was what he wrote good or not? Are there no standards? This is one of the most effective and insidious destroyers of a writer's fragile ego, one of the methods by which cynicism and bitterness are created.

Only fortitude, a thick skin, and an absolute, unconquerable determination will save the new writer, or the veteran.

Fortunately or unfortunately, however, very few novices are ever faced with the situation described above. The new writer is at home writing his script on speculation, not developing it step by step under the critical eyes of producer, editor, and network executive. The script the beginner writes is either accepted or not. What happens to it after it's accepted, *if* it's accepted, is of course another matter. We will discuss that happy contingency in later chapters.

The Network Executive

The network executive in episodic drama usually oversees and is responsible for one or more series. If the series are long running and have satisfactory ratings he does not normally interfere to any great extent; but in a new, untried series every idea, outline, and script must have his approval. He represents the network and will accept only the material that, first, he—and/or his superiors—think will have a high rating and, second, will not be too controversial in either subject matter or treatment.

Who is the executive who oversees series drama on behalf of the network? Often he too has been a writer. For an important part of his responsibility is to make sure the scripts selected are written well and contain the necessary ingredients for popularity. At his best, the network executive should certainly have the qualifications of the producer when it comes to spotting problems in a script and how to overcome them. Nevertheless, he rarely meets with the writer directly.

Questions and Answers

In the projection room now Walter Hyer is talking to John Bright and the other writers about the pilot they just saw. He wants them to note that one of the leading actors who plays a continuing character—the younger of the two detectives, Ginigen—has been replaced with a new and very exciting actor whom the studio brought out from New York. In their stories they can give him a lighter, more humorous touch than in the pilot. He was a hit in Neil Simon's latest comedy on Broadway. Also, play down the violence. There's too much in the present version. The network wants softer stories and more humor. Also, more sex. Don't overdo it—but if you can keep it light and bright like the old romantic movies Cary Grant played in, especially those directed by Cukor, we'll all be very happy. Otherwise, what you saw here is the basis of the kind of stories we need, what the series will be. Any questions?

There are a few: How many scripts is the studio buying? How many have they got? Is this a science fiction show or a detective show? Or what? If SF, what about production problems, costs, and how to deal with technical and scientific advances peculiar to the year 1999? People have different notions about that, based upon which crystal ball they happen to be looking into.

Hyer explains that the network has ordered thirteen scripts but the studio will probably assign three or four more as backup because several always fall out. Two are already being written by Bill

Picker here, who wrote the pilot. As editor he'll work closely with the writers, along with me. Don't worry about costs. Just write the best scripts you can. It's basically a detective show, except it's set in the future. Don't get involved in SF elements, except as they affect the detective-story plots. What the world of 1999 will be like—at least in this series—is contained in a "bible" or presentation that Bill has written and which we'll hand out now. If you have specific questions not answered in this presentation, feel free to call the office—and we'll try to get your problems solved as soon as we can.

After the presentations are passed out, Walter thanks the writers for coming in, suggests they go home and think, and the moment they come up with something to call him or Bill to set up an appointment. He hopes he'll see them all soon.

This chapter describes a typical method of acquiring scripts for a new series. There are other methods. Sometimes pilots are not made. The network orders a series on the basis of a presentation alone, plus the reputation of the company. In such cases the writers coming in to write for it don't even have a typical script, much less a pilot film as a guide. The struggle in such cases—always intense—to get the series into proper focus may be overwhelming; producers and editors are replaced without warning. Scripts are rewritten or thrown out. Ulcers and heart attacks become common.

For the new writer, writing an episode for a series on speculation—as your first script—is filled with pitfalls. It has been done; nevertheless, I advise my students against it. One reason is that by the time your script is finished the series may be off the air and the market gone. Secondly, writing for a series is technically more difficult than writing a straight anthology script. The leading characters usually must make the story move rather than the new, more interesting characters the writer has created. These continuing characters never change. They must be included in a certain percentage of scenes, no fewer, no more. They are often thrust into a story, not according to logic or believability but in accordance with the demands of the series. Only an extremely skilled craftsman can do this and make it acceptable to an audience. Also, without being in close contact with the producer and knowing what his specific needs are, it's difficult for the new writer to determine exactly what should go into his script. In addition, a series is always undergoing changes. What the new writer sees on the tube was written months ago and may not be what the producer or network wants *now*. Finally, the producer and editor who made the particular episode now on the air may have been replaced.

I suggest that the new writer *create his own teleplay, using his own plot and characters.* I suggest that he not concentrate on a particular market, but write what he feels most strongly about, whether comedy or drama. Only in this way can he truly show his own talent, originality, and craftsmanship. Only in this way can he put his best foot forward. Moreover, the completed script is his. He can present it to various markets, not just the series he wrote it for. Any qualified reader can tell from this sample script whether the new writer has the ability to take on a series assignment or not. If he has the ability, he'll most likely be given an opportunity, probably on a successful series.

5

The Premise

The next day or two John Bright spends thinking, making notes, digging into his files filled with newspaper and magazine clippings and ideas jotted down weeks and months ago for possibly just such an occasion as this. He envisions the two continuing characters of the series, Finn and Ginigen, in a variety of situations. He imagines how they would act when confronted by specific obstacles. How would they react to danger? How would they overcome the machinations and power of brilliant but ruthless "heavies" (villains)? How would they handle the charms of lovely ladies in distress, or in various states of undress? He considers the kinds of crimes his two heroes may have to solve, capers they may have to break up. How can he fit these creations of another writer into a world he knows very little about, that of the year 1999? He reads and rereads the material that Walter Hyer passed out. Maybe some of it can even give him a starting point for a story.

The Essence

What John is expected to come up with at this point is a *premise* for an episode of the series. If the producer likes his premise and it is approved by the network, John will be assigned to write the script.

But what is a premise?

A premise is a basic idea for a story, what the story is about. A *complete* premise contains the essential structure of the final script.

A premise is the seed of a story. Like a seed planted in the ground, it contains within itself all of the elements of the final growing plant.

It is the story told in the fewest possible words, from beginning to end. It is the plot distilled to its essence.

A ruler of the ancient Greek city of Thebes seeks to rid his people of a terrible plague caused, according to the Oracle, by the unsolved murder of a former king. The action of the play is the search for the guilty party by the present ruler. At the climax the ruler discovers that he himself is not only the murderer but has married the dead king's wife, his own mother. In horror, he puts out his own eyes.

This is the premise of one of the greatest plays ever written: *Oedipus Rex* by Sophocles.

In an early live television play of mine, *Love, Marriage and Five Thousand Dollars,* a thirty-five-year-old man gives up his secure but unsatisfactory post office job and marries the woman he loves when she offers to lend him $5,000 to buy a photographic shop he desperately wants. However, she doesn't have the money. Shocked, angered, he leaves her. But in the climax he realizes that her lie gave him the courage to quit his job and be free—and at the end he accepts his new insecure but more fulfilling life with her. (Note: Part of this script is reproduced in Appendix C.)

From the examples just cited, it is clear that a good premise is not merely an "area" or an "idea" or a "concept." It is an area that has been brought into focus. It is an idea or concept that has been thought about, whose thrust and central characters have been considered from many angles. It is a story problem that has been solved, even though the details still have to be developed.

Purpose of the Premise

A good premise does several things. It tells who the main character is, what his/her main conflict and/or emotional involvement is, and what the opening scene (often called the *hook* or *teaser*) is (we'll discuss openings later); it gives an idea of how the story will be resolved (what the climactic scene will be).

A premise is the first step required in the writing of a dramatic episode for a series; it is the first step in the writing of any professional script on assignment. This is what the writer must submit *orally* before he is given a contract to go ahead with the development of a teleplay. The novice should take this step in constructing his television script as well—even though he may not have to submit it to anyone—for a good premise clarifies a writer's thinking about his script at an early stage. Here flaws become readily apparent. At this stage fuzziness, lack of focus, and other problems can be more easily corrected than later, after the teleplay has been written.

Although a premise is not presented on paper by the professional, the new writer should write out his premise carefully. This is for his own benefit, to clarify his own thinking. After he's written it down as briefly as he can—not more than a page or two—he should test it to see whether it contains a believable protagonist, a central conflict and/or emotional relationship involving the protagonist, a good opening scene, and a resolution, or climax. These concepts will be expanded and clarified in succeeding chapters.

Obviously the writer should be willing to put a great deal of thinking and planning into the creation of a premise.

However, for the experienced professional, much of the work that goes into developing a good premise is done shorthand. Putting together the basic structure of a story becomes almost automatic. Certain steps are skipped or taken for granted. Much of the thought process is probably intuitive.

Moreover, depending upon the reputation of the writer and his relationship with the producer and the kind of series involved (some are more complex and difficult than others), he may be given an assignment on less than a fully worked-out premise. He may even be advised *not* to come in with a complete premise. An interesting "heavy," an exciting or unusual background or "area" may be enough (examples of this will be given further on), but only if the producer has great confidence in the writer and/or he needs the script urgently. It rarely happens on a new, untried series, and never with a new, untried writer.

Furthermore, finding a good premise for a teleplay takes for granted a certain level of understanding on the writer's part of what a story, plot, scene, conflict, and climax are—concepts that we'll discuss fully in Chapters 9, 12, and 13. As we come to them now in our further treatment of the premise, however, we'll try to explain their meaning briefly.

Putting It Together

To see how a premise is put together, let's return to John Bright and try to follow his thought processes as he actually works one out.

Where does he start?

Since this is an episode for a series, he starts with the continuing characters, Finn and Ginigen. They're detectives, which means that they will be involved in the solution of some crime. Since they're *private* detectives, it's a crime that will not (at least initially) involve the police or another law enforcement agency . . . perhaps a crime that has not yet been committed . . . a crime—or problem—that someone doesn't want the police or public to know about. Perhaps someone's in danger and needs protection. . . .

John decides at this point not to get involved with the science-fiction aspects; he'll work out the premise first as if it were a contemporary situation.

But as he thinks about these possibilities, John remembers the pilot. What were those who made it trying to establish for the series, in a general way? Was the crime merely a puzzle in the manner of Agatha Christie, or was the pilot trying to create gritty but romantic reality a la Raymond Chandler? The pilot, John thinks, had a kind of sensational undertone, something resembling Chandler's *The Big Sleep,* set in the future. It was nothing like Agatha Christie.

Okay—John gets a flash, an idea, not actually an idea yet. A character. A woman. A beautiful young woman. Rich. Married. The wife of a businessman, an industrialist, a banker perhaps . . . based on several things he's read (and clipped from the newspapers for his files), plus a combination of several women he's known, as well as an actual case a police officer once told him about several years ago when he was doing research for another show. Women—housewives—who spend their days, while their husbands are out, working as call girls. (But he doesn't want this to be a trite, sleazy story.)

Immediately several questions present themselves: Why would a wealthy woman become a call girl? Clearly she doesn't need money. John thinks about making her poor, or even middle class. Maybe inflation is so bad in the year 1999 women have to do such things to supplement the family income. Maybe people are so squeezed economically that morality has gone out the window. But no, John is looking for something else, something more interesting, offbeat, a more psychological, provocative motivation. Keep her rich. Yet keep her working as a part-time (at least) call girl. Why does she do it?

He's not sure yet, but as he thinks about it, he decides to call her Sylvia from the song/poem by Shakespeare, "Who Is Sylvia?" The mystery, John decides, is one of character. Who is Sylvia? is what the teleplay will be about—that is, why does this beautiful woman who has everything money can buy—and a successful husband—become a call girl? He will also call the teleplay "Who Is Sylvia?" even though he doesn't even have the premise yet. He, the writer, will find out who Sylvia is as he works out some kind of story involving her and his detectives.

And since it is a detective story, the plot must involve some crime, or threat of crime. Certainly suspense.

Suppose someone is trying to harm—even kill—Sylvia. She can't tell anyone, especially her husband, because she's afraid that the threat is related to her "other life," her life as a call girl. Her would-be murderer comes from that other, secret life.

John decides to make her husband a banker—because a banker's reputation is more vulnerable, and the consequences to him, her, and their marriage would be greater if she were exposed.

Let's make her husband the archetypical banker, a man who works hard, who is brilliant in his handling and understanding of money, but whose emotional life leaves a great deal to be desired. His morals are rigid. He believes in the letter of the law, not its human qualities. He has no feeling for his wife's emotional needs, which doesn't mean that he doesn't love her. He may have passion but can't express it. Although he shows his love for Sylvia in the only way he can love—by buying her presents—his involvement with his work twenty-four hours a day has shut her out of his life. John decides to name him Roger.

Sylvia lives isolated in a large, lovely home. Shy, artistic, brought up as a princess by a wealthy aunt, Sylvia's need for love, for passion, is intense. This need motivates her secret afternoon life.

But let's go a little further. Is it possible, John asks himself, for Sylvia to repress her afternoon activities? Even from her own consciousness? Without making her psychotic? In other words, suppose she lives two lives, is two different people—one person not knowing what the other is doing. Maybe she has emotional problems. Maybe she's neurotic. But she's still lovely, warm, desirable—and above all, sympathetic. John knows his important characters, especially the leads, should be people the audience relates to, feels strongly about, identifies with; but most important of all, they must be believable. Can John make his audience believe that Sylvia could block out half of her life, without having them think she was "crazy"? Is it psychologically sound? He thinks so, but to make sure he'll have to do some research. Check with an authority, a good psychologist. (We'll discuss the nature and methods of research later in this book.)

Okay, John thinks, we have Sylvia, her husband, Roger, and the two continuing characters, Finn and Ginigen. How do the detectives get involved?

Sylvia is in danger. Someone has tried to kill her—several times. She's frightened. She calls Finn because she knows he is discreet, and she feels she can trust him (How? Well, she met him once six months or so ago at a wedding and was charmed by him), and because she's desperate. What about Ginigen? How can we make him fit into the show? That's the trouble with series TV, John complains to himself—extra characters whom the writer has to squeeze logically into a plot even when there is no reason for them to be there. In this episode he decides to make Ginigen Finn's sounding board—but let's get back to him later.

John Bright, at this point, feels his idea is developing well. But something important is missing: the heavy—the one who wants to kill Sylvia. Why does he want to kill her? Also, what is Sylvia's afternoon life like?

She meets men. Where? Not at her home. At a bar. At the exclusive bar of a top Beverly Hills hotel. Her clients are all wealthy professionals or businessmen. Although they pay her well, she is not doing this for money, but rather to fulfill a deep emotional need, to fill an emptiness inside her.

This is where she met the man who is trying to kill her.

But why does he want to kill her?

(Notice all the "whys." As a writer begins to develop a story, he is constantly searching for and checking the motivation of all the actions of all of his major characters. Remember: In a good plot everything that takes place and everything that your characters do has a reason. But we'll get into this more deeply when we discuss story and plot in Chapter 9 and character in Chapter 10.)

At this point John is in pretty good shape. He has the main characters of his story, the central conflict, the main emotional involvement. He even has the opening scene: Sylvia's life is threatened by someone we don't see (*who* is threatening her is part of the mystery and will not be solved until near the end). Perhaps she's playing tennis at her club and as she finishes and drives back home alone in her sports car through lonely curving mountain passes, a truck follows her ominously, trying to run her down. As she speeds away, her brakes fail and her car goes hurtling down a steep road out of control, finally crashing into a tree. An exciting kickoff, full of action and tension. Who is trying to kill this lovely woman? Why? Has he succeeded? A good "teaser" or "hook" immediately involves the audience and asks the main dramatic questions of the drama.

In scene two we're at a party at Sylvia's home. Among the guests are Finn and Ginigen . . . or perhaps at this point only Finn. Sylvia has called him ostensibly because he's an old friend of Roger's (he could be; perhaps they went to the same college or they were in the army together) but really to ask him to help her . . . without letting her husband in on her precarious situation. The scene ends with Finn taking on the case. His objective is to find out who and why someone is trying to harm/kill Sylvia, to protect Sylvia's life. The deeper mystery, of course, is: Who is Sylvia? Why is she involved in "the life"? How will this discovery affect her relationship with Roger? (At this point, of course, the audience doesn't know what she's involved in—only that she's anxious and that her dealings with Finn are surreptitious. What's going on? Stay tuned.)

In terms of a premise that John can present to the producer, all that is necessary to know at this point beyond what he has already developed is who is trying to kill Sylvia? And why? This, of course, is a fundamental question, for its answer involves the climax—the solution of the plot.

The would-be killer, John decides, must logically be someone Sylvia has met during her secret afternoons at the hotel bar in Beverly Hills. Most likely he'd be a wealthy businessman, a playboy, perhaps. Perhaps he gambles. Perhaps his money comes from illegal sources. Could he be a drug dealer? Why not? Sylvia became involved with him as she has with other men. During one of their "dates" she inadvertently picked up certain information that, in the hands of the police, could destroy this particular lover. She doesn't realize that what she learned was damaging. The would-be killer, however, does. That's why he wants to kill her.

He is stopped, of course. At the climax Finn and Ginigen find out who he is and either kill him or bring him to justice—but at the same time Sylvia's problem and motivation are also uncovered—and she finally faces her relationship with Roger. It will not be a "sweet" ending, but it will offer hope, the possibility that the couple will eventually work out their relationship satisfactorily.

One more step is still necessary before John Bright can present this premise to Walter Hyer. How do his characters and his story fit into the world of 1999?

Perhaps in the opening scene Sylvia is driving a personal space vehicle powered by solar or nuclear energy rather than an old-fashioned automobile. Perhaps the crime of the man who wants to kill Sylvia has nothing to do with drugs. Perhaps it has to do with the smuggling of an exotic twenty-first-century fuel. Perhaps the new family relationships of that time and the changed morality make Sylvia's emotional situation even more precarious than now. How? Well, John will think about that later. He's already developed his idea into a very well-thought-out premise. He hopes that Hyer likes it, because the plot is almost all there, and the teleplay will be a snap to write.

6

Story Conference (1)

Three days after viewing the pilot, John Bright calls the producer of *Naked Stars* for an appointment. By now he has developed three additional premises, none of which he's worked out in as much detail as "Who Is Sylvia?" the one he likes best. As a matter of fact, one of the three is not even a premise at all; it's merely a vague idea that he has no real handle on, and which he'll bring up only if all else has failed—as a last resort.

Although he may make some notes for himself, John will not submit anything on paper at this stage. That would be "speculative writing"—an act prohibited by Writers Guild of America rules, subject to disciplinary action and/or a stiff fine. This rule was created some years ago to protect professional writers from a certain type of ruthless producer who milked the writer's brain, paid him nothing, and used his ideas for his own (the producer's) advantage. Or the producer would ask a number of writers to come in with their ideas or premises written out without informing any of them that he was doing this. Then he'd pick out the idea he liked—which meant that the writers whose ideas were rejected had worked for nothing. (As explained in the previous chapter, however, the novice is well advised to write out his premise, for his own benefit.)

John Bright arrives at the studio the following Wednesday. There is a visitor's pass at the main gate in his name. The guard tells him where to park and points out the location of Walter Hyer's office.

The studio or lot contains offices, barnlike sound stages, projection rooms, editing rooms, costume and scenery rooms—everything necessary to produce motion pictures for theatrical or television viewing.

John drives to the parking area, locks his car, finds his way into a small building nearby, and enters Hyer's office at precisely 10:00 a.m., the time set up for the story conference. Hyer's secretary provides him with coffee and this morning's copies of the trades while he waits; then, even before he's had time to read the first page, the buzzer sounds and John is shown into Walter's ballroom-size office. Both producer and editor welcome him graciously, make him comfortable, and give him their full attention. Bill Picker will be taking notes.

Well, what does he have?

The Art of Spitballing

John now relates his first story idea or premise—"Who Is Sylvia?"—as clearly and as interestingly and with as much enthusiasm as he can. This process, which in television vernacular is called *spitballing* or *pitching,* is usually crucial to the selling of an idea, the first step toward writing a teleplay. Any writer who wishes to be successful in television must develop the ability to tell a story orally, simply, getting to the point in as few words as possible. Often writers who can speak well, who can improvise rapidly, get more assignments than their sometimes more talented colleagues who don't have this ability. This salesmanship may, in a sense, have nothing to do with the art of dramatic—or any other kind of—writing. Nevertheless, in the collaborative world of television (and motion pictures as well), it is fundamental.

And it can be learned. It can be learned through practice. I require my students to submit their ideas and premises orally exactly as in studio procedure. After a while, even the shyest students become proficient. For those learning on their own, I suggest the use of a tape recorder. Talk your story into the recorder, then play it back. See if it makes sense, if it is clear, if it still intrigues you. Try to be objective. Play the tape—or better, tell your story to a friend. Does it interest him? Does he want to know what happens next? Does your listener understand your story? Does it seem logical?

Does the end satisfy? Do this over and over. As with everything, practice makes perfect.

In order to tell your story well, it first must be clear in your own mind. Are your main characters real, well motivated, believable? Is the opening of the story exciting; does it immediately arouse the listener's interest? Is the central conflict well focused? What about the resolution and the general structure of the narrative? Does it hang together—even if most of the scenes are still missing? These points will be discussed in forthcoming chapters.

Quibbles

After John finishes, both Hyer and Picker ask questions about his premise. Both can see how Finn gets involved in the story, but if he's a friend of Roger's, why would Sylvia trust him with her case? If Roger found out, her marriage would be on the rocks. Also, the company is paying the actor who plays Ginigen a lot of money . . . certainly not to stand around with egg on his face. What does he do? What is his role in the solution of the mystery? Also, it's a good idea to put the leads in jeopardy, especially in a detective show. It makes for audience involvement. Where and how are Finn and Ginigen in jeopardy? Sylvia is interesting but a fuzzy character at this stage. Is she or isn't she psychotic? How can she not be if she's completely blocked out the memory of one-half of her daily life? Furthermore, the climax doesn't seem quite clear. And finally, this seems like a contemporary detective story, not one set in the future.

John thinks all these objections are quibbles. He answers them as best he can, talking swiftly, elaborating on what he's already told them, improvising, and trying to sound even more enthusiastic. This is a story he'd love to do. He has strong feelings about it and knows he can write the hell out of it. But Walter and Bill refuse to be impressed.

It is not because they don't want to be. They want a script from John almost as much as John wants to provide them with one. Hyer's job is to get thirteen good teleplays, the best ones he can. His own career depends upon his ability to do this. He knows that John can write the kind of script he wants. But he objects to this premise, though he agrees that it might work out into an interesting script, because he doesn't feel (a) it's the kind of thing the network will wax enthusiastic over, or (b) that it has what it takes to attract a large enough audience.

Anything else?

John narrates his second premise.

More questions, more discussion—but still the reaction is less than favorable.

Hyer looks at his watch and begins to rise and politely dismiss John, suggesting that if he comes up with another notion to give him or Bill a ring. John, already on his feet and halfway to the door, desperately blurts out his final premise—which is not really a premise but a fragmentary, half-formed concept dealing with the murder of a ninety-seven-year-old philosopher by a computer that is the leader of a youth cult of the future. Actually, the idea is so wild and so poorly thought out that John is almost too embarrassed to mention it. But he has to take this gamble because if he doesn't, the first thirteen scripts will probably be assigned before he has a chance to come back again with several newly developed premises—and all his thinking and planning will have gone down the drain.

John scarcely waits for Hyer or Picker's reaction, since he's sure it'll be negative. Instead he thanks them for listening to him, reaches unhappily for the doorknob, and is about to depart, when suddenly the two men call him back.

Their interest clearly has been aroused. They push him into his seat. Now they don't simply ask questions, they express ideas. Creative sparks begin to fly.

Great youth-age conflict, says Hyer, beaming. I know just the actor for the part of the old philosopher.

Man, you sure hit on something, having a computer lead the young punks, Picker fairly shouts.

Right. Computers—machines—express kid-thinking exactly, Hyer adds.

But we've got to have an interesting murder, Picker goes on.

Could be disguised. The authorities don't realize it's a murder. After all, the philosopher is ninety-seven years old.

Right. But he's got a daughter . . .

A granddaughter.

A granddaughter, Picker agrees, who doesn't accept his death as natural.

She calls in our boys.

Finn thinks she's a flake . . . like everyone else.

But Ginigen digs her.

She's young, beautiful, sexy, scatterbrained . . .

But not really—or how could she suspect murder when nobody else does? Hyer asks.

Right. She's really brilliant. Listen, Walter, do you think the network'll accept an affair between her and Ginigen?

I'll call them and find out.

John's eyes swing back and forth from Walter to Bill as the two excitedly build the elements of a story from his vague notion. He attempts to make a few weak contributions of his own, but is politely ignored. Paper and pencil are shoved at him. Soon he's the one making furious notes.

An hour later the conference is over. Does he think he's got everything? Hyer asks. Maybe we should've taped it.

No, it's okay, John says. I've got enough.

Do you like it? Bill wants to know. Do you feel good about it?

John grins as enthusiastic a yes as he can muster—but inside he has doubts. What they improvised doesn't seem half as exciting or well thought out as his own first premise, "Who Is Sylvia?" But if this is what they want, he'll do his damnedest to make it work.

Okay, great, the producer is saying. But don't start writing yet. He'll get back to John this afternoon or first thing in the morning. He's got to check with the network for approval. Always a problem with a new series. But he's sure they'll like it.

Man, they'll love it, Picker agrees, laughing. It's gonna be a great show.

John shakes hands with Hyer and Picker, thanks them again and leaves feeling good, but still not quite sure he has an assignment.

The Deal

The phone rings that evening while John is eating dinner. It's his agent telling him he just got a call from "the dealmaker," an executive who handles financial matters at the studio, and that he has a contract.

Then the network okayed it, John mutters.

I don't know what you're talking about exactly, but they must've. . . . The details are standard, so we don't have to negotiate terms. All I can advise is, write a good script.

Don't I always . . . ? John's laugh is a little hollow.

Right, the agent snaps. Get back to you later.

John slowly and thoughtfully replaces the receiver, but immediately the phone rings again. This time it's Walter Hyer.

Did your agent call you?

I just hung up.

When can you get the story in?

Well, I don't know . . .

Listen, John, we've worked together before and you know I don't like to put pressure on my writers. Normally all I ask for is a great script. Usually I'm willing to wait. But this time I'm under the gun myself. I want the script great, but I also want it fast. The network's got a lot going on this show. It's the Wednesday night lead-in.

As Walter is talking, John's mind is working. Two weeks, he suggests.

How about ten days? Walter responds. The whole thing's practically worked out.

I'll try.

Do it, Hyer says. I've got you down for April first, ten days plus one weekend from now. Okay?

Okay. John's voice is weak.

Good. I'm counting on it.

The Contract

John Bright has a firm deal to write an episode for the new series *Naked Stars*. What does that mean? It means that he is contractually bound to perform certain writing services for which he will receive a set amount of money. Every time anyone writes anything for television, a contract is involved, legalizing a previously negotiated verbal deal. (In episodic television the writer receives a standard fee, negotiated between the WGA and the producers' organization in the same way that contracts are negotiated in any union-company situation. Movies for television, specials, etc., however, are negotiated individually between the writer's representative and the company. Although there are minimums, fees vary widely depending upon the reputation of the writer. These will be discussed in detail later in the book (see Appendix E). Usually the writer does not receive or sign the contract until well after the deal is made, often not until he's almost finished with his script. Nevertheless, when an oral deal is made in the TV-motion picture industry, it is binding on all parties.)

But what, specifically, does the contract say? What is John required to do? What writing services will he have to perform? And what will be his compensation?

As of this writing,* a professional writer such as John Bright should receive $14,318 for the script of a sixty-minute episodic, high-budget television film (one in which the negative costs—or production costs—equal or exceed $52,250). He would also receive residuals amounting to 100 percent of the applicable minimum for each "in season" airing of the program. For "out of season" reruns—the period from May 5 to August 31—compensation is 80 percent of the applicable minimum if the program is shown on prime time. Residuals continue for the writer on a sliding scale—10 percent of minimum after the eleventh showing and only 5 percent after the thirteenth.

*February 1985

But John Bright doesn't receive this money all at once. Nor does he write the teleplay all at once. He writes and receives payment in installments.

This is called a *step-deal*. The installments are the steps in both payment and writing. Most freelance writing assignments in television are step-deals.

According to the contract, after the premise is approved the writer must first write an outline (also called a *story*, or *treatment*). This is a scene-by-scene narration of the development of the story, usually written in the present tense. The treatment indicates action and the substance of essential dialogue, but no actual dialogue is used. It describes the characters, their relationships and motivations, and indicates the locations of all the scenes. It usually runs from about eight to twenty pages or more double-spaced, though there is no set length. (A *step-outline* may sometimes be required. This is a shorthand version of the same thing, a scene-by-scene breakdown of the treatment in which each scene is described in a sentence or two.)

Clearly this first step is by far the most difficult part of the assignment, since a good treatment is, in essence, the script without camera directions and dialogue. And as the nineteenth-century French playwright, Eugene Scribe, once said, "When my story is good, when my scenario is clear and complete, I might have my play written by my janitor!" The people who employ the writer know this only too well and have arranged it so they pay about one-third of the total price of the script, $4,959, for what invariably turns out to be the major portion of the work.

John Bright will work hard constructing this treatment. The fact that the producer and story editor have concocted a rough story for him has not made it easier. If anything, it has made the job more difficult. The next morning when John analyzes his notes, he finds that the exciting improvisations of Hyer and Picker contain some major holes. Next, he knows he has to write a story that will satisfy a concept visualized in someone else's head. In other words, he might turn in a very good treatment that, nevertheless, could be rejected because it does not conform to an image the producer had in his mind. This inhibits John's creativity. He's like a good tennis player who is psyched-out and loses to an inferior opponent. Sometimes, in the course of constructing and writing, he becomes angry and asks himself why he's in this miserable business which everyone outside it seems to consider so glamorous. At moments he's ready to chuck the whole deal. But because he's basically a sensible fellow who has a family to support, he will complete his assignment on time, hand it in, and then start to worry. Because the producer, or the executive producer, or the network people may not like what he wrote and reject it for any number of reasons, which would mean that John is "cut off" at story. That is, he is paid for the treatment, but that's all. The option to write the script—included in the contract—is not taken up. In monetary terms he's lost the opportunity to make another $6,500 or so, plus residuals that would add up to another $10,000, plus the opportunity of having a sole credit on the air, plus the chance to possibly write another script—and perhaps more—for the series, plus a loss of face where Hyer, Picker, and everyone else connected with the show are concerned . . . and a good chance that none of them would want to hire him again, at least in the near future.

Thus John has cause for anxiety. The rejection of this treatment and a consequent cutoff could be, if not disastrous, a serious blow to his ego, his fortunes, and his career.

Dramatic Construction

Before we go any further with John Bright as he racks his brain trying to complete his treatment for an episode of *Naked Stars*, let's step back a bit and consider his overall objective: the writing of the entire teleplay.

So far, with the "help" of his producer and editor, he's developed an idea, or premise. Now, based upon that premise, he's writing a treatment. Only after that treatment has been approved will he be granted an option to write a teleplay.

Do you, the new writer—not bound by any contract—have to go through these same steps?

No law, no edict says you must. But most dramatic writers for the theater in the past and most professional television writers today would strongly advise you to. I certainly would.

Why?

To answer that question we're going to discuss *dramatic construction*—which, after all, is the heart of this book and which is what we've been alluding to throughout.

TV as Theater

We have defined a teleplay as a dramatic story written to be performed on television.

We've also said that *television is theater.* It is not an outdoor amphitheater like that of ancient Athens, nor the "wooden O" indoor playhouse that Shakespeare wrote for, nor the one with the constricted picture-frame stage that dominated Europe and America during the last century. It is electronic; its audience is everywhere, in homes throughout the nation and the world; and it's changing rapidly. But we must always keep in mind that television is theater. Thus, the men and women who write for TV are dramatists. Just as Sophocles was and Shakespeare, just as Ibsen and O'Neill and Tennessee Williams. It follows naturally then that some of *the same ingredients that make a good play must also go into a good television script.*

It follows further that there are common approaches and practices that dramatists have found to be successful in the past which can also work for the television dramatist today.

What are some of these approaches and practices? What ingredients make a good play? A good teleplay?

Let us remember, first, that a television drama—all drama—appeals to the emotions, not to the intellect—at least not basically. George Pierce Baker, the great teacher of playwriting at Harvard and Yale, described a play as the "shortest distance from emotions to emotions." The emotions to be reached are those of the audience. The emotions conveyed are those of the people on the stage—the actors—or of the dramatist.

Secondly, let us not forget that a television dramatist tells his story basically through what his characters *do* and what they *say*. A teleplay contains only dialogue and a description of the action—plus certain camera and sound directions. (Through pictures, however, it is possible to show a character's thoughts—to a limited degree, memory—in flashbacks, and even events that will happen in the future, in flashforwards. Later some of these cinema techniques will be explained in some detail.)

Remember: Dramatic writing is not the same as narrative or descriptive writing. A playwright approaches his task from a perspective very different from that of a novelist, short story writer, or essayist. He also has different objectives.

Writing for television is, in essence, a collaborative effort. We've already seen how, from the very inception of the idea, the writer is involved with others (producer, editor) in developing that idea. But even after the script is complete, others may revise and change it. Furthermore, a director, a cameraman, actors, and many technicians will interpret it so that it will have become, by the time it is on the tube, not quite what the original writer conceived. Sometimes it will be better. More often, not as good. But always it will be different, to one degree or another. Furthermore, there is the audience. The audience is part of the collaboration—a fundamental part. Without it there is nothing.

The primary goal of a play, said William Gillette, a popular American playwright, actor, and theatrical manager whose career spanned the early decades of this century, is to "seize and hold the interest, sympathy and admiration of an audience. Otherwise, no matter how admirable its basic idea, no matter how well the author knows life and humanity, it will fail and be worthless; for a play is worthless that is unable to provide people to play to. . . ."

George Pierce Baker, among whose students was Eugene O'Neill, agreed. The common aim of all dramatists, he said, is first "to win the attention of the audience"; and second "to hold that interest steady or, better, to increase it till the final curtain falls."

The reader of a novel may lose interest or become bored and skim or skip pages. He may set the book down at any time and return to it later. He may take days, weeks, even months to finish the story. There is no hurry. While reading he may look into space or close his eyes and think about something else.

If the audience in a theater loses interest or becomes bored, the play fails. The result is disaster for everyone. Every playwright is aware of this danger and constantly struggles to avoid it.

For the television writer, holding and keeping the interest of his audience is, if anything, more important and more difficult. We've already discussed the relative ease with which a person in front of a TV set can push a button and change a channel. We know what happens when ratings fall. We also know that *to write a script which will attract and hold an audience requires craft, technique.*

Construction and Planning

What does craft involve? How does John Bright actually go about writing his script?

John would say that, unlike the novelist, he *constructs* his script rather than writes it, at least in the early stages. He might even say that the construction is more important than the actual writing (if by that is meant writing the dialogue and action and camera directions). Or he might modify that extreme statement and agree finally that writing a television script *is* constructing it.

Aristotle described the playwright as an artificer, a highly skilled craftsman. To him a play was not written, it was wrought. He referred to the dramatist not as an author, but as a "poet or maker . . . a maker of plots."

Making a plot means building a structure. This implies *planning*.

A novelist sometimes begins a book without knowing where he is going. He may, having no more than a mere idea of what his story will be about or who the characters are, sit down at his desk and start writing. Walter Scott and George Sand were famous novelists who wrote that way. A more recent example is Thomas Wolfe, author of *Look Homeward, Angel.* (Wolfe studied with George Pierce Baker at Harvard but could never learn to write a play—because he could not construct or plan.)

A television writer may also begin with nothing more than a character he may want to write about or an incident that appeals to him. But before he starts writing one word of dialogue, he must work out the dramatic significance of that character or incident. He must conceive, invent, motivate his characters and incidents into a logical progression, a story or plot. He must develop a plan.

Most of the work, the most important work, involved in writing a drama (whether for stage, film, or television) is developing the plan.

"A plan is to a play what it is to a house," said Eugene Scribe, the most commercially successful playwright of nineteenth-century France, the Neil Simon of his day, who was instrumental in creating the concept of *the well-made play.* He continued:

A dramatic story must first of all be *clear*. Without a plan there can be no clarity. *It must proceed without a stop to a defined goal.* Without a plan such a progression is impossible. A dramatic story must assign to each character his proper position; each action must be placed at an exact point. Without a plan there can be no due regard to proportion. Each scene must not only be the logical outcome of the scene which preceded it and be integral with the one which follows it, but it must transmit its own momentum to the next scene so as to push it forward without interruption and in that way to reach, stage by stage, the final goal, the denouement or climax.

The plan, as Scribe describes it, is, in TV terms, the outline, or story, or treatment.

The treatment is the most crucial step in the construction of the teleplay.

It is completed *before* the writer begins writing the dialogue.

It is not only the most important but the most difficult part of the overall task.

It contains the essential form and structure—the complete skeleton—of the teleplay.

How John Bright actually creates his plan, or treatment, in specific terms, how he works with and uses the basic blocks—scene, development, character, climax—that make up his final structure will be dealt with at length in forthcoming chapters. But at what point does he begin? Does he start his outline at the beginning, with scene one?

When we talk about constructing the outline, we're talking about the construction of the teleplay itself. This never follows any apparent rule of logic. The writer may have a character or a setting or an incident that has impressed him. Or, as John Bright had when he began to think about *Naked Stars,* he may have a couple of continuing characters and a particular kind of action they're going to be involved in, a suspense-detective story set in the year 1999.

Constructing a premise is integral with constructing a treatment. The treatment, or outline, is merely a further, more detailed extension of the premise.

In John Bright's original premise, after he has his main character or characters—in this case Finn and Ginigen, who are part of the package, and Sylvia, whom he created—he searches for an *action,* a *dramatic action.* The kind of series he's writing for demands suspense, mystery. Thus, there must be a murder, or a threat of murder—someone is in jeopardy. In John's first story it is Sylvia. Finn and Ginigen, recruited to find out who wants to kill Sylvia and why, try to forestall her death. Who wants to murder Sylvia will become clear at the climax of the story.

Finding the Focus

John's next step, as he works with his characters and situation, fumbles for scenes, and tries to create real relationships that hang together in some sort of logic, is to find the *focus* of the story. This will be the *solution of the mystery* of who wants to kill Sylvia and why. The solution of the story will be revealed in a *climactic scene* in which the intended murderer is uncovered by one or both of our detectives.

Eugene Legouvé, a playwright-critic and colleague of Scribe who also participated in the creation of the "well-made play,"* insists that

> One of the first laws of the dramatist's art is to make the dénouement   the logical and enforced consequence of the characters and/or events of the play. *The last scene of a play is often written (conceived) before the first,* because till that last scene has been found there is virtually no play, and as soon as the author has got his dénouement   he must not lose sight of it for a moment; he must subordinate everything else to it.

In 1878 Henrik Ibsen opened his notebook and scribbled a few notes for a new play, as follows:

> NOTES FOR A MODERN TRAGEDY.
> There are two kinds of spiritual law, two kinds of conscience, one in man and another, altogether different, in woman. They do not understand each other; but in practical life the woman is judged by the man's law, as though she were not a woman but a man. The wife in the play ends by having no idea of what is right or wrong; natural feeling on one hand and belief in authority have altogether bewildered her . . .
>   . . . She has committed forgery and is proud of it; for she

---

* The *well-made play* is a method of dramatic construction originally created by a group of French playwrights in about the second and third decades of the nineteenth century to attract and please an easily bored middle-class audience whose increasing prosperity and mediocrity demanded artificial and brittle theatrical entertainment and diversion. This technique, perfected by its practitioners to a high polish and used mainly to reinforce conventional and shallow but popular attitudes in the boulevard theater, was transformed later in the century by Ibsen into a vehicle of power and poetry. The *well-made play* method of construction has been the mainstay of the commercial theaters of Broadway and London's West End at least since the end of World War I. It has also been the basis of most Hollywood films and network television drama. But there have been counterpressures from experimental and innovative American dramatists since at least the time of Eugene O'Neill, and in Europe long before that.

did it out of love for her husband, to save his life. But this husband with his commonplace principles of honor is on the side of the law and looks at the question from the masculine point of view . . .

The play, of course, into which Ibsen developed these notes, was *The Doll's House.* More than a year would pass before the play was completed, but already he was feeling for the end, the climax, the inevitable result of his basic concept.

So with John Bright. As he begins to think about his characters and story, he is already searching for a solution, or climax. He wants to find it as soon as possible because, as Legouvé says, until he finds it he has no play. Who wants to kill Sylvia? Why?

The person trying to kill her is a drug dealer, a man probably into other areas of crime as well. Certainly a man like this could logically inhabit the world where Sylvia dispenses her favors. As a matter of fact, it is very likely that he'd hang out at the bar of the hotel that is her base of operations. He's met Sylvia. In the course of the teleplay we learn that he has discovered she has inadvertently picked up information that could ruin him. What does she know? Something to do with drugs. The time and place of a shipment. How did she find it out? While making love to him in his office one day, she overheard a cryptic phone conversation. She doesn't understand the meaning of the conversation, but it haunts her.

Finn and Ginigen, our brilliant detectives, finally and not without difficulty, decipher the conversation and, in a dramatic scene, save Sylvia and capture or kill the drug dealer. That scene is the climax. It is the solution of the drama, the focus of the plot. From this point John Bright works backward, motivating his characters so that they fit logically into that climax.

The actual construction is never as simple and clear and sensible as all that. It's a painful job of juggling and changing and crossing out and going down the wrong path and then having to do it all over again, and still finding out it's wrong. But this is essentially the process. These are the kinds of steps the writer consciously or unconsciously looks for.

In another chapter we will explore the climax in all its aspects, but for now all we need to know is that it is the focal point of the teleplay, its principal part, the scene that is conceived by the writer as soon as possible when he begins the work of constructing his drama. Once the climax has been determined, the direction of the story's movement becomes clear. Everything in the story becomes subordinated to it.

When John Bright finds his climax, the solution to the puzzle of who has been trying to kill Sylvia and why, he now works backward to develop and motivate the preceding action toward this point. Everything in the story will relate to and lead toward the climax. Someone is trying to kill Sylvia, right from the opening. She calls our detectives in order to protect herself. She can't call the police or tell her husband, because if he knew what she did every afternoon it would destroy her marriage. She loves her husband. She wants to protect her marriage. This adds to the pressure she's under. But what she does every afternoon relates to both her relationship with him and her own nature. *Who is Sylvia, What is she?* is the real mystery of our drama. It relates directly to the reason she lives the kind of life she does and has put herself in danger. The solution to the mystery of the plot becomes integral to the solution to the mystery of her character. When one is solved, so is the other.

Everything in a good script is related. Everything fits together like the mechanism of a fine watch. All nonessentials have been discarded.

To sum up: John begins to construct his teleplay by constructing, from a character or an incident or a setting that interests him, first a premise, then a plan, or treatment.

In developing his premise, in constructing the treatment, the first thing he tries to find, as he works with his characters and thinks about the situations and conflicts they will go through, is the climax. This takes time, is never easy. Often the first few climaxes the writer finds turn out to be false.

But after he finds his climax, where does he open his drama? What is the first scene?

Can he start anywhere?

To answer this question, we must now examine the concepts of *story* and *plot*.

Story and Plot— Causality

"I n drama," said E.M. Forster, "all human happiness and misery does and must take the form of action. Otherwise its existence remains unknown, and this is the great difference between the drama and the novel."*

To put it another way, in a drama—in a television play—all the characters' emotions result from some sort of action. They do not spring from a secret life in which there is no external evidence, as is possible in a novel. The characters of a teleplay can't just sit there and think or remember or fantasize as they do in a novel. They must *act*.

Plot versus Story

A story, according to Forster, is "a narrative of events arranged in their *time sequence*.

"A plot is also a narrative of events, the emphasis falling on *causality*."

He gives examples: " 'The king died and then the queen died' is a *story*.

" 'The king died and then the queen died *of grief*' is a *plot*" (all italics mine).

---

*Forster, the author of *A Passage to India, A Room with a View*, and other distinguished novels, discussed his profession in a series of lectures at Trinity College, Cambridge, in 1927; these lectures were later collected in a book entitled *Aspects of the Novel*. Although he spoke primarily on writing the novel, several of his ideas are of crucial importance to the television dramatist.

In a plot, there is a *reason* for what happens. There is a reason for the death of the queen, a cause-and-effect relationship between the death of the king and queen. This causality—grief (love?)—connects the king and queen.

Forster continues: "Or again, 'The queen died, no one knew why, until it was discovered that it was through grief at the death of the king.' This is a plot with a mystery in it, a form capable of high development."

Looking at it from another point of view, he asks us to think about the death of the queen. If it's a *story,* we ask what happens next? If it's a *plot* we ask *why* it happens. That *why* is the fundamental difference.

An audience for a *story* is merely *curious.*

A *plot* demands from an audience both *memory and intelligence.*

In terms of drama, a *story*—using Forster's definition, that is, a sequence of events *not* connected by causality—is *episodic,* as, for example, *The Arabian Nights.* The narrator of each story, or night, merely relates a series of fantastic events unconnected by any sense of logic or causal relationships. Coincidence and accidents proliferate. The narrator begins and ends each episode almost arbitrarily. The reader is held merely by curiosity.

Long experience has proven that, in the theater or on television, episodic plays do not work. They do not hold an audience. An audience in a theater will usually become bored with a drama of this type and walk out (mentally, if not physically) long before it is over. And the television viewer will switch to another channel.

Why?

Because curiosity is not enough.

A theatrical or television audience needs some sort of suspense or mystery to hold its interest—even if the suspense or mystery is merely, What's going to happen at the end? How will it all work out?

Suspense, mystery—drama—requires plot. The element of causality helps to give a television script structural unity. It is the glue that holds any kind of play together.

The Causal Connection

Let us consider Forster's example of a plot, "The king died and then the queen died of grief," once more.

It's a plot because there is a causal connection between the deaths of the king and queen. The queen died *because* the king died. The *cause* of her death was *grief.*

Let us suppose that this is a premise for a teleplay, or the first step in the development of a premise. It has the basic structure. The opening scene might dramatize the death of the king. But let's take it another step and suppose he's not a king but an ordinary man, a salesman.

How, in that opening scene, does he die? Under what circumstances?

If he's a salesman, a traveling salesman let us say, it would be logical to suppose that he might be driving somewhere. Perhaps he's driving along a highway to an appointment with an important client. He's late and is driving fast, beyond the speed limit. Suddenly he hears a police siren, panics, and is stricken with a heart attack. The car goes out of control and crashes. The salesman is killed.

To make this opening scene more believable, the writer will motivate the anxiety of the salesman, his reason for speeding, and the smashup. One way to do this is to develop his character. He's a nervous, anxious man. His financial situation is precarious. His job is in jeopardy. He's had a previous heart attack, or at least warnings. He's extremely law abiding, suffering from a guilty conscience about something, the police frighten him—all of which will be revealed *later* during the course of the play. (In other words, action becomes character and character, action.)

If the salesman (the king) dies in the first scene, the leading character, the protagonist, must be his wife (the queen).

Now let's skip to the final scene, the climax, which might take place some weeks or months later. In Forster's example, the queen— the salesman's wife, the protagonist—dies of grief. Unable to cope, she takes her own life or perhaps dies of a broken heart (psychologists maintain this is possible). Her death—which must be dramatized—results, directly or indirectly, from her husband's death. The drama would show her struggle to try to survive, to exist without him. That struggle can take various forms and go in various directions, depending upon the ingenuity and imagination of the writer. Whatever obstacles she may overcome, she finally fails; and *why* she fails is what the story is really all about. Not merely the incidents of the drama but her character will have to be examined thoroughly. However, having a clear idea of what the climactic scene is, the writer can now work backward, as we saw in Chapter 8. Everything in the teleplay—every scene and character, especially that of the protagonist—will be developed to answer the question dramatized in the climax: Why does the salesman's wife fail to cope? Why does she die? Moreover, there is a causal connection between the opening scene—the husband's death, which sets the plot in motion—and the climax, the wife's death, which resolves it.

That connection is absolute and necessary. When we break that connection, we break the structural unity of the plot, and we're in trouble—unless of course we have the talent of a dramatist like Moliere or Shakespeare or Neil Simon. Sometimes comic brilliance, melodramatic effects, the excitement of the basic material, or acting or directorial genius can overcome structural flaws in a script; but a writer who depends upon any of these elements is swimming in shark-infested waters.

Getting Started

This leads us to our earlier question: If the climax is of fundamental importance in the architecture of any drama and is causally connected to the opening, how do we find the opening?

How and where do we start? Which characters do we involve? What is our first scene? Can we begin arbitrarily, anywhere?

No, we can't. There is nothing arbitrary in a well-constructed teleplay. Every scene, every character is there for a purpose. The opening is especially vital.

The first scene is determined by what takes place in the climax.

The first scene not only sets up the mood and feel of the entire piece, but it presents the dramatic problem. The last scene—or climax—resolves it. (The climax is not always the final scene. Sometimes there is a kind of epilogue, called a *tag*, usually a short scene to wrap up the loose ends of the plot. But normally, once the climax has been reached, the play is over.)

For example, the typical episode of a police or private-eye series usually opens with a crime, or a suspenseful action, often a murder. This scene's purpose is not only to thrust the plot into motion but to grab the audience's attention. Often the scene is played without any, or very little, dialogue. An audience's interest and emotion are more quickly and easily aroused by physical action than by dialogue, especially physical action that also develops the story or illustrates character, or both.

In John Bright's premise, "Who Is Sylvia?" some mysterious person was following Sylvia as she left the tennis club, trying to run her off the road and kill her. Immediately we are intrigued. We see the action. We don't need any dialogue. We want to know who this lovely but overly tense young woman is. Why is someone following her, clearly trying to harm her? Who is it?

The task of the detective—in this case, Finn and Ginigen, the continuing characters—is to find out. This is the struggle or action of the drama. For clearly there is opposition to our heroes' efforts. This opposition creates *conflict*. And *suspense*. Suspense derives at least in part from the puzzle contained in both plot and character. In "Who Is Sylvia?" as in most good melodrama, we see the world through the eyes of the protagonist(s)—in this case, two private eyes who pit their knowledge, intelligence, intuition, bravery, and tenacity against the forces of evil responsible for the crime about to take place.

Often in this type of melodrama the hero is in danger. Often he's led up blind alleys. Usually he goes through intense emotional involvement and physical stress (no matter how "cool" he's supposed to be). A point comes near the end when all seems lost. The odds seem insurmountable. But finally, in an exciting climax (in filmed drama it may well involve a chase), our hero overcomes the opposition and solves the crime. In the process he may win or lose a lover; he may discover something he didn't know about life, society, himself; he may even die (though of course continuing characters never do). But if the show is good, we are satisfied. We've been held, excited, moved—and the mystery set up in the first scene is explained at last.

Of course this is a very simple example.

But in a really superior melodrama of this type, in addition to the basic puzzle—whodunit—there are other mysteries. The question of motives. The mystery of character, as in "Who Is Sylvia?" The mystery of human emotions, even human existence.

A Touch of Mystery

The element of mystery is essential to any plot, and therefore to any drama.

In *Oedipus Rex* a plague has fallen upon the city of Thebes. Its citizens have come to their king beseeching him to find some way to lift the curse that, according to the Delphic Oracle, has been caused by the unpunished murder of Laius, the former king. Who killed him? Oedipus offers rewards to anyone who will reveal the culprit, and he threatens with dire punishment anyone who conceals or protects him.

Thus the great tragedy opens with a mystery: Who killed King Laius? The action of the play—like the plot of any good police or private-eye show—is Oedipus' quest for the slayer. But unlike the pursuit of the detective in search of the criminal, Oedipus' quest, in the words of Francis Fergusson (*The Idea of a Theater),*

> . . . becomes a quest for the hidden reality of his own past; and as that slowly comes into focus, like repressed material under psychoanalysis—with sensory and emotional immediacy, yet in the light of acceptance and understanding—his immediate quest also reaches its end.

In the climax, as we know, Oedipus discovers that the guilty one is himself. And as he cries out in a terrible shriek that echoes across the centuries, he tears out his eyes. Thus the mystery is solved; the curse is exorcised. Thebes is at last free of the plague, and the now blind Oedipus can finally truly see.

As in *Oedipus,* the mystery in *Hamlet* is who killed the former king, Hamlet's father. This is the curse causing the corruption in the state of Denmark. As the play opens, the ghost of Hamlet's father comes to Hamlet in the night and accuses his brother, Hamlet's uncle, the present king, of being the murderer and of also "incestuously" marrying the queen, Hamlet's mother. He demands that Hamlet avenge his death by killing the present false king.

Although *Hamlet* is a much more complicated drama than *Oedipus,* with several subplots, its central action is Hamlet's quest, first to find the truth: Did his uncle truly murder his father and marry his mother? And, if so, second to avenge his father.

At the climax he discovers, through the performance of his play, that King Claudius had indeed murdered his father. Finally his revenge is accomplished, and Hamlet also dies—but in the process the curse is lifted and Denmark, like Thebes, is freed of the evil that had corrupted its soul.

In Peter Shaffer's play *Equus,* Alan Strang, an adolescent boy, has blinded six horses with a metal spike. The play opens as Martin Dysart, a psychiatrist, is called in to find out why. The mystery is one of motivation, of character. What led the boy to do this strange and horribly fascinating thing? Dysart's task is to find out, to solve the mystery. His quest, like that of Oedipus and Hamlet, is a search into the purpose not only of Alan's life and relationships but of his own life and, by implication, of the lives of all so-called intelligent and sophisticated people today—all of us—who are out of touch with the passion and poetry of our own deepest primitive feelings.

In the climax, Alan, under Dysart's treatment, relives the moment when he blinded the horses. In a painful scene that takes place on two levels, past and present, the boy tries but fails to make love to his girl, Jill. Both are in a stable, naked. Jill is more than willing. Alan is unable to make love with her because the horses, which to him have become archetypical images of judging, punishing gods, are watching, their eyes disapproving, their hooves and their weird whinnying terrorizing him. Unable to bear the anguish, Alan finally leaps at the animals and slashes them. And in his hysteria, as he collapses to the floor, attempting to stab out his own eyes as well (shades of *Oedipus*), the pain of his illness is expelled. The dramatic answer to the opening mystery—why he blinded the horses—is revealed. Now, cured, he can achieve a life of normalcy and peace.

Ironically, however, the thematic statement that we expect (implicit in the climax) is reversed. For to Dysart (and the author) normalcy is a kind of slavery. He had respected, even envied, the "sick" Alan who had blinded the horses. Now, made "well," but deprived of his passion, the boy is like a tethered animal, a tamed beast. We have all traded in the ecstasy of belief, of the primitive identification with gods, Shaffer says, for servitude.

Variations on a Theme

We can apply Forster's basic approach in other ways. Instead of a king and queen, or husband and wife, our central characters might be friends, or lovers—anybody. Let's use the example of a father and a son. In the opening scene we find the father breaking down emotionally ("the king dies"). He is divorced or a widower and has recently met a younger woman who has fallen in love with him. She is concerned about him and wants to help him; among other things, she feels she must find out what produced his breakdown. While caring for him she finally learns of his tremendous love for and dedication to his son, a brilliant and attractive boy who was stricken with leukemia and, after a long, terrible illness, died. The father had invested his total emotional life in his son. The boy's death—the final blow in a series of reverses—drove the older man to the point of despair.

This discovery—dramatic revelation—is the climax. The hope, of course, is that the young woman's love for the man will eventually help pull him out of his breakdown/depression. Now, in a reversal of roles, the man who had spent years caring for his son becomes the patient—and his young lover becomes his nurse.

Or, by changing the resolution, the same story could begin earlier. The son is still alive. The father is caring for him. He has met the woman and likes her, but he cannot allow himself to become too deeply involved—even though she loves him—because of the physical and emotional needs of his son. The story opens with the son dying and the father emotionally shattered. He begins to go into a depression. The woman, loving and supportive, struggles to save him, to give him a new purpose and the will to go on. At the climax in a dramatic scene, there is a reversal: She succeeds. Through her love, he is now able to take the first steps back on the long road to health.

In both versions the structure works because the opening scenes clearly set the plots in motion by creating a mystery that is not solved until the climax. In the first version the mystery is: Why is the man suffering? In the second: Will love be strong enough to help pull him out of his depression?

We can use this basic structure, or framework, to build almost any kind of workable plot. The death of the "king" in the first scene does not have to be a real death. It may be symbolic. That is, the person we are presenting doesn't actually die but reaches a point in which he can no longer function in his normal manner. He loses his job.

He leaves his lover or spouse. He abandons his teenage daughter. He changes his lifestyle. In *Streetcar Named Desire,* Blanche arrives in New Orleans to stay with her sister and brother-in-law. In the movie *10,* the protagonist, suffering a middle-age crisis, sees a vision of a young girl. At the opening of "Who Is Sylvia?" Sylvia is almost killed. She cannot go on as before. She must call in outside help. The climax then may result in a symbolic discovery of "life," of affirmation, as in the two examples of father and son cited above, rather than the "death" of the protagonist, the one who has been abandoned.

Or consider a tragic love story, *Romeo and Juliet.* It opens dramatically with two simultaneous lines of action: first, the conflict between the Capulets and the Montagues, and second, the meeting of Romeo and Juliet. The immediate, powerful, overwhelming passion of the two young lovers, unable to find normal fulfillment because of the conflict between the two families, leads causally, through many complications, to the tragic end.

A Balance of Forces

Another way to approach this aspect of structure is to think of the opening scene or sequence as an action that *upsets the prevailing balance of forces* and by so doing sets the drama in motion. In *Romeo and Juliet,* the balance of forces is upset by the meeting and falling in love at first sight of the young hero and heroine. Their object and struggle is to fulfill their love in the face of the violent, bloody family feud that separates them.

In the usual TV medical series drama, the balance is often upset by an illness (analogous to a crime in a police show). As our story opens, for example, a young girl with great talent is training to be a ballet dancer. She seems to have the ability to become a great ballerina. A perfectionist, she is rehearsing hard for her first important performance. The ballet master, her mother, and other students are watching with admiration. Suddenly, whirling on her toes like a lovely bird, she collapses to the floor, her leg limp. Unable to move it, she can feel no sensation. The others crowd around in shock and horror. Thus the opening scene, or teaser, ends and we, the audience, are hooked. The balance of forces has been upset in a riveting manner—and we immediately ask ourselves, What happened? Why?

The mystery deepens in the next scene when the doctor-hero examines the girl and finds nothing physically wrong with her leg.

The upset of the balance of forces leads step by step to the denouement as the doctor investigates the life and character of the patient, including all her relationships. Will she dance again? What's wrong with her? How is her inability to dance affecting the rest of her life?

At the climax, the solution of the mystery is unravelled in a dramatic scene involving both doctor and patient (the protagonist must be involved in the climactic scene). The young dancer has not been able to move her leg and dance because of a deeply buried guilt connected with a long-past tragedy involving her younger sister—also a child dancer—whom she was unconsciously jealous of and whose death she feels she caused. The doctor has, through struggle mainly against the resistance of the patient, brought her to the point where she is able to face her guilt—and, in an emotional resolution, relieves her of it. Now the paralysis is gone. She can dance again, free of her burden. The climax restores the balance of forces, but on a new level.

But remember: As the writer begins work on his material the first element he looks for is the climax. Once he finds that he has the focus of his play. Now he can seek incidents, scenes, reasons to justify it.

At the end of *The Doll's House*, Nora, the dependent, childish housewife, leaves her husband, home, and family, an act that shook the foundations of middle-class marriage when the play was first presented. Ibsen's task when he set out to write the play was to justify that act, to show why it took place, dramatically. As the play opens Nora has already taken the first step. She's secretly borrowed money for the benefit of her husband, an act that is contrary to his rigid morality and the accepted morality of that time. This leads *inevitably*—causally—to the resolution. Nor is any character or any action included in the play except to serve the needs of Nora's story and, in the final analysis, to justify the climax.

Arthur Miller, writing about *Death of a Salesman* in the introduction to his *Collected Plays* (1957), says the same thing in another way: "The ultimate matter with which the play will close is announced at the outset and is the matter of its every moment from the first." In fact, all he knew when he began to think about *Salesman* was how it would end.

> The play was begun with only one firm piece of knowledge and this was that Loman was to destroy himself. How it would wander before it got to that point I did not know and resolved not to care. I was convinced only that if I could make him remember enough he would kill himself, and the structure of the play was determined by what was needed to draw up his memories like a mass of tangled roots without end or beginning.

Knowing only the resolution, the playwright could forgo "suspense and climax" and "the usual preparations for scenes"—and still the play would work. He did not have to write a "well-made play" with obvious machinery as he did with his first success, *All My Sons*. He could experiment with form and allow it to emerge from content. Not only would it work on the stage, but it would work brilliantly, because the one element he did not dispense with, no matter how he moved back and forth in time or shifted from reality to imagination, was *causality*.

As Miller was very well aware, the resolution of his play—"its ultimate matter," the climax—is announced at the opening. It is what the play deals with in every scene, at every moment. No character appears who is not involved dramatically in its outcome. The beginning relates causally to the end.

Dangerous Traps

There are two dangerous traps beginners often fall into. They are the opposite of causality: *accident* and *coincidence*.

In a well-constructed television script, nothing is accidental or coincidental.

Accidents and coincidences must be justified dramatically; that is, they must be prepared for, motivated. An automobile "accident," for example, may be motivated by a driver being drunk, or under great emotional tension, or self-destructive. Karl Menninger, in *Man Against Himself,* explores human accident at length and gives many examples for which he finds clear psychological causation. He agrees that, psychologically speaking, there are no accidents. In one of my writing workshops a student was doing a script about a model and her relationship with a photographer with whom she was living. On the eve of an important photographic session she discovered she was pregnant—a situation that could have serious ramifications for both their careers, unless she had an abortion, which was what the story was about. But the immediate question involved her pregnancy. Was it merely an accident? If so, that fact would take away a great deal from the drama, her character, and her relationship with the photographer. In fact, as the story developed, a vital unconscious motivation for the pregnancy was revealed in the climax. This actually made the teleplay work much better and gave it greater depth and impact.

The elimination of causality, whether through accident or coincidence, inevitably reduces believability; once that is gone, you've lost your audience.

Of course there are exceptions. The history of drama is strewn with successes that have broken all the rules. But there are no arbitrary rules. Rules are merely what has worked in practice over a long time for most dramatic writers. The exceptions that work are few and far between. To attempt to write a script for TV, film, or theater without causality—especially for a beginner—is to swim against a current made up of the experiences of most dramatists over the centuries.

10
Character

A s John Bright struggles with his teleplay—or rather the outline or treatment, the *plan* of his teleplay—he is also developing and creating characters.

When we see a good play or film or television drama, we usually remember afterward not the convolutions of the plot or individual scenes, but the characters. Do you remember the plot of *The Merchant of Venice?* Or *King Lear,* or *The Doll's House,* or *Death of a Salesman,* or *A Streetcar Named Desire?* How about *Annie Hall? Breaking Away? Norma Rae?* What about *Holocaust,* or *Roots?* Probably not. But even if you do, you surely remember Shylock and Lear and Nora and Willy Loman and Stanley Kowalski and Blanche DuBois and Norma Rae. You must remember the leading characters in *Holocaust* and *Roots*—the Jewish doctor, the young German husband who became a careerist in the Nazi hierarchy, the black boy kidnapped from Africa and made a slave in America— perhaps the most memorable television dramas of the 1970s.

Chicken or Egg?

How does a television dramatist create and develop his characters?

Does he work out his plot first? Or his characters? Does he sit down at his desk and create a detailed biography of each character from birth to death? Does he attempt to include all the complexities and contradictions that constitute actual people and fit them into his story without change? How does he introduce and reveal a character?

First let's talk about real people. How do we discover the true character of any individual?

By the way he dresses? By what he says? By peculiarities of behavior? One person loves cats. Another enjoys gardening. A third is afraid of heights. A fourth is always jolly. A fifth, nervous.

These aspects of an individual may (or may not) be *clues* to his character. But they do not constitute the character himself. For instance, how a person speaks and what he says may actually hide rather than reveal his true self. A loud, macho bully actually may be a coward. A fast-talking comic who's always "on" before an audience may be, in reality, a shy, morose person. Dress also reveals or hides aspects of a man's or woman's true self. Peculiarities of behavior are no more than a facade of the real person.

How, then, does a human being reveal himself? How do we judge a person?

Not by what he says or by the way he looks, but by what he does. By the way he *acts*.

By the way he acts *instinctively and spontaneously in a crisis*.

The same is true of characters in drama—especially television drama. They are revealed to an audience not by dialogue, not by what they say, but by what they *do* and how they *act*—especially *under pressure*.

Aristotle said it first: "All human happiness and misery takes the form of action."

In television drama today—just as in Aristotle's time—character is revealed in action.

Character is action, and *Action is character.*

What does that mean in the creation and construction of a teleplay?

It means that the characters are not preconceived. They evolve as the plot evolves, out of the main incidents of the story. They grow and change in accordance with the demands of the plot. At the same time, however, the characters affect and change the plot. In other words, as John Bright constructs his outline, he is also searching for reasons—motivations—for the actions of his characters in order to make them fit believably into his plot. In the creative process of dramatic construction there is a constant interaction between the development of the characters and the development of the plot.

When John Bright conceived of his main character, Sylvia, he placed her in danger. That was necessary in terms of the series he was writing for and the plot he was developing. Someone was trying to kill her. That's why she called in Finn and Ginigen. Why was she in danger? Who was threatening her? Someone she met during an afternoon rendezvous. But in order to motivate Sylvia's other life, John had to characerize her, make her a certain type of person—a person who would go to a hotel bar every afternoon and meet men. But to give her sympathy, John had to find understandable reasons for her doing what she did. How did he do this? As we have seen, he first created a husband, Roger, who was unable to meet her emotional needs. He was rich, involved in business. He gave her things, and kept her in a magnificent mansion—which merely added to her isolation. John still felt he had to develop additional background information for Sylvia to motivate her actions more fully. He had to deepen her character. Sylvia would live in a world of fantasy. She had been abandoned emotionally even as a child. Deprived of warmth all her life, she had powerful needs for emotional fulfillment. She satisfied those needs in the only way she could. Her developing character resulted in her taking actions that affected the plot. But at the same time John carefully motivated her in a specific direction so that she would fit believably *into* the plot.

What Do You Want?

When a writer conceives and builds his character he usually starts with a rough feel of some person, probably someone he's known. As he's developing the incidents of the plot he tries as quickly as possible to find the line, the "spine" of the character, the character's basic direction.

He does this in terms of goals—what the character wants.

Every human being, consciously or unconsciously, wants *something*. There is a goal to everyone's life, whether it's merely that of staying alive or of reaching the top in his career. To be loved, to be rich, to be famous, to be part of a happy family, to be accepted, to be respected—these are general life-goals. They are common not only to characters in life, but to characters in drama. In addition, the characters in our teleplays also want something specific *in terms of the story itself.*

Oedipus wants to find out who killed King Laius. Hamlet wants to find out if his uncle really killed his father and married his mother and, if so, to exact revenge. In a typical television police drama the central character—a police officer or detective—wants to catch the criminal and solve the crime. In a typical medical drama the doctor wants to cure the patient. In *A Streetcar Named Desire* Blanche wants to find a home with her sister, a place of refuge. In *Equus,* Dysart tries to find out why a boy put out the eyes of six horses. In *The Miracle Worker* Annie Sullivan tries to help Helen Keller, blind, deaf, and dumb, to communicate. In John Bright's premise "Who Is Sylvia?" Finn and Ginigen want to find out who is trying to kill Sylvia and why, in order to protect her.

To show more specifically how goals are used to define and develop a character, let's go back once more to our discussion of story and plot, using E.M. Forster's definitions and his example: "The king died and then the queen died of grief." Substituting Bill and Mary, an ordinary middle-aged couple, for "king" and "queen," let us suppose that Bill dies in the opening scene. Mary then would be the protagonist of our plot.

As we develop the plot and the character of Mary from this sketchy framework, first we ask ourselves what Mary wants. What does she want specifically in terms of our teleplay? What is she struggling for?

The moment we ask and try to answer that question we begin to create a character.

For example, if we see Mary as a middle-aged housewife with no skills or training, and if her husband dies without any—or with very little—money, Mary's struggle might be to survive. Her survival would most likely depend upon her ability to find work. She would have to face the job market and the cruel world alone, without any kind of support. Her struggle toward specific goals—some sort of training, her education into the "real world," the conflicts she would face—are not merely the stuff of drama. How she faces and over-comes, or fails to overcome, her obstacles would be a true test of her character. The various incidents or scenes—her confrontation with the job market, with banks and loan agencies, possibly with the threat of eviction from her home, her attitude toward having to pawn valued family heirlooms, the way she handles or mishandles one or more emotional relationships—would all reveal important aspects of her true self.

Action, Struggle, Conflict

Not merely does Mary struggle *for* a specific *goal* but, as we've seen Mary struggles *against* various *obstacles*. Struggle implies the presence of obstacles, most of which will be human. Struggle also implies *conflict*.

Character is revealed *in action, in struggle, through conflict*.

That struggle is intense. In most television series drama the issue is one of life and death.

Whatever the struggle, whether it's life and death or not, as the teleplay progresses, the central character becomes obsessed. His goal becomes overriding, the *only* purpose of his life. Everything else in his existence becomes subordinated to that goal. If we were to abruptly extract the protagonists from the second or third acts of most dramas, we'd have a bunch of raving maniacs on our hands, men and women powerfully, totally obsessed with escaping from a prisoner-of-war camp, finding a mate, getting a part in a play, achieving the next step up the career ladder, avoiding a death threat, becoming a king, winning a battle, escaping the law, saving a loved one's life, winning a husband or wife back to the hearth, or freeing oneself from the domination of parent, teacher, dictator, church, or any of a hundred other forces.

This obsession of the central character takes place in the gentlest of comedies as well as in the most powerful of tragedies.

The *spine*—the central line or direction—of the main character is defined by his struggle or goal, whether he achieves it or not.

The *issue*—will he succeed or not, and how—is solved at the climax. Every scene and incident in the drama leads in a direct, ascending line to the climax. The protagonist's struggle is the force that pushes the action toward the climax.

In a well-constructed teleplay, the spine of the protagonist and the line of the plot coalesce, become one. There is also a dénouement, a climax, a turning point in *both plot and character*. These two climaxes, the one of plot and the one of character, become fused, indistinguishable from each other, one and the same.

Another way to think of this struggle of the central character toward a climax is to imagine him having a "blind spot." This blind spot, or false goal, is removed in the climax. Something he was not aware of, something he didn't see or realize before—that the clue he overlooked is the vital one, that love is more important than success, that money isn't worth all this struggle—is revealed. Now, in the most intensely emotional scene of the play, as he comes face to face with whatever he's been struggling against, the issue finally comes into focus. In other words, the main character is always pursuing a false goal. He cannot, or refuses to, psychologically recognize it until he is forced to by the logic of the drama in the climax. (See Chapter 13.)

Maxwell Anderson, one of America's leading, most prolific, commercially successful playwrights during the 1930s and 1940s, puts it this way:

> The mainspring in the mechanism of a modern play is almost invariably a *discovery by the hero* [protagonist] of some element in his environment or in his own soul of which he had not been aware or which he has not taken sufficiently into account [the blind spot]. . . A play should lead up to . . . a central crisis [climax], and this crisis should consist in a *discovery* [removal of the blind spot] by the leading character which has an indelible effect on his thought and emotion and completely alters the course of the action . . . (italics mine).

Anderson goes on to say that the leading character must make this discovery himself. I would add that he makes this discovery in the climax—which implies that *the leading character must be present in the climax.* A climactic scene invariably includes and involves the protagonist. A climax in which the protagonist is absent is most likely a false climax and should be reexamined.

One and Only One

A television drama should have only one leading character. This means that there is only one central story. All other characters and all other stories (subplots) are used only to answer the demands of and give added meaning to the main character's story.

In John Bright's premise "Who Is Sylvia?" the main character is Sylvia. Every other character was created (except Finn and Ginigen, of course) to help move Sylvia's story along. Roger is there not only to reveal Sylvia's character but to explain why she has to steal away every afternoon. Roger's presence makes it necessary that Sylvia be secretive; it creates urgency for her, and it explains why she has to call the private eyes rather than the police in the first place. And of course the relationship between Sylvia and Roger is the main emotional focus of the story. The detectives are called in by Sylvia to solve the central question of the plot: Who is trying to kill her and why? The drug dealer is essential simply because he was plotting her death. To find him, the detectives must find out about Sylvia's secret life. Their discovery at the end (removal of the blind spot) is who Sylvia really is. Sylvia's blind spot is her inability to see the cause of what she is doing. She discovers (removal of the blind spot) that she herself unconsciously got involved in this kind of life in order to be exposed—to cause a sensation and jar her husband into removing his blinders and seeing her emotional needs for what they really are. Simply, it is a roundabout and desperate way of telling him what is hurting her and what she needs from him.

Make Characters Real

Although television is changing, many of the characters, especially the leads of series, are still heroes. And many of the individuals they're in conflict with are heavies. And many of the plots are melodramatic. How do we make both the hero and heavy in a melodrama exciting and believable human beings? Or as believable as we possibly can?

When creating a heavy, or villain, try to make him important—strong, sensible, persuasive. The more powerful the antagonist, the greater the victory for the protagonist.

Of course, age, sex, occupation, class, and personal idiosyncrasies are all vital. You should know as much as you can about every character in your teleplay, but at the same time don't cling too rigidly to your preconceptions.

Moreover, in introducing your characters, remember that first impressions are important. Usually the core or essence of a character in a teleplay is apparent the first time we meet him. If he's a leading character or the protagonist, that first impression should be a strong one. That, of course, doesn't mean that characters can't change, or that our first impressions can't be wrong. But in either case you must clearly motivate all character changes—and if our first impression is incorrect, you must show us why.

Carlo Goldoni, an important and prolific eighteenth-century Venetian dramatist, said that "in order to bring out a character, I have always thought it necessary to place it in direct contrast with another whose nature is the opposite of it." Contrast is an effective device you should not hesitate to use, where applicable, to define your characters.

Also, always motivate your characters. Why does the heavy act the way he does? Every character, no matter how seemingly evil, is not without his good side and certainly not without a good reason for behaving as he does. Most murderers (unless they're maniacs— and maniacs don't count because they're out of touch with reality and hence make lousy villains; they're okay as evil forces, like a hurricane or a shark or an epidemic, but that's all) have logical, sensible, in a way almost sympathetic reasons for taking a life. In John Milton's epic, *Paradise Lost*, even Satan himself became a real, identifiable character because Milton gave him certain enduring human qualities. Above all, Satan's actions were motivated (unlike the demon in the film *The Exorcist*, who represented pure evil and had no redeeming characteristics).

As for heroes, try not to make them stiff goody-goodies. Find their weaknesses. Find their flaws. Even let them fail sometimes, if possible. Without taking away their heroic stature, allow them to behave as human beings. Motivate your heroes too. Often this is more difficult to do than with villains; villains are usually more interesting. Milton made Satan more interesting than God. Milton's God had no faults. He had no weaknesses. But Shakespeare, whose heroes and villains are almost always interesting, powerful, complex, and above all, believable, rarely failed in this area. His characters have specific goals, and we can understand everything both his heroes and his villains do. For this reason they transcend their heroic or villainous natures and become memorable human characters in their own right.

11
Progression

You should realize as we arrive at this point in our story that John Bright is still building the structure of his teleplay, still working on his outline or treatment.

Not a word yet about dialogue, camera technique, or teleplay format . . . .

We've seen how he develops his plot, the fundamental importance of causation, how he searches for the end, or climax, first. As soon as he finds it, he has his focus: he knows where his story is going. Then he works backwards. We've seen how, in a good plot, the choice of an opening scene is not capricious. It is not an arbitrary decision on the writer's part, but is related causally to the climax. After he has found his climax, the nature and content of his opening scene become almost inevitable.

As John works on his plot, he simultaneously creates and develops characters. The creation of his characters in turn affects, and changes, and develops his plot. We can't talk about characters without talking about plot, or plot without characters. The two concepts constantly overlap because character *is* action *is* plot.

All right then, you have the climax of your still-to-be-written teleplay, the first scene, your central character or characters, the emotional line, a rough feel of and some of the incidents of the plot. But most of it is still missing. How do you make the teleplay progress from scene one to the climax without losing your audience?

Drama is the art of crises. The crises develop through conflict. As the story progresses, each crisis becomes more intense than the preceding one. The last and most powerful crisis is the climax.

This series of mounting crises is perceived by an audience through what the characters in the teleplay do (action) and say (dialogue). In a certain sense action is dialogue, or at least *dramatic action* is dialogue. But neither all speech (dialogue) nor all action is dramatic. We will discuss the dramatic importance of dialogue later, but now let's try to find out when action is dramatic and when it isn't.

Dramatic and Nondramatic Action

Action that brings forth an emotional response in an audience is *dramatic action.*

Dramatic action is human and psychological.

Two cars colliding is *not* dramatic action. But if a man or woman we know is hurt in the accident, or causes the accident, we're involved emotionally and the action *is* dramatic.

A man walking down the street to get a loaf of bread at the supermarket is *not* dramatic.

A man walking down the street to get a loaf of bread at the supermarket for his starving child *is* dramatic.

Idle, unmotivated activity is not dramatic. This kind of action may keep an audience interested for a limited period of time, but if carried on very long it becomes boring.

Action that matters in a television script is dramatic action. It matters because it creates an emotional response in an audience. When people are responding emotionally they are not bored; the story they're watching holds their interest. And that is our goal as television writers.

The Importance of Unity

But dramatic action by itself is not enough. To hold an audience from the beginning of a television play to the end, dramatic action must have *unity.*

"The structural unity of the parts [of a play]," Aristotle said, "is such that if any one of them is displaced or removed, the whole will be disjointed and disturbed. For a thing whose presence or absence makes no visible difference is not an organic part of the whole."

The incidents, the scenes, the crises of a well-crafted teleplay not only contain dramatic action, but these incidents, scenes, and crises relate to each other organically. Causally. The dramatic action has unity.

In order to achieve unity, the writer must select only those incidents that keep the story moving toward the climax, that relate to the main character's struggle toward a predetermined goal. He must eliminate everything else.

"Ask anyone who has crowded too many events into his play what the reason for this fault is," Voltaire wrote. "If he is honest he will tell you he lacked the inventive genius to fill his play with a *single action*" (italics mine).

A single action means there is one main plot, one protagonist, one central conflict, one central emotional line, and one climax, which is the focal point of both the plot and the struggle of the main character.

Thus each incident the writer selects must move the protagonist a step further toward his goal. All other incidents, no matter how exciting or dramatic, must be dispensed with.

In the same way, each of the characters is there only to advance the main character's story. There should be no others. Moreover, *that story will be told largely from the protagonist's point of view.*

A writer writes out of a lifetime of experience, impressions, hearsay, books he's read, films, plays, and TV he's seen, education he's had, and out of his invention and imagination. A dramatic writer must select from these billions of images and sounds and incidents and people one limited group of scenes and characters. He must arrange them into a structure in which they relate causally to each other. He must discard everything else. In the process his incidents and characters will change. They may change radically. They will most likely become transformed, if they're based on reality, into something so different from their original concepts that the new creations will be scarcely recognizable. Sometimes in the process of creation a leading character is eliminated and a minor one becomes a protagonist. Scenes and incidents are shifted, transformed, cut out. The writer keeps backing and filling, plunging into the last part of his teleplay while he's still thinking about the first. If he's done a good job the final product will be more real, with greater depth, than the original concept. It will have reverberations invisible to the casual observer. The final product, moreover, will still contain the essence of the original reality and will be true to the original premise. In other words, the completed drama will comment upon the incidents and characters the writer has *not* included, as well as those he has, and will express a larger truth about the human condition.

A good play on television, screen, or stage is like an iceberg. Most of it is under the surface. We see only the tip.

But *how* does a dramatic writer select, eliminate, condense?

It is a process as difficult as the creation of the characters and the plot. The ability to do it is developed partly from training and experience; the rest comes from intuition and talent.

Perhaps the best way to illustrate the process of selection is to examine the way dramatic writers have handled it in the past.

When Sophocles wrote *Oedipus Rex,* he had, to start with, a complicated story that included many characters and many incidents extending over a long period of time, almost as much narrative material as is contained in a three-decker nineteenth-century novel like *War and Peace.* This story was the myth of Oedipus.

Sophocles' task was to adapt and shape this material into dramatic form. We will discuss adaptation further in Chapter 21, but actually, in a sense, all dramatic writing is adaptation. The writer must select, eliminate, and condense—adapt—from a mass of material (his experiences, his life) only those characters and those incidents that he can develop into a unified plot, which will effectively go toward making up a dramatic story.

How did Sophocles do it?

First, he started his play very close to the end.

When the play opens, the plague has already descended upon the city of Thebes, which Oedipus and Jocasta have been ruling with great success for a number of years.

The action of the play takes less than a day.

Oedipus' goal in the play—his quest, his struggle—is to find Laius' slayer.

In order to do this he questions the Oracle, the prophet and seer Tiresias, and a series of other witnesses, ending with the old shepherd who gave him to the king and queen of Corinth. Each witness and every event withdraws a veil from the past, and almost every scene develops contrary to the expectation of the audience. The events are disclosed in almost complete inverse order to that of the temporal sequence. At the end, Oedipus is unmistakenly revealed as the murderer.

The play is constructed like a contemporary murder mystery. Oedipus is the detective or district attorney, and when he refuses to give up his quest, thrusting ahead against all advice and caution, and at last convicts himself, we have the powerful solution, the climax.

Sophocles selected from the complicated myth only those incidents in Oedipus' life that would, when put together in a certain way, dramatically and inevitably prove that Oedipus himself was the murderer of his father and husband of his mother.

But how did Sophocles know where to place each incident? Why, for instance, didn't he place the scene with the old shepherd first instead of last?

The scene with the shepherd is the final piece of evidence that sums up the "case for the prosecution" against Oedipus. The shepherd's testimony proves that Laius' and Jocasta's son Oedipus didn't die as an infant as everyone believed and therefore could well have done everything that the previous evidence suggests he did, such as murdering his father and marrying his mother. The person who the Oracle said would commit the horrible crime, the son of Laius and Jocasta, was not dead. It was Oedipus himself. Placing the shepherd scene first would have been like telling an audience watching a modern murder mystery who the murderer is before the end. There'd be no further reason for the audience to remain in the theater.

When Sophocles knew his climactic scene, the solution of the mystery, he had his opening: the citizens of Thebes beseeching their king to find some way to rid them of the plague. Oedipus enters to reassure them, and we hear through the report of the Delphic Oracle that the cause of the plague is the unpunished murder of Laius, the former king. Oedipus promises his people that he will uncover the criminal and free them from the mysterious disease.

These first brief scenes immediately establish the situation, introduce the protagonist, and tell the audience all it needs to know clearly, succinctly, and dramatically.

The Art of Exposition

Planting information in the audience concerning the characters and events that have taken place in the past, before the curtain rises, before the scene fades in, is called *exposition.*

Because most modern plays take place in a limited period of time and space, exposition has become an art, reaching perhaps its highest peak in the works of Ibsen.

The modern dramatist's problem (it was also Sophocles') is often to impart a great deal of necessary past information to an audience but at the same time not to bore it. Ibsen's solution was to keep the drama moving and the plot developing while he subtly dropped pieces of information here and there—all the necessary facts.

Exposition is less important to the television dramatist because most television plays begin much further from the end and cover much more space (many locations or scenes) than do modern plays written for the theater. Consequently, the TV writer has much less of a load of previous information to convey.

When exposition does become necessary, the television writer should try to make it seem natural, to let the facts emerge indirectly out of conflict and character relationships. In addition, he should use every possible visual device he can. (See Chapter 16 for a discussion of film and other visual techniques.)

Let's see how exposition is used in series television.

Most television episodes, as we've suggested earlier, start with an action that sets the story in motion.

In the first scene of John Bright's premise "Who Is Sylvia?" Sylvia is followed in her car by a mysterious small truck. She is almost killed as she speeds away down a mountain pass and crashes when the brakes fail to function.

This opening scene immediately involves the audience in an action. Now that he's got the audience's attention, the author must reveal what the situation is, what's happened up until now—and he must introduce his other main characters dramatically. How does he do it?

In the next scene John Bright has Sylvia invite Finn and Ginigen to a small party in order to explain her predicament. Since Finn and her husband, Roger, were in the army together and knew each other well, she has an excuse to invite the detectives that will not arouse

Roger's suspicion. During the party she will surreptitiously take Finn aside and nervously tell him just enough to involve him. He of course will in turn question her about the facts in the case, why she's called him rather than the police, and why she must keep everything secret from her husband. Thus this exposition will emerge naturally, out of a real situation, with dramatic tension and suspense.

In the story we developed out of Forster's concept, "the king died and then the queen died of grief," the "king" became, in our version, a traveling saleman who smashed his car in the opening scene and was killed.

Scene two would probably take place at his funeral. Central to the scene would be his wife, the protagonist, in shock. But now she is told by his lawyer about her husband's debts, that unless payments are made she will lose her house. How will she survive? What is she to do? Necessary past information again emerges naturally, dramatically. The situation is clarified, and now we want to know if and how the wife will cope. The second scene has taken us a step forward and makes us want to go on to scene three.

In the medical series illustration we presented previously about the young ballet dancer, you'll remember that in the opening scene she collapsed during rehearsal on the eve of an important performance.

In scene two the young dancer is brought to a doctor, the hero-protagonist of the series, who, while examining her, asks her necessary questions about herself and her life situation—facts about the past the audience needs to know. In the process family members are introduced, and it is revealed that the tests show nothing physically wrong with her leg. What is the cause, then, of her paralysis? Again, as the scene ends, we want to go on to the next one where we'll find out more as the conflict and urgency increase and involve us even deeper. What is the cause of the ballet dancer's paralysis? Will she be cured? How?

Leak Before Sinking

The mirror image of exposition is the art of *preparation*. A startling action must not be sprung upon an audience out of the blue. A murder weapon to be used in the climax of a teleplay must be shown earlier. And if you show a pistol in Act I of your script, the audience expects you to use it before the conclusion.

If you're going to sink a ship in the last act, you'd better let the audience know it's leaky in the first—and also that a hurricane is on its way.

A man who suddenly leaves his wife at the end of a television drama must be shown to have a good reason for taking this action.

As we have seen earlier, every scene and every character in *Death of a Salesman* was used by Arthur Miller to prepare for Willy Loman's suicide—the climax.

To prepare the audience for a scene or an action usually means showing motivation for it.

In a good plot, exposition, preparation, and motivation often overlap. But the main purpose of all these techniques is to make the audience "suspend its disbelief," to make the viewers accept the actions of the characters in your teleplay as true and believable.

Preparation is also used to produce *suspense*.

To create suspense in your story means simply to make your audience worry about what is going to happen next. Suspense is a necessary ingredient of every script. It is a handmaiden of mystery.

Earlier we said that a good plot begins with some sort of mystery. Suspense makes your audience concerned about everything that happens in the story until the mystery is finally solved.

If we see a man with a gun and have been shown earlier that he's a killer, and if we see him pursuing his next victim, we are anxious. Suspense has been created. Will the killer be successful again? The suspense increases if we know who the intended victim is, if in addition we like him and identify with him. Each step the murderer takes toward his victim tightens the screw one more notch. Suspense is heightened as we watch the murderer's preparations and see the intended victim walk unseeingly toward the trap.

In other words, we are producing suspense by preparing, motivating, characterizing—letting the audience see who our characters are and what is happening to them.

Be clear at all times, and don't keep your audience in the dark. Don't lie to it or confuse it. But don't give everything away all at once, either. Feed the audience necessary information gradually, one item at a time.

Related to suspense (and often confused with it) is *surprise*. Surprise causes excitement—but only for a moment. Suspense lives on and on and is the very stuff of drama.

What is the difference?

Alfred Hitchcock, the great motion picture director and master of suspense, gives an example of each. In the first example, a group of people are seated around a table having dinner, laughing, talking, enjoying themselves. Suddenly a bomb explodes underneath the table blowing them all to smithereens. That is *surprise.*

In Hitchcock's second example, the same group of people are seated around the same table eating, talking, laughing. But as they do we, the audience, see a bomb ticking away beneath the table. We see the second hand moving closer and closer to the zero point that will set off the explosion. We see the people at the table totally unaware of the catastrophe about to destroy them. As the bomb continues to tick, we begin to bite our fingernails. Why doesn't one of them look under the table? We want to shout and warn them. But they're enjoying themselves too much to hear even if we did. We watch, the knots in our stomach tightening. That is *suspense.*

The difference is simply that to create suspense we let our audience in on what is happening: we *show* our viewers what is about to take place. We *prepare* the crisis.

With surprise, we take the audience unaware and merely shock it. We don't prepare. We don't let our viewers in on the situation. We keep them in the dark. There is no nailbiting, no anxiety.

Suspense is much more effective dramatically than surprise. Always try to create suspense rather than surprise.

Preparation has other uses; it is accomplished by other means. In "The Castaway," an episode for the series *The Swiss Family Robinson,* I wrote a story about the loss of innocence of the youngest member of the Robinson family, Ernie, age eleven. The time is one hundred years ago. The family has been shipwrecked on an uninhabited island in the Pacific. The story involves Ernie's relationship with a seaman who is cast by a storm onto the island in a tiny makeshift raft. The man, a fast-talking criminal, is capable of any kind of underhanded act. But he tells everyone, especially Ernie, he's a sea captain and regales the youngster with tales of his own bravery and daring. In the painful and emotional climax, Ernie discovers that his idol not only has feet of clay, but is indeed an escaped felon who has committed murder, and, what's more, is trying to exploit the Robinson family for his own benefit.

To make the story more effective dramatically and to create the proper amount of suspense and urgency, I first let the audience—but not Ernie or his family—know who the castaway named Johnson really was. Showing him to be a criminal and a murderer placed among this honest, hardworking family and this adoring young boy, would have been analogous to showing the bomb under the table in the previous illustration. If I hadn't let the audience know who he was and allowed them to find out only at the climax when Ernie and his family did, I would have opted for surprise rather than suspense—and the inner tension of my whole plot would have been dissipated.

In order to reveal Johnson as a criminal and a murderer to the audience—but not to the family—I included a brief expository scene near the opening of the show (actually the second scene) in which I showed Johnson and another sailor on a flimsy raft not far from the island but just out of sight of any of its inhabitants. I had Johnson wrestle a bucket containing the last bit of water from his weakened partner, gulp it down, then coldly throw him overboard.

The relationship between Ernie and Johnson was the basic, emotional story line of the drama. Every character and incident in the teleplay related to this single issue. It was resolved in the climax when Ernie discovered who Johnson really was and what he was trying to do.

The *basic story line* should always be the *emotional line* of the script. Don't make the basic line the social or philosophical or political comment of the script. If you do, it'll become a propaganda piece. Drama is concerned only with emotion. But if your story or characters carry other values or ideas, good. It adds another dimension to your show. But that's all it is, a dimension.

Time, Place, Action

As we consider the basic story line and the emotional line of a script, we turn again to the subject of unity, the unity of time, place, and action, all associated with the ancient Greeks. These unities developed out of a specific historical period, a specific theater. Greek tragedies were acted in one set. The actors, standing on stilts and wearing masks, half-chanted and half-sang the great poetic lines of the playwrights. The audience, seated on hard stone benches, was too far away to see a great deal of physical action, so there wasn't much of it. Thus, *unity of place* became a necessity for that kind of theater. But when the theater changed, unity of place became an anachronism. Now, of course, television drama, whether on tape or on film, can go anywhere. Teleplays normally contain many sets or locations (except situation comedy, which uses few sets).

Unity of action—which means an organic cause-and-effect relationship between all scenes and characters from the beginning to the end of a play—is a goal of dramatic writers, no matter what medium they're working in. In television drama it's essential.

Unity of time was also a necessity for the Greeks, since their plays had only one set and no intermissions. Greek writers could not omit or skip over a passage of time. If a drama ran an hour and a half of real time, the action of the story covered an hour and a half of stage time. Later, however, as the theater changed, as intermissions were introduced, stage time could be extended. A dramatist could easily end one act at a particular time and open the next act an hour or a week or a year later. The intermission was the device that made this possible. And in films or television, a writer can cut from one scene to another, one place to another, one period of time to another in a fraction of a second. Time has become fluid.

How, then, does the television writer handle time, practically speaking?

You should try to concentrate on the time period your story covers, at least as much as possible or feasible.

A story that covers many years, that extends over the entire lifetime of an individual, runs the risk of being episodic. Causality is difficult to maintain when you jump over long stretches of time.

We've seen how Sophocles telescoped time when he adapted the legend of Oedipus for the stage. He boiled down a story that originally extended over many years to a drama which covers less than two hours in the theater. These methods work for the modern television writer as well.

But the main point to remember when dealing with time is to make sure your causality holds. That means if your teleplay has an organic unity, a unity of action, a cause-and-effect relationship from scene one to the climax, the time problem becomes relatively unimportant. Fine teleplays—witness *The Autobiography of Miss Jane Pittman,* Emmy winner of a few years back, a memorable show—have been written that covered long periods of time. In *Jane Pittman* the flashback technique was used. There have been other biographical dramas that told their stories in sequence from beginning to end that worked. Be warned, however, that it's a difficult method with many pitfalls, especially for the new writer.

A dramatic device, the *time lock,* is often used in television scripts to create additional tension. A time lock exists when a predetermined action is set to take place at a specific time. An example of how a time lock may be used brings us back to our time bomb. Except in this new situation, the bomb is not under a table. Instead, a terrorist group has set it to explode in an office building in mid-Manhattan in three hours. Unless their demands are met, many will be killed. Can the authorities find and defuse the bomb in time without giving in to the terrorists' demands? The point where the bomb is set to go off is the time lock against which everyone else in the drama is pitted. In other words, time is so concentrated—locked—it becomes an element of suspense in itself.

Another example is the traditional "heist" story that was central to the plot of the classic film *The Asphalt Jungle* and many others. Can the would-be bank robbers get in and out before the alarm goes off? Almost the whole picture was a breathtaking, nerve-wracking race against the clock.

Many good teleplays contain a time lock. In our earlier story about the young dancer, a time lock can be used if we make the date of her performance vital to her success. If she doesn't dance on that particular night, she'll never get a chance again. Let us say the date is two weeks off. Can the doctor cure her in time? The drama, then, races against time; the "lock" is the night of her scheduled performance.

Beginning, Middle, End

In arranging the incidents in your teleplay, it is a good idea to keep in mind the beginning, middle, and end as the three major sections or parts. As you structure your treatment, think of it as falling into three acts.

(This does not conform with the actual act breaks in a television drama as aired; these are quite artificial. Their purpose is merely to produce time for commercials. The usual hour-length episodic drama has four acts and sometimes a teaser and/or epilogue. There is a commercial at the end of the teaser and each act, and before the final credits. A two-hour TV movie usually has eight acts. But these are arbitrary—developed after the film is shot. None of this has anything to do with the structural acts we're now discussing.)

At the opening of Act I an incident will thrust your plot into motion. At the end of Act I, approximately one-third of the way through the script, there should be a high point of action or dramatic tension, leading to a confrontation between the opposing forces and the beginning of a new development. By now all the major characters will have been introduced, the plot lines established, and the drama well under way.

By the end of Act II, two-thirds of the way through your teleplay, a high point of dramatic tension should have been reached, the highest so far. All seems lost. The hero has no chance. There seems no way for the lovers to ever get together. The detective is completely stumped, all clues having led to blind alleys. The doctor is about to lose his patient.

The climax—the point of highest dramatic tension in the script, where the hero makes a discovery, where the removal of the blind spot takes place, leading to a new course of action, where the theme of the story is revealed—comes at the end of Act III. We will discuss the climax in detail in Chapter 13, but first let's examine the building blocks of the plot, the scenes and sequences.

12
The Scene

We have referred to the scene a number of times in our discussion of the construction of a teleplay. Now we're going to stop and examine the subject a little more closely.

When one thinks of a scene in a play one often thinks of, dialogue. Scenes contain, consist of dialogue. Dialogue is part of what a scene is. Right? Wrong—at least as far as television and motion pictures are concerned. Many scenes in motion pictures contain no dialogue at all. This is also true in filmed television drama. Think of a chase, or a fight, or a lovemaking scene. Even certain intimate emotional scenes may not need words.

John Bright (and, I hope, the reader of this book) is still working on the *construction* of his script—the treatment—and has not yet written one line of dialogue. In John's case he will not be given the go-ahead to write the dialogue until his treatment has been approved. Nevertheless, at all stages in the process of building his treatment, John is constructing scenes. Even at the earliest idea stage, as we have seen, he had already begun to think of his plot in terms of scenes.

What Is A Scene?

The dictionary defines *scene* as one of the units of a drama.

In the theatrical sense, a scene is a change of setting.

For our purposes, let's say that *a scene is the basic structural unit of a teleplay*. Scenes are the essential building blocks from which a television drama is constructed. When the writer finally begins to write his teleplay, he writes scenes. Certain memorable scenes (as well as characters) are what we remember from the best television dramas. Scenes are of the utmost importance in the final teleplay. In television, a scene does not necessarily change with the change of a location or setting.

Let us imagine, for instance, a scene between a young man and woman. They've just met. He tries to persuade her to go out on a date with him. She is reluctant at first. The scene might start in an elevator. It continues as the couple emerge in a lobby and then walk out to the street. It ends when the young woman flags a cab and leaps in. But as she does, she smiles and hurriedly gives her consent, telling him to call her. In the last shot, the young man stands there smiling, looking after the disappearing cab.

The same scene could take place in a single setting. But *dramatically*, the effect is the same. A man asks a woman for a date. At first she demurs. After a certain amount of persuasion on his part, she gives in.

The issue of the scene is: Will the woman go out with the man? The conflict is between the man who wants something and the woman who resists. The scene is resolved when the woman consents.

That is drama. The *filmic* description of a scene is somewhat different. In the production of a television film one needs to change the position of the camera for every shot in a new location. This change of position implies a new scene. But that has very little to do with dramatic construction. For your purposes, as you write, think of the scenes as units in your teleplay.

Making a Scene

In a structural sense, a scene is a miniature of the overall teleplay.

What does that mean?

Like the complete teleplay itself, each scene has a *beginning,* a *middle,* and a *climax,* or *resolution.*

We've spoken of drama as the *art of crises.* The crises are contained in the scenes.

Each scene not only has a *crisis* (a small climax), it also contains *conflict.* The crisis grows out of the conflict (as in the scene just mentioned between the man and woman).

Moreover, each scene in a well-constructed teleplay *advances the plot through conflict and crisis.*

Each scene *moves the story forward.* It ends one step further along in the plot than where it started. It reveals at least one additional element of necessary plot information.

In an episode of the series *Hawaii Five-O* called "Elegy in a Rain Forest," everyone on the Five-O squad is looking for an escaped killer. In an early scene, two of the detectives cruising along spy a derelict named Sancho, whom they know, emerging from a cheap bar. They pick him up and inform him that his old pal, Lucan (the killer), has escaped. They want information. Sancho, evasive and nervous, at first refuses to say anything. The detectives threaten him. Finally Sancho succumbs to their pressure and fearfully gives them a name.

The scene opens with action: the two detectives cruising. They see Sancho, and there is a brief chase. They catch him. The issue, the *conflict,* is: Can they get Sancho to give them information? They pressure him. Sancho resists, but finally they succeed—Sancho gives in and reveals a name. This is the *crisis,* the resolution of the scene. The scene is over.

A new piece of information has been provided and a new scene can begin. The previous scene has advanced the plot. The detectives now have a clue they did not have before, leading toward their eventual confrontation with and capture of Lucan, which will be the climax of the teleplay.

The scene just described is very simple and direct, but it clearly illustrates how a scene is constructed and how it works within the script as a whole.

Another function of a scene is to *reveal character.* In "Courage at 3:00 A.M.," an episode of *Ben Casey* (see Appendix B), character, conflict, and the advancement of the plot emerge together in a somewhat more complex manner. The central emotional line is the relationship between Ben and Liz Wilson, a biochemist who works in the hospital lab. Liz has cancer. She is also working in what she considers the army of scientific researchers in the war against cancer. She has already made what seems to be an important breakthrough. She needs to go on. She feels she doesn't have much time.

However, the pain of her cancer is so overwhelming it affects her work.

She has just seen Ben perform an extremely delicate operation on an older man to remove the nerves in the region of the brain where the idea of pain is localized. In this scene, at the beginning of Act III, Liz asks Ben to perform the same operation on her. Ben, the cold objective neurosurgeon, doesn't want to. He doesn't want to because he's in love with Liz. Not only do we see another side of Ben's character here, the emotion that he's capable of, but we see the tremendous, obsessive dedication of Liz. She is willing to risk the consequences of a life without the ability to feel or recognize pain—one of the most vital means of protection her body has—in addition to the risk of the operation. Ironically, Liz Wilson, whose work is her life, whose dedication to science is why she lives, is very similar to Ben Casey. Both are dedicated to saving lives. But in this scene, Ben is the one who exhibits emotion.

The scene reveals Ben's and Liz's characters. It is built on an intensely emotional conflict between the two. The issue is: Will Ben perform the operation? The scene reaches its crisis when Ben informs her of the consequences of the operation even if it's successful. Liz will be one of the walking wounded for the rest of her life. Her life will constantly be in danger. Yet she insists. Ben finally gives in an inch by telling her he'll consider it. He'll let her know tomorrow. By that statement the scene also advances the plot because it moves the events of the story one step closer to the climax—the operation itself.

The Length of a Scene

No law governs the length of a scene.

Scenes may be any length, from just a few seconds on the screen to many minutes.

Most plays written for the stage, however, have fewer scenes than the average teleplay, and the scenes are longer. They are developed more fully and work to their crises fairly slowly, mainly because they consist almost totally of dialogue and appeal to the audience's ear. The audience needs time to digest what it hears. It is even necessary for the dramatist to repeat certain information. At the same time, a longer scenes usually requires greater exploration and depth of character and theme. Scenes in live and taped television dramas also tend to be longer—and there are fewer of them—than in filmed teleplays.

In theatrical motion pictures there are usually many scenes, and they're generally much shorter than scenes in plays or even teleplays. This is partly because motion pictures are more visual. We can absorb what we see more quickly than what we hear; thus, some scenes may last only a few seconds on the large screen. If they seem truncated in comparison to scenes in plays or teleplays, they are. Often a motion picture scene is cut so that when we see it on the screen it has already begun—we're well into it. And the editor or director will cut away from it before the crisis, before the scene is really over. In other words, a scene may be written showing only its beginning, middle, or end. In contemporary writing for theatrical films this method is often used. It helps move the plot more swiftly than the long, slow scene developments of the past.

The length of scenes in filmed teleplays lies somewhere between that of theatrical motion pictures and plays written for the stage. Television is both a visual and an aural medium. We can watch and absorb a dizzying array of visual images in a commercial or a montage sequence that runs for a minute and a half; we can also sit entranced before our home screen held by a long, intimate scene between two characters that consists mainly of dialogue.

If you're concerned about the length of a scene in your filmed teleplay, I'd say that normally you should keep it under five pages. One page is not too short. But remember, this is not a law, and if your scenes run longer they may be fine. The nature of the teleplay and the scene itself will determine its length. Keep these questions in mind: Does the scene advance the plot? Does it reveal character? Does it contain conflict? Is it structured properly with a beginning, a middle, and an end, or resolution?

If you answer "yes," keep the scene. If you answer "no," cut it out.

The Sequence

Sometimes a writer—often in motion pictures but also in television—may need more than a single scene to do the job that a scene normally accomplishes. For instance a chase, or a wedding, or a fight, or a party, or a bank holdup. In such cases he will combine a group of scenes. A group of such scenes clustered together having a common purpose or action is called a *sequence.*

You might think of a sequence as a unit of dramatic action held together by one central idea, an expanded scene. Like the scene itself, the sequence has a beginning, a middle, and an end, or resolution. It also may be thought of structurally as a microcosm of the plot.

One of my students began to develop a story about a young woman who, upon the divorce of her parents in Ireland, is sent to a relative in Florida. The relative, a woman in her late thirties, has a ten-year-old child and a forty-year-old husband. The action of the story actually begins with the young woman's arrival at the airport in Florida, but it was important to show why she had come. Instead of using dialogue to handle this exposition, it was decided to use an opening sequence—a series of short dramatic scenes with little or no dialogue—showing first the young woman in a Dublin courtroom between battling parents, her father with his mistress and her mother in a state of hysteria; then, the young woman boarding a plane in Irish fog as her separated parents watch from two different cars; then a shot in flight, the young woman's sad face in the rain-streaked window; then the Florida airport, sunlight, flowers, and smiles, as her new family welcomes her.

In "Elegy in a Rain Forest," the episode previously described from the series *Hawaii Five-O,* the opening consists of a sequence of very short scenes showing the escape of a handcuffed prisoner, Marcus Lucan, from a van in which he's being transported from a holding facility to a state prison. We see first the coastline of Oahu, the van making its way across a remote stretch of highway, the nervous driver, a uniformed prison guard.

Then we see Lucan in the rear, handcuffed, being watched by two armed guards.

Lucan strikes one of the guards, using his hands as a club; grabs his shotgun; points it at the other guard; and forces him to call the driver over an intercom to halt the van.

The driver stops the vehicle, comes around to the rear, unlocks the heavy doors to see what's wrong. As he does this he's met by a shotgun blast from within the van.

Lucan jumps out. We see that the two guards have been clubbed down. Lucan now takes the keys from the dead guard, locks the others inside the van, and runs off.

In a nearby rain forest Lucan stops and, using his teeth to hold the keys, unlocks his handcuffs. On the tube this sequence runs three minutes.

Remember, each scene consists of a specific incident involving a specific issue, a specific conflict; there is something at stake leading to a high point or a crisis. A discussion about the past, even one in which the characters disagree and argue, is not enough to make the scene viable, unless that discussion, that conflict, relates to a specific action in the present.

By the same token, a scene merely illustrating character that does not advance the story must be either changed or eliminated.

A television treatment or script then consists of a series of scenes. Each scene is like a link in a chain. It contains conflict, develops character, and moves the story one step forward. As you develop your plot, check each of your scenes. Does it accomplish its purpose? Does it contain the necessary elements? Is it essential to the overall drama?

Remember, finally, that a television script is only as strong as its weakest scene.

13

The Climax

The climax . . . is the principal part of the play and for which . . . all the machinery of planning and constructing has been set in motion . . .

—Carlo Goldoni

Until the last scene has been found there is virtually no play, and as soon as the author has got hold of his *denouement* he must not lose sight of it for a moment: he must subordinate everything else to it . . ."

—Eugene Scribe

So long as one has not reached the end of his play he has neither the beginning nor middle. . . . This part of the work is obviously the most laborious.

—Eugene Labiche

As soon as John Bright conceived the idea of "Who Is Sylvia?" he began to look for a climax. Even before completely working out his premise he had discovered, at least in a general way, what his moment of crisis or resolution would be. He wasn't locked into it permanently, but at least now he had a point toward which his story would lead: an end, a focus. Now he could construct an opening and work backward, juggling, inventing, transferring, changing, tearing his hair trying to find the proper moves his characters would make, and in the process developing and refining the structure of his plot.

He's worked hard and now he's beginning to see the light at the end of the tunnel. Now it's time for him—and us—to reexamine the climax.

We've stressed the fundamental importance of the climax a number of times in previous chapters and analyzed it in some detail. I believe the failure of so many recent films and plays is the result of false, confused, or nonexistent climaxes. The writers may not have truly understood or faced the real meaning of what they were trying to say. Or the problem may be the way motion pictures are made today—the script often being of less importance than the star or director. Or it may simply be a lack of knowledge of dramatic construction.

Although it does happen, failure in dramatic construction is much less prevalent in television, especially TV series, than in either feature films or plays produced in the theatre. It happens less often, I believe, because most television drama is fairly simple melodrama; also because the writers and producers who create television films week after week have done it so often and have so much practice that they've generally become highly skilled practitioners of their craft; and finally because almost everyone involved in the creative side of television realizes the importance of the script.

The Well-Structured Climax

As you examine the climax of your treatment, you should remember first that it consists of a scene or a sequence.

Essentially, the climax is the scene in which the mystery or problem presented at the outset of the story is finally faced and resolved.

It is the scene in which the protagonist reaches a final confrontation with his antagonist (if there is an antagonist).

It is the scene in which the protagonist's blind spot is removed and he comes to some new understanding. You may think of the blind spot as a false goal. Throughout the story the main character has been struggling for something that he *thinks* he wants—but he finds out in the climax, as a result of his struggle and confrontation, that he actually wants something else. The values he's lived by, the dream he's worked for, no longer apply.

For instance, a man is struggling for fame and fortune but discovers he's really been striving for love without realizing it. This is a profound emotional discovery; it fundamentally affects his life and changes his course of action. The leading character must make a discovery in the climax of a play that affects him emotionally and completely alters the direction of his life.

Thus, the climax involves both plot (action) and character (the hero). The plot is resolved, and the hero makes a discovery. These two actions are interconnected; the resolution and the discovery take place simultaneously and are seen as one and the same.

If the leading character makes a profound discovery in the climax, then it is obvious that he must *appear* in the climactic scene.

The theme, or purpose, or central idea of the teleplay also is revealed in the climax. Why? Because the purpose *must* be revealed if the protagonist comes to a new understanding. *That new understanding is the theme.*

In the climax, then, three things take place: *the plot is resolved; the protagonist comes to a new understanding; and the theme emerges.* These three occurrences interconnect and take place simultaneously.

In the premise of a man struggling for fame who discovers he really wants love, for example, the theme is that love is more important than fame.

In "Powder Burn," an episode of the short-lived but well-done police series *Eischied,* the main character (along with Chief Eischied, the continuing lead of the series) is a woman detective, nicknamed Sam, who comes from a wealthy family but joined the force because she wasn't satisfied with her previously empty life. In the course of the plot—which turns on the efforts of the police under Eischied to stop 1,100 illegal handguns, hijacked from a delivery truck, from hitting the streets and causing untold havoc—Sam shows herself to be a brave and efficient detective. But she also commits a grave personal error that she is at first unaware of or refuses to admit. She is so intent on doing her job—uncovering the boss of the operation—that she allows a colleague to be murdered. At the climax the guns are found and she leads the police to the source of the crime, but she is almost killed. Eischied risks his life to save her. In the process it is shown to her—and us, emotionally and dramatically—how important it is for police officers to trust and rely upon each other in their work. The case one is working on is *not* more important than a fellow detective. Sam emerges from her ordeal a changed person.

In an episode of another well-written and -produced series, *The Paper Chase,* entitled "Bell and Love," the central character, Bell, a somewhat naive law student, has a brief, platonic but intense and romantic relationship with a young married woman who's run away from her husband. He learns that what a person wants or needs to believe can blind and distort his perception of the facts in a situation. Bell's discovery is made in a climactic scene when he realizes that the young woman with whom he's fallen in love never really loved him, that her love was instead a product of his own desperate fantasy. As a result Bell has learned something important. In fact, he's able to apply his new knowledge to a case he and the other law students are contesting with Kingsfield, their brilliant and authoritative law professor. Thus the teleplay, in the broadest sense, states that education doesn't always come from books, and is another version of the loss-of-innocence theme.

In "Bear Bondage," an episode of the *BJ and the Bear* series, the chimpanzee, Bear, a mascot and friend of BJ McKay, a truck driver (the series lead), is sick because he made a pig of himself and ate too much junk food. BJ takes him to a veterinarian hospital. The hospital happens to be a front for a scheme in which animals are sent off by the evil owner, a woman named Dr. Niven, for experimentation and dissection. Although Janet, a young student vet who works in the hospital but is not part of Niven's operation, is sure Bear only has a stomach-ache, Niven overrides her. Niven takes Bear for ostensible overnight testing but actually kidnaps him and tells BJ the next morning that his mascot is dead. BJ is crushed. Janet meanwhile checks on Bear's symptoms. When she complains about Niven's procedures, the head of the hospital and her assistant, Dr. Mason, drug her and decide to kill her. Before they do BJ discovers what's happening. The main thrust of the story involves BJ's efforts to find Bear and rescue him. In the process he must also free Janet. Bear, meanwhile, is revealed as a clever and resourceful chimpanzee in his own right. In the climax BJ overcomes Niven's henchmen, rescues Janet, and frees Bear—but not before Bear releases all the animals in the hospital—brought there for the same purpose. They overwhelm their tormentors, Niven and her cohorts, in a seething, howling, furious finale.

Simply told, the story opens with Bear being kidnapped. The main struggle involves BJ's effort to find and rescue his mascot-friend. The urgency develops because we know Bear is to be sent away and killed for experimental purposes. Can BJ find and rescue him in time? In the climax BJ overcomes the heavies. But Bear brilliantly participates in his own escape. A simplistic theme emerges: Natural goodness will overcome materialistic goals, which are essentially antihuman and antilife. The removal of the blind spot or discovery made by the leading character, BJ (who never changes), is that his mascot and friend, Bear, and the other animals are tougher and more clever and more human in the long run than many inhuman human beings.

Satisfaction

No matter what complications or subplots are introduced in the three episodes from the three different series just cited, their basic plots are very simple and clear; moreover, the stories are all told in terms of their climaxes. The first and third stories—from *Eischied* and *BJ and the Bear*—are played out in a melodramatic framework; but the episode of *Eischied* tries to explore character and theme, as does the one from *The Paper Chase*, a series that rarely relied on melodrama. Despite their differences, however, all three episodes have well-structured climaxes that develop directly out of their basic situations and are satisfying, at least in terms of their own modest intentions.

Among the greatest dangers facing a beginner are false climaxes, missing climaxes, and anticlimaxes. A false climax fails to evolve logically and causally from the basic situation set up in the first scene. A missing climax leaves the basic situation presented in the story unresolved. An anticlimax is a false climax. It is usually indicated by a falling off of intensity in what should be the climactic scene. In other words, the preceding scene or sequence is more powerful. The climax fizzles out. Incorrect climaxes leave audiences dissatisfied and cheated—like being made love to by an unskilled lover. All leave the audience unhappy afterwards.

False climaxes usually result when quite unexpected and unrelated—accidental—events take place that materially alter the development of the plot. The Greek dramatists had a device which they used to help them out of difficult story complications. It was called the *deus ex machina,* the god from the machine. The god was sent onto the stage in a machine to extricate the characters from a situation the author couldn't otherwise solve. Writers still do this. But instead of using gods, they use accident. They manipulate the characters instead of allowing the characters to develop according to their own natures. The plots then become unbelievable and the climaxes are forced and illogical.

A satisfactory climax develops causally and inevitably from the opening scene. A satisfactory climax is the scene containing the highest point of tension in a drama. It may be compared to water brought degree by degree, step by step to a boiling point. The beginning of the tension (or drama) takes place when heat is first applied to it. The boiling point is the climax. As the water is being heated, as it becomes hotter and hotter, the changes in degree, in *quantity,* become apparent. Think of these changes as scenes increasing in intensity. The climax involves a qualitative change, a change in quality. When the water boils, it changes into steam.

When a drama reaches a climax, the essential conflict or struggle is over. A discovery is made. The balance of forces is realigned. The story is ended. The viewer can switch off the set or turn to another program, satisfied.

14

The Treatment

In the last six chapters we have described John Bright's (any television writer's) methods of constructing a plan, or treatment (sometimes called an outline, or story). This treatment, when it is complete, will contain the basic structure of the teleplay he expects to write. (Treatments for teleplays—movies of the week and episodic scripts—and for feature films are essentially the same.)

It should be clear by now that the main work in writing a teleplay, the most difficult part, is in constructing the treatment. This is where writers, from novices to Emmy winners, stumble the most.

What does John have so far? By now he should have everything necessary to actually write the treatment: the opening, the climax, the protagonist, the main conflict, the central emotional line, all the necessary characters, and the essential structure and content of every scene from beginning to end.

He has this information in the form of notes or a rough kind of outline on several sheets of paper, or possibly on 3x5-inch cards.

Many writers use cards in the development stage of the treatment. Each card contains a shorthand description of one scene.

In "Who Is Sylvia?" the first card might read "Sylvia, followed by a small truck, crashes." The second scene might take place at Sylvia's home. She has invited some people to a party. Among the guests are Finn and Ginigen, the detectives. The second card would read "Sylvia's house. She tells Finn (and Ginigen) about her problem, the accident. Wasn't just an accident. Brakes didn't work. Surreptitiously she hires detectives. Introduce her husband."

Scene three might take place at a garage where Finn and/or Ginigen is talking to the owner about what happened to Sylvia's brakes. Deliberate sabotage. The mechanic who worked on Sylvia's car, however, has disappeared. The card would read "Garage. Finn finds evidence of deliberate sabotage to brakes—but mechanic missing. Where is he?"

Step by Step

The development of all these cards in a step-by-step order detailing a brief description of every scene from beginning to end doesn't just happen. It involves a lot of work, thought, imagination, invention, and creative energy.

The work may be seen as two overlapping processes.

Process number one involves the gathering of the material. This means that after the climactic scene and the opening scene have been found, all the other steps, or moves in the development of the plot, must also be decided upon.

Each of these steps involves many choices by the writer. Every possibility the writer can think of or invent will be jotted down. One idea will lead to another. But one or a whole series of moves may eventually be discarded, and the descriptions on the cards erased or crossed out. (Don't throw them away, or you'll be buying many, many packs of cards and wasting a lot of money.)

This first process—gathering material, inventing possible steps or scenes, and then discarding or changing them—will be repeated ad infinitum. Don't hesitate to change or eliminate scenes. As we said, this is the hardest part, the real work. It can drive you crazy or to drink or a lot of other silly things—but at the same time it's a very exciting process, because here is where the creativity takes place. This is the heart of constructing a teleplay. When the right steps or moves or combination of scenes begin to form in your mind and on paper, your entire being will come alive. You will want to laugh and yell and jump with joy.

How do you know when the steps are right?

First, by intuition, which is based upon experience.

But never trust intuition by itself. The steps can be tested objectively. But we'll get to that in a minute.

Now let's mention process two. After the specific moves of the story are decided upon, they must be placed in the correct order as we suggested: scene one, scene two, scene three, to the climax.

Remember: the two processes overlap. Which means that while you are inventing scenes, you are also trying to place them in the proper order. And as you order them, new ideas will come to mind, new steps.

The point of cards is that they're flexible. You can lay them out in whatever order you please on your desk, a table, a bulletin board, the floor—or you can thumbtack them to a wall, if you have a wall you don't mind filling with holes.

Eventually, after shuffling the cards like a gambler, shifting their order hundreds of times, and adding new ones and discarding others, you will finally arrive at an order that feels right.

This may take days, weeks, even months. You're a new writer. It's a difficult process. It takes time. It's not easy for any writer, even an experienced one. But an experienced writer can usually do it more quickly, because in time and of necessity he becomes more skilled at it.

You will use everything you have learned so far in this book.

Nor is it necessary to use cards. You may find that you can visualize the material better on regular 8½x11-inch sheets of lined or unlined paper. For many writers cards are easier to handle and work with, but use whatever works best for you. And don't worry about the cost of settings or character actions. Are they logical? Do they work into your plot? That's all you should concern yourself about.

Put It to the Test

You've finally got your shorthand scenes or steps in what intuitively feels like the correct order.

How, then, do you test it?

Does every scene carry the plot forward one step? Are there any that don't? Be ruthless. Throw them out.

Are there steps or scenes missing? Scenes that should be there to move the plot? That is, are there jumps between one scene and another so wide that you need something to bridge the gap, some explanation of what happened, some visualization?

Find the missing scenes; note their contents briefly; insert them into the proper place.

Remember, scenes you get rid of tell you what scenes you need. By the process of elimination you will find out what works.

As you go forward from card to card, from scene to scene, ask yourself, does the story grow in dramatic intensity? Is the urgency increasing? You can judge even at this early stage.

Do the cards lead you, each in turn, in a cause-and-effect development toward the climax? Are there detours, sideroads? Cut them out. Are there scenes that sound exciting but don't move the plot forward? Get rid of them.

Check every scene to make sure that it relates causally to the one preceding it and the one following it. If you can't find a relationship, something is wrong.

Remember always, you're constructing, not writing.

Is there conflict in every scene?

Is every scene constructed in terms of its own little crisis?

What about the protagonist? Is he struggling for something specific, which everyone watching can understand?

Is his conflict clear?

Is his emotional involvement continuous? Does it develop logically, dramatically, from one card, one incident to another?

Is the story told from the point of view of the protagonist? (This point of view doesn't have to be exclusively the protagonist's, but the plot must be developed largely through his eyes or consciousness.)

Is the blind spot removed in the climax? Emotionally? What does he discover?

What about the climax? Does the climactic incident resolve the dramatic problem or mystery set up at the opening?

Writing the Treatment

Back to John Bright. He has tested his structure. It feels good. He can find no holes or problems with it. At this point he could start writing the script.

But because of his contractual requirements, he must write a treatment first.

The treatment is a scene-by-scene narration of the entire plot of the teleplay from beginning to end.

It is written in prose, in the present tense.

A treatment may contain some dialogue. I believe, however, that direct dialogue in a treatment should be avoided. I learned years ago that any line of dialogue in a treatment may jar some reader or executive, rub him the wrong way, and cause him to quibble with it and reject the entire story. Don't give them anything specific to reject until you have to. Hold off on dialogue until you actually write the script.

In a treatment, all dialogue should be indirect. For example, don't write " 'I want you to go to the store,' John tells Mary." Instead, write: "John tells Mary to go to the store." Not: " 'I love you,' she murmurs." Instead: "She murmurs that she loves him."

Small but significant differences.

Treatments can be of any length. On the average they run somewhere between eight and twenty pages for an hour-length episodic script. But they could be shorter or longer. For a two-hour TV movie they're twice as long. (See Appendix A for an example.)

John writes his treatment for the most part in clear, simple, declarative sentences. He writes visually. (Visual writing is developed by first learning to see, and then to reproduce the visual images as directly as possible on paper. The novice should read and reread the early Hemingway, then practice.) John doesn't overload it with excess description or fancy writing. The fancy or literary writing will impress no one. He knows that what finally *counts* is *not* what's on the paper, but what is seen on the tube.

When he finishes, he reads it over carefully, checking once more to make sure everything hangs together logically, causally, and believably. He remembers something he once heard about Menander, a prolific Italian dramatist who wrote a century or so before the birth of Christ, and Racine, one of the most important classical French playwrights whose main works were produced about a half-century after Shakespeare's. Both answered a question as to the work they had in hand by the assertion, "My play is done; I have now only to write it."

John feels the same way. He turns in his treatment with relief.

15
Story Conference(2)

John has completed his treatment and turned it in. As the days pass and he hears nothing, his anxiety increases. He knows from past experience that if the producer doesn't get back to him quickly it probably means trouble. He calls his agent. The ten-percenter is in conference. He leaves his name. His call isn't returned and he has the jitters all day, resolving first to fire his agent and second to give up writing for TV altogether.

He is about to explode when the phone rings. He grabs the receiver, barks hello into the mouthpiece.

It's his agent.

John informs him that he handed in his treatment a week ago and has not heard a word from Hyer.

The agent tells him to relax. This is a new series, and they're having the usual problems. Nobody knows what they want or in what direction the show ought to go. There's been a shakeup of the top generals at the network, and everybody's feeling insecure, waiting for things to settle down. Meanwhile he's trying to set up an appointment for John to see a couple of new pilots that are scheduled for showing next week.

John hangs up feeling only slightly better. He tries to think about other things. He puts on his jogging suit and runs three miles. This clears his mind and calms him down. He takes a shower, goes to his desk, pulls out the notes for an original screenplay he's been fooling around with off and on during the last year, and is soon deeply involved in the material. It feels good. He's already begun to make further notes when the phone rings, startling him.

Yes?

It's Hyer's secretary. Her boss would like to see him as soon as possible.

He asks her what's going on.

She tells him she doesn't know anything, but the studio is going crazy. A lot of network brass are in from New York. Can he come in tomorrow morning? Nine?

When John steps into Walter Hyer's office the next morning, a steaming cup of coffee in his hand, he finds the producer and story editor strangely subdued, possibly even embarrassed.

Hyer immediately tells him that the network has changed its policy about the direction the series will take and does not want to proceed with the treatment he submitted.

John's throat goes dry. You mean I'm cut off?

Yes, the producer answers apologetically—but you did a good job.

A very good job, Bill adds quickly. It wasn't your fault.

But I'm cut off, John repeats hollowly.

Actually they want to go ahead . . .

. . . Go ahead?

. . . With the first idea you suggested, Hyer states.

The first idea . . . ?

Right. "Who Is Sylvia?"—how about developing that?

But that would require an entirely new treatment, John mutters. I'd have to start all over from scratch.

True, Walter answers, but you'll be paid. We'll handle it as if it were a brand new deal. You keep the money for the treatment we're not going to use. We'll call your agent right now. Okay?

John nods, his mind working. He stands to make $9,972 for the new treatment and script (if all goes well) plus the $2,417 that he's already received for the treatment he turned in last week, not counting residuals—which is a lot better than he had expected.

Do you—do they—have any problems with the premise? John asks. Any suggestions?

You seem to have it well in hand, Walter answers. Why don't you write it the way you feel it. You know our show.

Fine, John says. I suppose you want it yesterday.

Right, Walter grins. But to be serious, how about two weeks?

No problem, John assures him.

Thus, with a new contract for a new script, John goes home and writes another treatment. This time, because it's his own idea, an idea not out of somebody else's head, an idea he feels comfortable with, it's easier. Because he knows what he's doing, he's able to complete the seventeen-page story in eight days.

The day after he submits it, Hyer calls, telling John he likes it, the network loves it and thinks it'll make a great episode.

Go ahead (which means the option to write the script is exercised), but first Walter has a few notes for minor changes he'd like to give John over the phone.

Happy and relieved, John takes down the notes—most of which are more quibbles—and the next morning starts writing the script.

16
The Teleplay— Format

Now that he has a good, solid, well-structured treatment as a basis, John finds writing the first draft of his teleplay comparatively easy.

It usually takes him about half as much time to write his teleplay as it does to construct his treatment. Two-thirds of the time he needs to complete his script is normally spent on the premise and outline. The other third is spent writing the dialogue and directions, the actual teleplay.

What is involved in writing the teleplay?

First, it must be neat, well typed, and have the proper form or format.

An amateur-looking script gives a producer or editor an excuse not to read it. Don't give anyone that excuse.

Just as a stage play is presented in a certain way on a page, so is a television play. Television form is very simple. Novices worry about it, but there's no need to.

There are two basic forms for television scripts. One is essentially for *filmed drama*. This is similar to the *screenplay form* and is used for practically all dramatic series scripts, television movies, and most dramatic specials. (Appendix B contains an actual example of this format.) The other is for *live* or *taped drama*. This is the form used for most situation comedy scripts, daytime serials, variety shows, and some dramatic specials. (Appendix C contains an actual example of this form.)

What's in a Teleplay?

What specifically does the writer write in a teleplay?

To repeat: what the characters say—the dialogue—and what the characters do—the action.

Plus some—very few—camera directions, and even fewer sound directions. Only those necessary to tell your story most effectively.

In this chapter we're going to look at the form for television films, by far the most widely used in the industry simply because, as of now, most television drama is on film.

The form was originally borrowed from motion pictures, since motion pictures and television films are made—as we've seen—in almost exactly the same way. The only difference is that television films are produced faster and cheaper.

In the old days of Hollywood, during the 1930s and 1940s when the big studios controlled everything, the cameras were large and clumsy and production was an assembly-line process. Then the writer wrote down every camera angle, described every shot, and most directors worked mechanically from the completed script, shooting the movie very much in accordance with what the writer had written.

The era of mass production ended with the breakup of the large studios, the growth of location shooting, and the introduction of light, mobile, hand-held cameras. The director now decided how to approach each shot according to factors that no writer could foresee. These were, in fact, often last-minute decisions. Thus, the detailed use of camera angles and shots in a script became unnecessary. Camera angles and detailed shots are rarely included in motion-picture scripts anymore.

Television films are somewhat different. They are still made mainly by an assembly-line process. The director in television doesn't have the time to change what the script contains or fully develop his own interpretation of each shot. The television writer, therefore, must give him a more detailed guide than the screenwriter gives to the motion-picture director.

Thus, in writing a television script it's okay to include some essential camera directions. But a good writer will use them sparingly and only when necessary.

What a Teleplay Looks Like

Let's examine the form of a filmed television script. The following is the opening of "Blues for Sally M.," an episode of the series *McMillan and Wife* that I wrote with Oliver Hailey.

MC MILLAN AND WIFE

BLUES FOR SALLY M.

ACT ONE

FADE IN

1   INT. BUZZ SIMMS - APARTMENT - NIGHT - BEDROOM   1

The room is illuminated only by a couple of lamps. There is a king size bed, bureau with a tape recorder atop it, a desk and a sitting area -- small couch and coffee table. The music emanating from the recorder will later be identified as "Blues for Sally M." It plays loudly. Too loudly. BUZZ SIMMS, a handsome young man in his early thirties, sits on the couch looking through a scrapbook.

2   ANGLE ON WALL BY DESK   2

On the desk are the usual accessories -- desk blotter, letter holder, letter opener. A shadow of a hand reaches out, picks up the letter opener.

3   ANGLE ON SHADOW   3

as a figure, carrying the letter opener, moves across the room.

CUT TO

4   INT. CORRIDOR TO BUZZ'S APARTMENT - NIGHT   4

Mac and Sally are both dressed for dinner.

SALLY

You still think I've met him, don't you?

MAC
(an amused grin)

Did I say that? I don't believe I did.

CONTINUED

4   CONTINUED   4

                          SALLY
          I didn't say you said it. I said
          you're thinking it! I know your
          mind, Mac.

                          MAC
          My mind is thinking roast beef...
          maybe a little wild rice...a good
          salad.

                          SALLY
          You really believe me?

                          MAC
          Of course I do.

                          SALLY
          But how can you possibly believe
          me?

                          MAC
          If the situation were reversed,
          wouldn't you believe me? If a
          strange woman wrote a composition
          and named it after me -- and then
          sent us flowers and invited us
          to dinner -- and I told you I
          didn't know her -- and had never
          met her -- well, what would you
          think?

                          SALLY
          You know exactly what I'd think.
                    (she sighs with
                     exasperation)
          No wonder I'm riddled with guilt.
          Completely innocent and riddled
          with guilt.

     They stop at a door from which the same music we heard in
     the opening sequence is issuing.

                          SALLY
          Mac, listen. Do you suppose that's
          'Blues for Sally M.'?

     Mac presses the door buzzer. It sounds sharply.

                                        CONTINUED

4   CONTINUED   4

                              SALLY
                How can you ring a buzzer in the
                middle of it?

                              MAC
                Because we're here for dinner and
                I'm hungry.

       The music continues, but there is no reply to the buzzer.
       After a beat, Sally tries the door handle. It turns easily.
       Alarmed, she looks at Mac.

5   FAVOR MAC   5

       Sensing danger, he eases the door open and enters.

6   INT. BUZZ'S APARTMENT - NIGHT   TIGHT ON MAC, SALLY   6

       as Mac and Sally enter.

                              MAC
                Simms?

                              SALLY
                Mac!

7   MAC - SALLY'S POINT OF VIEW   7

       The living room is in shambles. It is clearly the apartment
       of a composer but has been ransacked. Musical manuscripts
       are scattered across the top of the piano, some torn. Record
       albums, most of them featuring Buzz Simms' name and picture,
       are lying all over the floor. Many have been broken and some
       of the furniture is overturned.

8   BACK TO MAC, SALLY   8

       as Mac moves to the bedroom door. The music continues.

                              MAC
                            (shouting)
                Simms!

                                        CONTINUED

8   CONTINUED   8

He tries the door -- it's locked. Muffled voices are heard
arguing, then a struggle and a cry for help. Mac puts his
shoulder to the door, breaks it open.

9   INT. BUZZ'S BEDROOM - NIGHT   9

as Mac crashes in. He glances around the darkened room.
A moan can be heard over the music.

10   MAC'S POINT OF VIEW   10

Buzz is lying on the floor beside the bed, the letter
opener beside him. As Mac kneels to examine him, Buzz
loses consciousness.

11   BACK TO MAC   11

as Sally enters the room.

                          MAC
                Call an ambulance, Sally ---

Sally rushes toward the phone as Mac moves to a window that
opens on the street.

12   EXT. APARTMENT BUILDING STREET - NIGHT - MAC'S POINT OF VIEW   12

A man is racing toward a parked car.

13   ANGLE ON MAC   13

as he exits from the apartment building.

14   ANGLE ON MAN   14

as he climbs into his car, starts it.

15   ANGLE ON MAC   15

as he races across the street, is almost struck by a passing
motorist, who honks at him angrily.

16   ANGLE ON CAR   16

       as it lurches away from the curb at high speed.

17   ANGLE OF MAC   17

       as he moves into the path of the car, waves an arm.

                                    MAC
                      Stop!

18   MAC'S POINT OF VIEW   18

       The car is roaring down on him.

19   BACK TO MAC   19

       holding his position.
                                    MAC
                      Stop!

20   CLOSE ON CAR   20

       as it swerves to avoid hitting Mac.

21   ANGLE ON MAC   21

       as the car just misses him. He turns for a final look.

FADE IN: This is the way every teleplay opens. Written in CAPS, it is similar to "The Curtain Rises" in a stage play. We go from nothing to something, from black to an image.

Two spaces below FADE IN is the first image or *shot*. Screenplays and filmed teleplays are written in shots. Shots are what the camera photographs. Each shot is written in caps. One or more shots make up a scene (in the film sense). The first shot in the scene will tell the reader whether the location is an interior (INT) or an exterior (EXT); specifically what the location is (BUZZ SIMMS—APARTMENT—NIGHT—BEDROOM), and whether it's DAY or NIGHT. Day shooting is different from night shooting and must clearly be indicated.

Two spaces below the locale is a description of the people, places, and/or action that the writer wants in the shot—the *content* of the shot. This description is written in lowercase letters, single-spaced from margin to margin. When you introduce characters, always capitalize their names, and if you describe them, be brief. ("BUZZ SIMMS, a handsome young man in his early thirties . . .")

ANGLE ON: indicates the viewpoint of the camera, what the camera is focused on, what we see.

Always center dialogue on the page. Write the name of the character who is speaking in caps two spaces below the shot description. The speech itself comes one space below the name of the speaker. It is always written in lowercase letters. More than one line of dialogue is single-spaced.

Directions tell what characters do within a scene, including their reactions. They're usually written single-spaced in lowercase letters and extend to the margins of the page, but sometimes they're placed in parentheses within a speech—especially if they're short. Dialogue may be broken up by directions, as in shot 4.

FAVOR MAC means that Mac is the main subject of the shot.

TIGHT ON means a very close shot on whatever is indicated, in this case Mac and Sally (shot 6).

MAC-SALLY'S POINT OF VIEW, or POV, means point of view, what the characters (Mac and Sally) see, how it appears to them. In this case the living room is seen from Mac's and Sally's point of view, as they are looking at it.

Remember though, all directions and descriptions are written from the camera's point of view. You will write your script from the camera's point of view—your plot from the point of view of the protagonist.

BACK TO: means we return from the POV shot of Buzz lying on the floor (shot 10) to Mac (shot 11), as Sally enters the room. Sometimes the word RESUME is used instead of BACK TO, but they both mean the same thing.

CUT TO: indicates the end of a scene (between shots 3 and 4). It means cutting, changing from one scene to another. The next scene takes place at another locale and/or time. (In many contemporary filmed TV scripts the phrase CUT TO is dispensed with. See shots 7 through 21. for examples. Cuts between shots and scenes are automatic and need not be spelled out.) The CUT TO between shots 3 and 4 was spelled out because we changed to a totally different situation. A DISSOLVE takes place when the image on the screen is fading out as a new image is fading in. CUT TO: to indicate a change of scene has replaced DISSOLVE, an older and slower method. Dissolves are still used now and then in slow shifts from scene to scene, in poetic and memory pieces, for example.

CLOSE ON CAR (shot 20) means a close shot of the car.

There are other camera or film terms that you ought to know.

ANOTHER ANGLE means a new viewpoint, looking at or shooting the subject from another camera angle.

VO means Voice Over. We hear a character's voice, but we don't see him. Instead we see the shot now on the screen. Sometimes OS—off-screen—is used instead. The person speaking is off-screen.

FADE OUT means the image fades to black. This, too, may indicate the end of a scene, but a fade out is used mainly at the end of a script. It's comparable to "The Curtain Falls" in a play. It indicates the END—of the act or the entire teleplay.

CLOSER ANGLE means that the camera takes the shot from a closer position than in the previous shot. CLOSER ANGLE, CLOSE SHOT, and CLOSEUP are often used for emphasis. A CLOSEUP, in which the camera is moved very close to a person or object being photographed, may also be used to tell the viewer something important—for instance, to reveal a clue in a mystery story. We show a closeup of fingerprints or a bloodstain, or whatever is necessary to elucidate our plot.

An ESTABLISHING SHOT is usually a long or wide-angle shot showing a particular location. This indicates to the viewer where the general action of the scene or story is taking place, such as OFFICE BUILDING, HOTEL, SUBURBAN AREA, RANCH.

DOLLY means to move the camera (on a dolly) in toward a subject or back away from it. The camera can also move along parallel with the subject, keeping the subject centered, or it can move back or forward as the subject moves in either direction. For example, two people are walking down a street talking. The camera keeps them in focus as it moves backward at the same pace.

A PAN is any shot in which the camera moves from one side to another to follow the action taking place in front of it.

Use a MOVING SHOT instead of, or to replace, DOLLY and PAN, which are not often used in contemporary scripts. The camera is photographing or following the movement of the subject. Or you may even write CAMERA FOLLOWS ACTION in a scene of action or movement, and let the director shoot it the way he wants to. He will anyway.

A REVERSE ANGLE is the opposite of a POV shot. For example, you could indicate John's POV as he looks at Mary and a REVERSE ANGLE of Mary looking at John, and the camera will show what she sees. Or in one shot John has his back to camera. In the next shot the camera is photographing his face, from the reverse position of the previous shot.

INSERT is a shot of something inserted into the scene—a letter, an address, a newspaper headline, a clock, etc.

All sound directions are written in caps. For instance: SOUND OF FEET MARCHING, SOFT MUSIC, DOG BARKING, CLOCK TICKING, etc. You will use sound directions only in terms of enhancing or heightening your drama.

Study these opening pages and the format of the script in Appendix B. Examine the indentation, the way shots are set up, how shots combine into scenes and scenes into sequences. Look, also, for the subject of each shot. In addition, examine the live or taped script in Appendix C. See how the formats vary. When you study this script, remember the three- or four-camera technique described in the Introduction and see how it applies.

In a filmed shooting script all shots are numbered, but not until the script has gone through all necessary revisions and is placed on the schedule for production. Since your script still has a long way to go before it reaches that happy point, you will *not* number the shots on the teleplay you're writing.

How do you learn to use the film-TV format so that it becomes second nature? Simply by doing it. Camera terminology may seem complicated at first, but as you work with it, it will become easier.

In the first place, do not let format bog you down. You are writing stories, dramas. That is your primary consideration. After you've developed your entire outline or treatment, then you'll begin to write the shooting script. To repeat: write it from the point of view of the camera, which is also that of the viewer or audience.

Meanwhile, for practice, look at my treatment in Appendix A, "The Redemption of Nick Lang." Try to write a script based on that treatment—or perhaps the opening five or ten pages—using the format and terminology we've just discussed in this chapter.

Do the next five or ten pages. Keep working on the process until it becomes comfortable and natural. If you're conscientious, you will discover that camera terminology and script format will become second nature to you sooner than you expect.

17

Dialogue

Up until now John Bright has been inventing and creating, imagining and building, shaping and changing, constructing the architecture of his plot—as you have been doing with your own plot.

Now he's writing the script.

First, of course, he uses the proper form that we discussed in Chapter 16.

And he writes what the characters say and do—from a visual or camera's point of view. But he does this without becoming bogged down with excessive camera directions.

He writes visually—objectively, not subjectively—without interjecting a lot of camera terminology. Writing visually means writing with the camera in mind, from the camera's point of view. Remember what you write will be seen on a television screen. You cannot describe what's going on in a character's mind as you would in prose, nor can you, the author, comment on the action taking place. You must write in terms of simple physical and dramatic action, movement, facial expressions, lights and shadows. What you write must be photographed. It must be acted by actors.

Finally John begins to write dialogue. His characters now start to speak, expressing their emotions in words.

A drama deals with emotion—emotions between people. These emotions grow out of needs, relationships, conflict. The characters in a drama act. They feel. They express their feelings.

They communicate—or try to—through speech, dialogue.

But remember that dialogue is only *one form* of communication.

On the stage, dialogue is the most important means of communication, of expressing emotion.

In film—which, never forget, started out as a silent, purely visual method of storytelling—dialogue is not necessarily the most important means of communication or of expressing emotion.

Nor is it in television drama.

The point of all this is that many writers new to television write much too much dialogue. They write long speeches in which the characters talk, saying only what the writer wants them to say. They don't communicate, or try to communicate. Their words give information, but they don't express feelings.

The characters don't communicate as people do in real life.

Listen to the way people speak. Often the words themselves do not express their real feelings. Nevertheless, you know what those feelings are. Drama must convey those feelings accurately, no matter what the characters say or fail to say.

Rarely do people talk in complete, well-formed sentences. In a normal conversation, especially emotional conversation, the sentences are broken off, incomplete; phrases and words overlap; there is repetition, inarticulateness. Television dialogue should try to capture this sense of living speech. But of course it takes careful planning and talent to accomplish this successfully and also to convey what the writer wants to say.

In television drama, dialogue is a method of communicating—*one* means by which the characters relate to each other.

Dialogue is *one* method through which characters express or hide their emotions.

Dialogue is *one* of the things that take place in a scene.

Guidelines to Good Dialogue

In every scene there is conflict, open or hidden. This is also true of dramatic dialogue. Conflict doesn't necessarily mean arguing or fighting. When two people first meet and begin a relationship, even if they immediately fall in love, tension develops as they get to know each other. Inevitably there are problems, no matter how minor. Each stage in the developing relationship must contain some kind of conflict, even if that conflict comes from outside the couple, as in

Romeo and Juliet. Thus, *good dialogue contains conflict.*

A scene, with or without dialogue, contains conflict and moves the story forward. *Dialogue also moves the story forward.*

A scene reveals character. *Dialogue reveals character.* In the normal course of events a factory worker will not speak in the same way a professor does, nor about the same things. Occupation and education are reflected in the way one speaks. Every trade has its own jargon.

Dialogue conveys information. We need to know certain facts that took place before the story began—exposition. This information is contained in dialogue, *if there is no other way to convey it.* Moreover, exposition must emerge out of conflict, as the story is being moved forward and as the characters reveal themselves through emotion. Dialogue in which one person simply tells another certain facts is dull and ineffective.

With very few exceptions, *speeches—dialogue—should be kept short.* Short speeches increase the action of the drama. Long speeches impede it. Long speeches, when necessary, should reveal emotional states rather than information. Of course, if information emerges from a character's emotional state, if the information creates—or adds to—his emotional state, then a long speech might work. For example, if a character is describing the death of a loved one and the emotion is overburdening him, and if the death relates to the plot, such a speech may be effective.

A corollary to the above is that if you can make your point visually instead of through dialogue, cut out the dialogue. *Visual action takes precedence over speech.* In television drama we rarely have time for characters to even greet each other with the usual "hello," "how are you," "you're looking well"; or introductions: "This is John Stanley, he's an accountant"; "Meet Leon Berney, husband of Mathilda." Let's introduce our characters in action.

Avoid stilted or literary dialogue. Spoken speech is often different from written, especially in stories and novels. Speech in stories and novels is usually not dramatic. It is often too long. It may look good on paper and read well, but it doesn't play well in a scene by actors. This is true even of Hemingway's terse monosyllabic dialogue.

Listen carefully to the way people talk. Try to get the feel of it in your dialogue. Practice writing scenes in dialogue—a scene of direct conflict, a love scene—anything. Read them aloud.

The following is from the opening scene of an episode entitled "A Material Difference" by Rogers Turrentine from the series *The Rockford Files:* (Note: The following does not represent the actual script format. For examples of format see Chapter 16 and Appendices B and C.)

INT. OFFICE BUILDING. WASHINGTON, D.C.

The room gradually darkens on a group of silent men conservatively dressed in business suits. A projector begins to flicker.

THEIR POV—A MOVIE SCREEN

On it is a 16mm film which has apparently been taken with a hidden camera and microphone.

We see a COWBOY seated at a table on a sunny patio of a Mexican restaurant sipping from a bottle of beer. Soon a sinister-looking black-clad figure approaches wearing sunglasses and leather gloves, conspicuously overdressed for the weather and locale. He's carrying a record album and looking around nervously. When he turns toward the camera we can see that it's ANGEL MARTIN.

> COWBOY
> (re: the record)
> Hey, you like the bluegrass, mister?

> ANGEL
> (flatly)
> I like all kinds of music.

> COWBOY
> I don't like jazz.

ANGEL
(a beat)
I don't either.

COWBOY
(looks him over)
You Jones?

Angel nods. The Cowboy gestures toward the seat opposite him.

COWBOY
Get a load off.

Angel sits. Periodically he glances about the room and pulls his gloves on tighter, stroking them down around his fingers, during the following:

COWBOY
You want a beer?

Angel shakes his head "no," then slaps at a fly on the table. As he flicks the remains of the fly off his glove:

ANGEL
Dulls the reflexes.

The Cowboy seems impressed by the professionalism. He slides a manila envelope across the table.

COWBOY
The name is Kramer. His picture's in there.

Angel weighs the envelope in his hand.

ANGEL
(suspiciously)
And the ten G's?

COWBOY
Five now and five on delivery.
(beat)
You can trust me.

ANGEL
(cold)
I know I can. Otherwise my next job'll be for free.
(beat)
You get the drift?

COWBOY
(nods)
There's an address on the back of the picture. I'll meet you at that address as soon as I hear it's done.
(beat)
And I want that to be right away.

ANGEL
Yeah. Well, you want in one hand and you spit in the other—see which one gets full first.

He slides the envelope toward the Cowboy, who is taken aback.

COWBOY
Hey, okay man. Take your time. Do it your way.

He refuses the envelope, stands up.

ANGEL
Just don't be tellin me how to run my business, understand?

A sharp glance, then the Cowboy moves on, out of the shot. Angel waits a beat then peeks anxiously in the envelope as the P.A. system calls:

HOSTESS VOICE
Rockford, party of two please.

Angel grabs a menu and tries to hide behind it as the Hostess leads Rockford and a lady to their booth. Rockford spots him anyway. To the woman:

ROCKFORD
You go ahead. I'll be with you in a minute.

They move out of frame. Rockford tips down the menu.

ROCKFORD
Angel?

ANGEL
Oh, hi, Jimmy. I didn't see you when I came in.

ROCKFORD
Just got here a minute ago.
(re his outfit)
Say, what are you anyway—a clone of Lash La Rue?

ANGEL
(huffy)

That's not funny, Jimmy.
He turns and leaves a puzzled Rockford as the tail of the film runs out.

The exchange between Cowboy and Angel meets all the criteria for good dialogue.
The dialogue is only one of the things that happens in the scene. Even though the two men don't refer to anything out of the ordi-

nary, there is immediate conflict, immediate tension. The short, monosyllabic half-sentences, which don't ever state directly what the issue is, create mounting tension and conflict. At the same time, character is revealed obliquely, first when Angel refuses Cowboy's offer of a beer because it "dulls the reflexes." Angel seems a hired killer who needs his wits about him at all times. Moreover, Cowboy is impressed with this refusal. So are we. Angel seems a professional at what he does. (Actually he is nothing of the sort. He's one of the continuing characters on the series, a "good guy," on Rockford's side; here he's pretending to be a heavy.)

Simultaneously, the plot is moving rapidly forward. The point of the scene, never mentioned as such but revealed by implication through ordinary conversation, involves Cowboy's hiring—or seeking to hire—Angel to kill Kramer for ten thousand dollars, five now and five later.

But to Cowboy (and us) Angel is not merely a pro. He will not be told how to run his business by Cowboy. Not only that, he finally refuses to do the job because of Cowboy's attitude and because Cowboy has not come up with the full ten thousand (but actually because he is not a killer; this is simply a role he is playing—which injects humor and another level into the situation). Angel's refusal is essentially the crisis, the turning point of the scene.

Rockford's entrance at the end of the scene is necessary to introduce the leading character of the series into the situation. Clearly he will be involved in the story. The fact that this is all on a film being watched by several men who clearly are heavies and a threat increases the tension and adds another dimension to the scene.

The Subtle Subtext

Every line of dialogue, even the most innocuous, expresses emotion—by seeking to hide it. The indirection and understatement add to its inherent drama.

This indirection, in which the real meaning of the scene lies below the surface, is called *subtext*. Subtext is the level of a scene (or of an entire script) that is *not* expressed in the dialogue. When a scene contains subtext—and most good scenes do—the dialogue becomes a kind of metaphor to its meaning.

As an example, a husband and wife, having reached a point of breaking up, come down for breakfast. They scarcely talk. But when they do, it's not about what is really bothering them. It's about eggs. The eggs are awful, he mutters. Can't she learn how to make eggs right, the way he likes them? Of course she can't, he goes on, when her mind is on something else. When she's always out of the house. What does he want her to do? she snaps. Spend all day learning to prepare eggs? Like his mother? Keep his mother out of it, he growls. Why? she asks sarcastically. Didn't she make good eggs either? But that's impossible. Maybe she ought to take a course, a correspondence course in egg making. From some chicken. She's very funny, he says. She ought to go on the stage. He could die laughing. What a beautiful concept, she laughs. If he'll promise to do that, she will go on the stage. But first she'll have to find him, he says, because he's not ever going to eat her eggs again. What is he talking about? she asks, staring at him. She'll find out, he mutters, and walks out.

The eggs were the metaphor. The eggs were what the husband and wife talked about. But the real issue was their relationship. That was the subtext of the scene. The crisis and turning point occurred when the husband walked out.

When you write scenes, try not to be too literal. As we pointed out earlier, people rarely say what's actually on their minds. Rarely do they talk about what's really troubling them. Often they don't know.

But the writer must know. He must let his characters speak and act as they logically would in a situation—confusedly, uncertainly, indirectly, and with emotion. Nevertheless, he must make sure that what they are saying and what they are doing is always clear and understandable to his audience.

Remember, in order to make your dialogue sound natural and your scenes come alive, you must not only listen to the way people speak, you must practice writing it.

Think of all kinds of situations. Develop them into scenes. Long ones, short ones, funny ones, sad ones; it doesn't matter. Write scenes based upon situations that have happened to you. Rewrite them. Read them aloud. Get a couple of friends and try to act them out. See how they sound. Keep writing, observing, listening, rewriting. It'll get better. It must.

18
Credits and Collaboration

The first draft of "Who Is Sylvia?" is completed ahead of schedule. John Bright brings it to the studio where Walter Hyer receives it happily.

After several days Walter calls John in for another story conference. Hyer, Picker, and John Bright now sit around a table and go through the script scene by scene, line by line. According to WGA rules, the producer can ask the writer to do one revision—which may be major—and a polish.

John accepts most of the producer's and story editor's suggestions, argues about others. On several points the producer and editor back down. The new writer must be aware of the fact that all scripts are changed. Plays are not written; they're rewritten. The professional can accept suggestions for improvement without feeling that his precious lines have been destroyed. Finally John takes the script home and makes the revisions—which may take from a few days to a week or two—and brings it in again.

Now all it needs is a polish: line changes and trims.

A few weeks or months later, according to a predetermined schedule, it goes before the cameras and John receives sole writing credit and 100 percent of the writer's share of the residuals. (He's been paid in full for the script within a week or so of turning in the final draft.)

Often, however, for one reason or another, the script is rewritten. The producer or an executive from the network may consider the script faulty or feel it's not quite in sync with the way the leading characters would act; or an important actor or director may not like it or feels he has a better way of doing it. Or the script may be too expensive to produce, or the original guest star has taken sick and been replaced, or the producer has been fired and the whole concept of the series changed, or because of any of a hundred other reasons. Sometimes the rewriting is done by the producer or story editor, sometimes by another writer not connected with the show who is hired to do it for a fee.

Whenever a script or treatment is rewritten by someone else it is sent to the Writers Guild for credit arbitration. Credits are important to a writer, both to his financial state and to his career. The assignment of credits based upon each writer's contribution to a script, therefore, must be as fair and impartial as possible.

The Writers Guild handles this problem by placing most of its active members on a continuing arbitration panel. When a script arrives for arbitration, three members are chosen from this panel at random, one of whom is appointed chairman, to form an arbitration committee. The members of this committee, unknown to each other except for the chairman, are asked to read all the material involved—outlines, scripts, revisions, and/or statements by the participating writers—whose names are deleted and the designation "Writer A" and "Writer B" substituted. (Members of an arbitration committee are not told the names of the writers whose credits they've determined.) Each member of the committee reads the material alone and then makes his decision based upon a carefully developed set of rules and standards approved by the members of the Writers Guild. For example, the final credits might read, "Story by Writer A, Teleplay by Writers A and B."

Whenever two or more writers share credit for a script, they also share the residuals; the percentage each writer receives is determined by his contributions. More money is paid to the writer who receives teleplay credit than the one who receives story credit.

Of course, when two writers collaborate on a script they share credits and money equally.

Collaboration

Dramatic writing for theater, films, and television is a collaborative art. Not only do many skilled and unskilled individuals participate in the making of a television film or tape, but rarely is the shooting script the product of one person.

In addition to the original writer or writers, the producer and editor help shape it from its earliest beginnings. We've seen exactly how this process takes place in the example of John Bright. Network executives determine the kind of material that will go on the air; their voices are felt especially in television movies and in the long form generally. These individuals, as well as production company executives, may also influence the writing at any or every stage. And of course the director has a large say in the final script. In motion pictures there is sometimes a close collaboration between the writer and director (a better product invariably results). This collaboration takes place in television as well, but to a much lesser extent.

Thus it is natural that two writers will form a team to collaborate with each other.

Most comedy writers work with partners. Writers bounce lines and ideas off each other as they would for an audience. As they create their one-liners they try to top each other—but always, in addition to the lines, they help each other invent humorous characters and scenes, constantly interacting, improvising out loud, essentially doing the same thing one individual writer does when he works alone in silence.

In serious drama writers also collaborate, but not nearly as often as in comedy. Some writers find they work best with a partner. Some can't write alone.

What happens when writers collaborate?

There are several approaches.

In some collaborations, one writer sits at the typewriter while the other paces the room throwing out ideas.

In some—at least in the early development stages—both writers talk into a tape recorder as they develop their story. A great deal of TV and motion picture "writing"—that is, the development of characters, situations, and construction of the story—is done aloud. In the story or outline stage the idea is often "talked." Collaboration can help spark ideas, situations, and characters through oral interaction of this kind.

Sometimes, in the script stage, one writer will write a scene or an act, and his partner will rewrite him. Then in the succeeding scene or act the first writer will rewrite the second.

If you decide to collaborate, try several methods until you find the one that feels best for both yourself and your partner.

To collaborate successfully, you must respect your partner's ability. You must be willing to compromise. And you can't let your ego stand in the way of what must be done to produce the best possible script.

Collaboration means to meld your own creative personality with someone else's.

It's like a love affair, or a good marriage.

It has advantages: You don't have to work alone, the blight of most writers' existence. But there may be conflict and emotional explosions.

Nevertheless, a good working collaboration in which two writers trust and respect each other can be creative and productive, containing more joy than sorrow.

Not every writer can do it, but some do it very well.

Is it for you?

Only you can decide.

19

Sitcoms and Soaps

Sitcoms and soaps, or daytime serials, are special areas of television writing that require special skills and abilities. This is particularly true in comedy, which demands a certain kind of talent. Comedy writing can be learned but often is either inborn or developed early in life, usually unconsciously.

Writing Situation Comedies

Everybody knows what comedy is in drama: a story acted on the stage, on film, or on television that makes you laugh.

Comedy—humor—is a serious and complex subject. A well-known television writer and producer, a friend of mine, once told me that the difference between a comedy writer and a dramatic writer is that the comedy writer sees things "funny."

Otherwise they do exactly the same thing.

Based upon my own observation and experience I agree with him—except that some writers can do both.

Moreover, sometimes comedy is extremely serious, biting, even hurtful. Classically, comedy has been one of the most effective theatrical means of attacking institutions, individuals, ideas. This tradition in comedy goes back to its beginnings in Athens, to the great satirist Aristophanes, whose *Lysistrata* and other plays still have a great deal to say to contemporary audiences.

So-called serious dramatic presentations often contain a great deal of humor—comic relief. Everybody remembers the drunken porter scene in *Macbeth*. Shakespeare introduced humor during one of the most suspenseful episodes of the play—the midnight murder of King Duncan—as a relief from dramatic tension and by way of contrast. The scene thus becomes more effective and is one of the classic comedy moments in dramatic literature.

In television, as anyone who watches the tube knows, most comic drama comes in a half-hour series format called situation comedy, or *sitcom.*

Situation comedies are usually produced live (on tape), often before a studio audience. Some of the best, however—including one of the top comedy series of the last few years, *M*A*S*H*—are done on film with canned laughter.

The live (taped) shows are done with few sets and few major characters, very much as live dramatic shows used to be produced back during the Golden Age (see Introduction).

Even those that are filmed are generally much less "filmic"—that is, they depend much more on character relationships and dialogue than do most dramatic series.

The style of sitcom humor stems from radio and the theater, where humor emerged out of "funny" dialogue and situations, rather than from classic motion-picture comedy, which was all visual. The tradition created by Chaplin and other pioneers is rarely found today in American television.

Each episode of a good sitcom is like a small one-act play. Many could be—have been— staged in theaters. In a sense they are a return to (or a relic of, at least in format and production methods) television drama of the 1950s.

A situation comedy script for a taped show follows the form of a script for a live drama and is quite different from that of a filmed script (see Appendix B for an example of a filmed dramatic format and Appendix C for an example of a live or taped format).

Like dramatic series, sitcoms have continuing characters. Each week these characters become involved in a story that is usually humorous and, in the better series like *Mary Tyler Moore* and *Rhoda,* often moving. Some series—*All in the Family,* for example— also deal with serious subjects such as racial prejudice, impotence, frigidity, growing old, divorce, obesity, but from a comic point of view. Rarely is satire an ingredient of this kind of show.

Sitcom characters are usually—but not always—ordinary human beings in real-life situations at home or at work. Unlike the leading characters in the usual hour-length dramatic series, they are almost never involved in life-and-death crises. Nor are they—as are the doctors, detectives, lawyers, police detectives in dramatic series—bigger-than-life heroes without foibles. Most characters in situation comedies are loaded with foibles. This is often the source of their humor.

The plot structure of a typical sitcom is exactly the same as in any other kind of drama. The craft and technique of dramatic writing apply equally to comedy.

Don't forget that the best and most enduring comedy is based upon character and situation rather than upon funny dialogue or jokes. An ordinary person in a ludicrous situation or a ludicrous person in an ordinary situation are basic sources of humor. Nevertheless, after he's created a good story with amusing characters and comic situations the successful writer of situation comedy tries to make each line as humorous as possible. Read a Neil Simon comedy or see one of his films. Almost every line he writes is funny in itself. Nevertheless, they don't work completely unless his entire script is structured correctly. What I'm saying is that no matter how funny the lines or jokes a writer may conceive, he will not write a successful comedy script unless he knows and can apply dramatic structure as outlined in this book.

As my friend the comedy writer-producer has said, situation comedy is what you should try to write if you see life "funny."

If you can do it successfully, you'll be in constant demand, for sitcoms are a staple of commercial television. Year after year, comedy dramas remain the most popular shows on the air.

Writing Soaps

Writing soap operas, or daytime serials, is not for everyone, especially not the neophyte.

Nevertheless, you ought to know how they're put together, because someday—after you're an experienced pro—you may find yourself involved in this special form of TV writing.

Like sitcoms, soaps are a staple of TV; they also became popular in the golden years of radio.

On television, afternoon serials are the only type of dramatic series still produced and broadcast live (not on tape—though audiences in a time zone different from New York, where most soaps originate, may receive them by tape-delay).

Until recently, each episode of a soap lasted one half-hour, but now many of them have been expanded to an hour, and some have even gone to the ninety-minute format.

Daytime serials are on the air every weekday of the year (except for a few holidays). Most of these shows have been running for a very long time. Several serials on the air today have been produced since the early days of television, and a few even originated in radio. They're called *soaps* because they originally were sponsored by soap companies. Many still are.

Perhaps the forerunner of the soap opera was the three-decker Victorian novel, consisting of a long continuous series of interwoven stories extending over many years. Whatever their origin, soaps are not only extremely popular, they are easy to get hooked on. Their structure is fascinating. It is quite different, however, from the usual television (or any other) dramatic fare.

In the first place, a daytime serial is more like a novel than a drama. It is more leisurely in the development of its plot and characters than the ordinary TV drama, nor do the stories develop to a climax in the same way those in the typical teleplay do. There is no removal of a blind spot, for example. Soaps consist of many small crises, and the characters undergo many small changes. Moreover, the plots used are without beginning and end. Characters are introduced, continue for a time, then disappear.

Thus, the overall series has no opening hook, or teaser, and no final climax. The dramatic structure is based upon each week's plot development. The big climaxes come at the end of each week, on Friday (to keep the audience's interest aroused until Monday). As in all drama, the scenes are connected causally.

The daytime serial tells its story slowly. In a dramatic sense it moves with the speed of a glacier. But what it lacks in physical action or suspense, it makes up in depth. In long scenes of dialogue, the characters interact on an intimate emotional level.

More than any other form, the soap opera uses television the way

I believe television drama should be used, the way it was used when it was live and dealt with the revealing moments in the lives of ordinary people, when it explored human relationships with "needlelike precision." Soaps may be maudlin, unrealistic, and bound by all sorts of clichés. But at least they exist in that dramatic area. And because the viewer gets to know the characters so well and becomes so intimately involved in their lives, he's easily caught up in their stories and comes back to watch again and again.

The men and women who write daytime serials are a comparatively small group who work on a contractual basis rather than as freelancers. Their contracts, which are renewable, usually extend for thirteen-week periods.

From the scripting point of view the daytime serial team consists of one or a pair of head writers and two to four regulars, dialogue writers.

The head writers normally write the "book," or "bible," or "long-term projection" of the show—a fifty-or-more-page narrative detailing the characters and plot complications that will develop during the next three or six months, or year. But sometimes someone else is hired.

When this projection is approved by the sponsor or advertising agency and/or network, the head writers break it down into weekly and daily outline segments. These are given to the dialogue writers, whom the head writers hire and pay out of the scripting fees they receive from their employers. (See Appendix E for fee structures.) Each dialogue writer then writes one or more of the daily segments of the serial—actually scenes, consisting mostly of dialogue—based upon that breakdown.

Head writers' yearly fees usually reach six figures. But they work very hard and are ultimately responsible for every script as well as the success of the series.

Many writers of daytime serials have previously written and published plays, stories, or novels. Some come from other areas of TV writing. To work successfully in this field you must prove you can write good, honest, human dialogue and strong, emotional, dramatic scenes about people just as a playwright does. You must also be able to create long, interesting, and complicated plots like a novelist.

For the writer, working on a soap means steady work and excellent pay.

Moreover, some of the most popular nighttime dramatic fare has included serials, from *Peyton Place* to *Dallas* and *Glitter*.

20
Writing the "Long Form"

For the television writer, the "long form" is the plum, the icing on the cake, the cherry on the sundae. It is the most fun, the most interesting, the most creative kind of assignment to tackle.

The "long form" includes any dramatic program that runs more than an hour and is not part of a series with continuing characters—television movies, miniseries, and dramatic specials.

If the drama's length is more than three hours, it probably will be shown in two parts. Some shows—like *Roots* and *Holocaust,* for example, or *Scruples, Shogun,* and *Masada*—extend over a number of hours. They're shown in several segments and are called *miniseries,* in contrast to regular weekly series that could conceivably last for many seasons, depending upon their popularity.

Television movies that appear regularly on certain nights of the week, however, are also considered part of a series; such series are known as *anthology series.* Anthology series differ from ordinary series in that there are no continuing characters and each drama is an individual unit completely separate from all the others. This is true not only as far as story, writer(s), and director are concerned, but each show is also made by a different producing organization.

Anthology drama goes back to the early days of television, to its Golden Age in New York. Every play on the major programs at that time—*Studio One, Kraft Theatre, Philco Playhouse, The U.S. Steel Hour,* etc.—was an individual unit of an hour's length. However, in contrast to TV movies, one producing organization mounted all the dramas for any one series.

There were also half-hour anthology series in those formative years—some on film. By the 1960s, however, anthology drama had seen its heyday and, except for an occasional attempt, or a special, seemed to have disappeared. They have since, of course, reappeared in the form of regularly scheduled TV movies.

Specials are a kind of TV movie or taped drama that have always existed and which are supposed to have a "special" significance, or star, or subject. Specials do not come under any series umbrella or time slot. Often they preempt regularly scheduled shows.

Getting the Assignment

Most—99 percent—of all long-form dramas are written on assignment. The writer presents his own idea, or concept for a show, or a published "property" such as a novel or play or article, to a production company. If the company likes it, it may take an option on the work and present it to one of the three networks.

If the network likes the concept, it gives the company the go-ahead for a step-deal. The writer then prepares a treatment in exactly the same way as he does for an hour-length episode of a series show. Approval or disapproval is made directly by the network executives. If the treatment is approved, a script is written. If the script is approved, it goes into production. But this is usually a long and painful process. A cutoff can take place (and often does) at any step along the way. There are only three markets for the long form—the networks. A production company's approval, in the final analysis, means nothing.

You can see how difficult it is to even get a concept under way, much less on the air, and what a monopoly the networks have over what is bought and what is shown to the viewing public.

Moreover, many of the ideas for the scripts that eventually become television movies originate within the networks. A network executive will inform the vice-president of a production company that the network would like to do a dramatization of a certain bestseller. He will also likely "suggest" the writer. And of course the vice-president of the production company hastens to comply. His organization needs to have as many shows as possible in the works and on the tube. That's where its prestige and profits come from.

What's In It for You?

Nevertheless, with these obstacles firmly in mind, I believe that this is the area where the new writer should try his hand.

Writing a television movie is done exactly as you would write an episode for a series, as we have watched John Bright do throughout this book.

You start with a character, a situation, an idea—a premise.

You develop it into a structure, a treatment.

After you complete the treatment (see Appendix A), you write the script.

Using the form described in Chapter 16 and Appendix B, a script for a two-hour television movie runs around one hundred to one hundred and ten pages. (For minimum fees, see Appendix E.)

Why do I suggest you try to write a movie of the week rather than an episode for an episodic series? I have already detailed the reasons why trying to break into and trying to write episodic series can be nonproductive. At the risk of repetition I will enumerate some of them once more. (1) By the time the novice finishes his teleplay the series may be off the air. (2) It is extremely difficult to construct series drama. (3) To write episodic drama one must have an intimate knowledge of the demands of the series. This is something that most beginners do not have.

Nevertheless, a few writers have broken into television by way of episodic series. How did they do it?

They may either have known the producer or editor, or have been known by them. The writer was most likely a successful novelist or playwright and was asked to do a script. In addition, the series was a long-running success, or else the producer would not have taken a chance with an unknown quantity. Or the writer wrote a script on speculation and sent it in and the editor or producer liked it and sent the writer a detailed "bible" of the show. Then the writer, having studied the "bible" and watched the show, somehow managed to put a script together that everyone liked.

The new writer, as I have tried to make clear throughout this book, must always put his best foot forward. He must always write as well as he can. No matter what he sees night after night on the tube, he cannot ever write down to it. He must prove his creative qualities and his technical proficiency by writing an exciting, powerful, honest script. It must have professional quality. His goal is to write better than what he sees on his home screen.

To do this, he must not worry about the themes that are supposed to be successful on TV, nor the material he thinks a producer will buy. I feel he must write, not an artificial series episode with all kinds of restrictions that he's probably unaware of about unreal cops or detectives or plastic doctors or lawyers, out of someone else's head, cut like salt-water taffy to fit the desires of some unknown audience, but something that he knows, that he knows intimately, something that passionately interests him.

He must write an original script out of his own heart and mind and experience—a script that is his from the first to the last page. The only area in which he can do this in television (and rarely even there) is the long form: television movies.

Sometimes an original is read, liked, and bought. Not often. But it can happen.

However, an original script is a calling card. It can be presented to an agent or a producer or anyone in a position to buy or hire as a sample of the new writer's work, of his ability.

Even if the script is not bought now, the novice may be hired for something else. The other script can always be sold later, and can be used as a calling card many times.

So, write that script. Make it professional. Write from your heart and brain, from your memory and dreams. Use the methods and techniques you've learned in this book to solidify and develop your craft.

As you develop the concept, check the overall structure. Is the beginning right? Does it point logically to the climax? Does every scene contain conflict? Does it move the plot forward? Are all the scenes necessary? Can you eliminate any? How about the characters? Is there a protagonist we can root for? Does the climax satisfy? Is the dialogue real? How about the emotional line?

Make your calling card *work* for you!

21
Research and Adaptation

Inevitably, if you become involved in writing for television, you will find yourself having to do research.

A writer must know what he's writing about. And you will often be called upon to deal with subjects outside your personal knowledge—medicine, law, police procedure, for example.

Why are facts necessary in fiction?

In the first place, if you present material that any portion of your audience knows to be incorrect, you lose that audience. Remember, your main task is to make the reader or viewer "suspend his disbelief"; that is, accept as true the story you're presenting, at least while he is watching. The moment that suspension of disbelief is lost, the audience is lost. It is no longer involved in what it's viewing. It switches to another channel and your drama has failed.

Secondly, it is important *not* to give the audience false information, because it could be potentially damaging. If your drama, in a medical series for instance, presented a doctor who cured his patient's cancer with aspirin, many people in the audience might take this to be literally true and follow this advice, with tragic results.

As a writer you have a responsibility to get your facts straight, to the last detail. Your work, especially on television, has enormous influence—for good or evil. Never forget it.

Research becomes necessary when you are called upon to write about something with which you are not personally familiar. Or even something you have experienced but which may have taken place some years ago, and you've forgotten certain essential details. Or perhaps you never knew them. You have to check. You need to do research, preferably by going to the source. If that is impossible, your next best avenue is to interview someone who has experience, an authority. Finally, you will explore the subject secondhand, through periodicals, books, photos, paintings, music, etc.

Primary Research

The most important type of research for the writer, however, involves going directly to the source. Medical, legal, and police series on television, for example, often hire consultants—experts whom the writers interview for specific stories and technical or procedural information. On the series *Police Story,* for example, police officers often participated with the writers in forming their scripts, contributing ideas as well as personal experiences. The police officers discussed their lives, their hopes, problems, joys, and sorrows. They took writers into the crime lab, the morgue, into their police cars during stakeouts. They gave the writers assigned to the series a true feel of what it's like to work as a police officer on and off the beat.

Several years ago I worked on a series called *The Eleventh Hour.* The continuing characters were psychiatrists. To write the scripts I was assigned, it was necessary for me to interview psychiatrists, visit mental institutions, and read many case histories. Every writer on that series had to do the same. This kind of research is always necessary for medical shows, legal shows, and most others.

Research may involve travel to exotic countries, or interviews with unusual and exciting people—from scientists and astronauts to clowns and prisoners.

Secondary Research

Your local library is a source of all kinds of information, a repository of statistics and history, of photos and music. There are indexes of periodicals in which you can find the sources of articles published on any conceivable subject, indexed by the year. There are dictionaries and encyclopedias, maps and reference works. If you can't find what you're looking for in your local public library, there are special libraries of law, business, medicine, science, etc. Your local newspaper has its own library, copies of the paper indexed back any number of years. There are also university libraries and larger central libraries in most major cities. Become familiar with them. Use them. If you can't find what you're looking for, ask the librarian. He is there to help you.

The Writers Guild lists sources in its monthly bulletin, numbers to call for accurate information or guidance in scriptwriting. To assist writers in the Los Angeles area, I've listed them below. If you live in another part of the country, perhaps there are analogous places to contact in your particular location.

Call these numbers on weekdays only between the hours of 10 a.m. and 4 p.m. These offices are not open on weekends.

Adoptions (PR Coordinator)	381-2761
Alcoholism Information	395-1419
Air Force	824-7511
American Humane Association	653-3394
Army	824-7621
Blind	663-1111
Board of Education	625-6766
(Work Permits, etc.)	687-4831
Bowling	276-1014
Boy Scouts	413-4400
Catholics	627-4861
Chicanos	224-2544
Christian Science	594-8769
CIA	(703)351-1100
Coast Guard	824-7817
Copyright Forms	688-3800
Credit Union	659-1745
Customs Service	688-5939
Deaf	885-2611
Epilepsy	382-7337
Fair Housing Council	781-6940
Family Counseling	Ext. 11, 465-5131
FBI	272-6161
Fire Department	485-5162
Food and Drug Administration	688-3771
Food/Hunger	449-2714

Forestry Industry	462-7278
Gay Task Force, L.A.	464-1376
Health Fund	659-7100
Handicapped	786-2752
Immigration/Naturalization	688-2780
Indians	747-9521
Italians	467-3656
Jews	Ext. 407, 852-1234
Kidney Disease	641-8152
Labor Department	688-4970
Law (ABA)	276-4974
Marine Corps	824-7272
Medical (AMA)	466-7225
M.P. Health and Welfare	873-5624
M.P. and TV Fund	937-7250
Navy	824-7481
Organ Gift/Transplant	641-5245
Pension Plan	659-6430
Police Department	485-3586
Population/Birth Control	273-2101
Probation	Ext. 2851, 923-7721
Psychiatric Society	271-7219
Red Cross	384-5261
Safety Council	385-6461
SCAN	(Your local library)
Script Registration	655-0809
Sexual Matters	999-1991
Sheriff	974-4228
Space Science	354-5011
State Department	688-3290
State Filming Information	736-2465
Telephone Matters	986-1460
Veterinarians	723-1746
YMCA (National)	783-5436

Remember, research is a vital part of writing. It is an area you cannot ignore. As a matter of fact it is often the most interesting, and sometimes the most exciting part of writing your script.

Adaptation

Adapting a novel, a play, a work of nonfiction, an article, a story, a "property" for television movies and miniseries is something most writers become involved in at one time or another.

Often the property is the source of the idea for the teleplay. *From Here to Eternity, Shogun, The Autobiography of Miss Jane Pittman,* and *Roots* are only a few examples of books that have found their way to the living-room theater through dramatization.

The adaptation of literary material for the theater has a long history. As we have seen, *Oedipus Rex* by Sophocles was an adaptation of a legend, as were most other tragedies by the great classic Greek dramatists. Many of Shakespeare's plays, including *Hamlet, Macbeth, King Lear,* and *Julius Caesar,* were based upon earlier plays or the works of Plutarch.

Anyone familiar with motion pictures is aware that in that medium, too, a large proportion of all the screenplays ever filmed were dramatizations of previous works.

The television writer, then, must understand how to adapt material into a screenplay.

Sometimes dramatizing a property is more difficult than creating your own original work.

Why?

Because you must try to (1) be true to the original work (especially if it's well-known and popular), and at the same time (2) write a drama that "works" on its own terms, a teleplay that attracts, holds, involves, and moves an audience from beginning to end.

Writing a drama that "works" is ultimately more important than being true to the original (if you can't do both), because if your teleplay is true to the original but is dull and turgid on the tube, no one will watch it.

Sometimes the property a writer is called on to adapt is so well-constructed he can use the original author's basic construction. Then the ideas, concepts, and themes of the property naturally flow into the dramatization. The job is easy and everyone is happy.

But usually, because the work is from another medium and has a different kind of construction, a great deal of thought and care must be exerted in translating it into a television drama. The original almost always undergoes some kind of a basic overhaul. Its structure must usually be revamped, at least to some degree. Sometimes it's necessary to create a totally new structure. In such cases all the writer can use from the original work is the basic concept. From this he may have to invent an entirely new plot. In the process, the basic concept may even change, almost inadvertently, and he's conceived an original, based on someone else's idea. His teleplay is "suggested" by the original novel or play. But he makes this kind of drastic change only when absolutely necessary—when there is no other way to successfully dramatize the work at hand for TV.

In adapting a property, the writer must work out a structure almost as if it were an original, using all the concepts outlined in this book relating to climax and scene, conflict and suspense, emotional line, story line, etc. This sometimes is more difficult than creating an original. The difference is that in selecting and arranging the incidents of the teleplay he will have less to invent, less to create than in an original—for the incidents will probably derive from the work he's dramatizing.

One of the greatest pitfalls in adapting a work for television is attempting to stick to a structure that may have been fine in its original medium but which is turgid or diffuse when transformed into drama. This is especially true in a very popular, contemporary work or a well-known classic. The adapter wants to stick to a structure which has achieved previous success. But he must be ruthless. Consider the vast changes made in transferring *Tom Jones* to film. The feel of the original was maintained, but the structure was condensed and altered greatly.

The main object of the writer in adapting any property for TV is always to create a drama that works, even at the expense of sometimes having to change and even distort the original material. The overriding question the writer must never lose sight of in doing an adaptation—or any other work—should always be: Will it hold a television audience?

If it doesn't, he's failed.

22
The Marketplace

Okay, you've written and rewritten your script too many times to count, making sure that the first scene set the story in motion and related causally to the climax; that each scene had conflict, its own little point of crisis, and carried the plot forward; that the characters were believable and clearly motivated and that everyone you introduced was necessary; that there was one emotional line, one main character, or protagonist; that there was one main story told largely from his point of view; that the protagonist made a discovery, had his blinders removed in the climactic scene, which was the point of highest tension or emotion in the drama and where the theme emerged. You've cut extraneous lines and scenes, sharpening, focusing, clarifying the dialogue, finding ways to substitute visual action for dialogue. You have typed your script neatly in the proper format, made at least five and preferably ten carbons or photocopies. You feel it's right. You've read it aloud to yourself or others. Their reaction was excellent. You feel good about it.

You should. You've completed your own original script. That's a big thing. Something to be proud of. You have a right to feel good.

But that's only half the battle. Now what?

Now a new and important stage begins. A stage so inextricably connected with the writing that you cannot ignore it: *the selling.*

In television, writing a good script is not enough. You must sell what you write. Because a script in your desk drawer is almost like no script at all.

Who is going to sell it for you?

You. No one else. You can't depend upon anyone else. A script has no reality until it's produced on television and seen by millions. *Writing it is only half the job.*

Whom do you give your script to, the script you've labored so long and with so much difficulty and emotional turmoil to complete?

First, do you know anyone in the television industry? Even slightly? A secretary? A grip? Someone who works in a literary agency? Even if you've only met him once, even if he's only an acquaintance of a distant relative or the friend of a friend, do not ignore the contact. Use it.

Call him. Write him.

Introduce yourself. Tell him you've completed a script. Does he have any advice? Would he read it? Could he give it to someone who might be in a position to buy, if he isn't in that position himself?

Before you can sell a script, you must get someone to read it; so don't be shy.

In Hollywood, no one likes to read scripts.

Especially a script by an unknown.

The Writers Guild

First register it with the Writers Guild of America, West. The Guild, founded back in the 1930s as the Screenwriters Guild, has gone through many changes in accordance with the changes in the industry and society. It is an important and necessary organization, an independent trade union through which writers in TV, motion pictures, and radio—like other workers, skilled and unskilled—band together to achieve better wages and working conditions. It has branches on the East and West Coasts, located in New York City and Los Angeles.

Registering a script is somewhat like copyrighting it. Write to the Writers Guild, 8955 Beverly Blvd., Los Angeles CA 90048, Attn: Registration Department. They will send you a form. Place your script (keeping a copy for yourself in case it's lost in the mail) and the completed form in an envelope along with the small fee required and mail it first class.

Registering a script is not 100 percent protection against plagiarism, but it helps to establish your authorship and ownership if there is ever a dispute. Usually in cases of plagiarism you need to prove "access," that is, that the person or company you're suing has seen your script. Lawsuits are long, complicated, and expensive, however, and usually the only one who comes out ahead is the lawyer; so try to avoid them.

The moment you sell something, you will be invited to join the Writers Guild. The Guild is a closed shop. There is an initiation fee and yearly dues paid in quarterly installments based upon your income from television writing. Until you sell something, however, you can't become a member, even if you want to.

Nevertheless, even for the nonmember the WGA can be helpful. In addition to the registration service, it provides a list of approved agents and a list of research sources (see Chapter 21 for the latter). Moreover, it publishes a television market list each month in the Guild newsletter, which is available to nonmembers. You may send your request to the Guild (Attn: TV Market List). The Guild sets up forums, craft meetings, a place to meet other writers from here and abroad. It has a Film Society (for members). The WGA Script Awards handed out in the spring of each year for the best writing done in films and TV are honored throughout the industry. Besides, its personnel are often available to help the new writer with myriad problems connected with writing for television.

Take advantage of it. It is totally open and democratic.

Someday, if you become eligible to join, you will find the Writers Guild to be an important and necessary part of your television writing career.

The Agent

You've registered your script, but you know no one in the industry. Or you've sent it to an acquaintance of a friend who's returned it with a polite note saying he can't help you.

Now what?

The next thing you do is try either an agent or a production company.

As I just mentioned, the Writers Guild provides a list of approved literary agencies in the Los Angeles area. Some will read the works of new writers—but don't send your script in cold. Write first, introducing yourself and describing the story in a few sentences. If you know a professional writer who is willing to recommend you, it'll be a big help in getting the agent to read your teleplay.

Agents come in various sizes and packages. There are very large agencies that handle not only writers, but producers, directors, and actors. These agencies are able to put certain television movies, specials, and series together—package them—because they control the necessary elements: writer (script), star, director, and producer. Many top producers, even heads of studios, were former agents. For the new writer, however, an agency of this size may be a poor choice because it's easy to get lost in an immense organization filled with a powerhouse of talent. And in any case, this kind of agency is very selective in its choice of new talent.

There are smaller organizations—some run by only one person, the agent himself—which might be better suited to your needs. But these are not necessarily easy to join, either. The agent will accept you only if he believes you have talent, if he thinks he can sell you and make money out of your success.

Although you will mainly sell yourself through your script, you should, in the Hollywood vernacular, also be able "to take a good meeting." That is, you must be personable and able to discuss your work knowledgeably and forcefully in a story conference.

Agents can be valuable. They can guide your career. Selecting an agent is crucial and should be done with care. If possible, you should meet with him personally to discuss your expectations frankly and openly. Of course, at this point in your career you may not have a choice and may have to accept any approved agent who is willing to handle you. But that is a good sign. As long as one person in the industry believes in you and is willing to work with you, it'll be a help. It may be a big one.

One word of caution here. *Don't* sign with an agent who is not recognized by the WGA. There are all kinds of charlatans out there lying in wait for unsuspecting, hungry novices. Don't pay an agent until he sells your work.

If you sign with an agent, he will get 10 percent of everything you get paid for (gross) whether he's had a hand in selling it or not. If you sell something yourself, he is the one who will "negotiate the deal."

Going It Alone

An agent is not absolutely essential for a beginning writer.

Many—probably most—television writers have sold their first efforts themselves.

It is only after they make a few sales that they take on an agent. By then they have some knowledge and clout. Under such circumstances the agent may be able to do more for them than when they were unknown.

When you submit a script to a production company or a network you will probably be asked to sign a release form. This is to protect the prospective buyer from a plagiarism suit. Sign it. Most companies and people in the industry are honest. They are not out to steal your ideas. Besides, you have no choice—because if you can't get anyone to read your script, how are you going to get him to buy it?

If the script is returned, be persistent. Keep sending it out. Meanwhile, start writing another one.

23
Epilogue—
To the New Writer

Now that you know something of what you have to face out there in the world of television, the exciting opportunities as well as the odds against you; now that you've been introduced to the techniques of dramatic writing for the small screen and are working on your own first script, these questions have been gnawing at you.

Will I make it?

Do I have the talent? How can I tell if I have talent?

What does it take?

Should I persist?

The first thing you must realize is that every successful writer was once an insecure, uncertain novice, just like you, a beginner who had yet to sell his first script.

What differentiates the man or woman who makes it, who becomes a pro, from the rest?

All successful writers have several characteristics in common. The most important is *determination*—the desire to write and to succeed at writing, above all else. The real writer has a drive that will not be thwarted, that must be fulfilled.

Along with determination, a writer who makes it in the tough, competitive world of television also has *persistence.*

Most professional television writers probably had doubts during their beginning years. They asked themselves whether they had the necessary talent and fortitude, and possibly wondered, just like you, whether or not they would ever sell a script. The one thing they did *not* do was give up.

Eventually, because they refused to accept defeat, because they persisted despite one rejection after another, because they hung in there when all doubted them—even when they doubted themselves—they sold their first script.

Facing Rejection

The fact is, every writer has faced rejection. Rejection goes with the territory. Even the most successful writers are rejected now and then, not only by producers, but by critics and audiences. Never forget that the greatest of all playwrights, William Shakespeare, had failures too; he wrote his share of bad plays.

Your work is part of yourself. When someone criticizes your script, when someone says he doesn't like it, you unconsciously feel he is criticizing *you.*

If need be, you must accept the fact then that some people may not like you, even though the script you wrote is *not* you. A writer who wishes to function in the sometimes heartless television industry must be able to accept criticism, even attack. He must accept failure. In the process he will eventually acquire a thick skin, which will become his armor. Tears and depression help no one. Failure must become a spur. Like a bleeding and groggy boxer knocked down for the count, he must rise from the canvas and come back tearing into his opponent with both hands.

Get Tough With Yourself

All right then, you have determination. You have drive. You're persistent. You will never be satisfied or fulfilled until you sell your first script. What else do you need?

You need *discipline.* The ability to work hard, to organize your day, and to be patient.

If you wish to succeed as a writer in television you're going to have to work every day, just as most other people do, whether they go to an office or a factory, whether they're butchers or doctors or bookkeepers or lathe hands. The difference between you and them is you have no boss. Your discipline must come from within, must be self-imposed.

Most working television writers—those in demand—write daily, on a schedule. Some work in the morning, some at night. Some work eight hours a day, a forty-hour week. Some work longer, especially if they have to meet a deadline. Some work much less. But all work with some kind of regularity. That is, they usually get to their desk at approximately the same time every day and work for more or less the same number of hours.

Writing must become a habit. For some writers the habit is so strong that when they take a day off now and then, they feel guilty. I don't recommend guilt; I merely cite this as an example.

A disciplined, regular work schedule is essential for every writer, especially the novice.

Even if you're supporting yourself by means of another job, you must find some time every day to write, preferably the same time. It may be only an hour or two, but if you do it regularly, after a month, six months, a year, you'll have written at least one script. You'll have begun to create a body of work.

Emile Zola, the great nineteenth-century French novelist who created a whole world in his many novels, wrote, "Work. Work. It all lies in that." His statement is as true today as it was when he made it.

Moreover, practice makes perfect. By writing consistently, you will improve. You must improve. Your dialogue will become smoother, your construction will become sounder. The best way to learn to write is by writing, by trying, by experimenting, by making errors, by seeing for yourself what works and what doesn't.

A book, any book, can give you only so much. It can guide you, set you on the right course, but in the final analysis you're going to have to do it yourself—by doing it—by writing.

The Talent Factor

Notice, I have not yet said a word about talent.

Is talent necessary?

A certain amount, obviously. But I take that for granted. You wouldn't be trying to write unless you had a certain facility or aptitude. If you don't have any, you're clearly in the wrong profession, and you'll soon find it out.

But even that statement must be modified.

In my classes students often ask me if I think they have talent. Should they continue? Should they make television writing their career?

If you have to ask that question, you're not a writer.

If you're a writer, you know you have to write. You know you will succeed. Nothing will stop you.

I've actually had many talented people in my classes who never made it, who never will make it. Why? Because they didn't want to badly enough.

On the other hand I've had students who seemed to have no talent at all, but who had determination. One young man seemed, when I first read his work, to have no sense of even basic sentence structure. He wrote awkwardly. He seemed "tone deaf" to the rhythm of dialogue as well as narration and visual description. Nevertheless, he had a feel for the way ordinary people speak and behave and a rough sense of character. Plus memory and imagination. More important, he wanted to write; he had things to say. He worked hard. He wrote and rewrote script after script. He wrote about real people, people he knew. The scripts were interesting but raw. As he revised and revised over a period of about two years, however, he began to learn structure. His style became smoother. He finally wrote a script that was beautiful in all aspects—honest, funny, perceptive, the work of an accomplished writer. He's already found a producer who wants to buy it.

If that young man could do it, so can you.

While writing this book I received a long letter from another student, which I'd like to quote in part:

> . . . It's about a year now since I took your great course at UCLA. . . .
>
> I thought I'd bring you up to date on what's happened thanks to some good screenwriting principles which I learned from you. [He goes on to mention in detail his progress in getting an agent and various producers' interest in his scripts; then concludes:]
>
> I mention the above details because of your own interest and possibly because you may wish to share them with your students.
>
> . . . Please let [your students] know that the screenwriting

principles you teach are really practical and reduced to their essentials, stripped of all baggage.

I keep applying them constantly as I think, plot, and write. Like a compass, they are a reliable test of whether I am on course or not:

1. Knowing beginning and end clearly.
2. Knowing what my character wants and what happens to him/her when he/she gets it
3. Making sure that every scene has conflict and ends on a note of conflict (avoiding scenes that only illustrate)
4. Filling in the plot between beginning and end before I write (structuring the story)
5. Keeping the emotional line (discarding what doesn't relate to it, no matter how interesting)
6. Building conflict till the story reaches a climax
7. Starting with the basic conflict, stopping once the climax has been reached

Those aren't too many rules to keep in my head—but they are the essentials.

I find it important not to start writing the script until all those things have been done—otherwise it's like driving on a freeway that hasn't been finished and you come to a screeching halt or plunge off.

Again, thanks for providing me with such good tools. They helped bring everything into focus for me.

> Best wishes and kindest regards,
> Rolf Gompertz

The television industry is hungry for good new writers and fresh ideas. Moreover, television is expanding, changing; it is in the midst of a tremendous technological explosion that will require more and more interesting stories than ever before.

In the wake of the technological explosion, we've also been undergoing a great cultural revolution. Writers today have the freedom to write about almost anything, as long as it's done well and in good taste.

Your obligation, then, and I can't repeat it too often, is to write a script. Not the kind you see every night on TV. A better one—more interesting, better crafted, more powerful, moving, funny, and more honest than anything you can now find on the tube.

As you write it, keep in mind that writing, real writing, is personal or it is nothing. Writing is revealing yourself, not concealing yourself. If you conceal yourself you are no writer. Writing is expressing what you are and who you are through other characters.

This script will then—as you know—be your calling card, your introduction to producers and agents—the proof that you can write, that you know and can apply your craft.

You can do it. Others have done it before you. Every day men and women are selling their first scripts. Every week the Writers Guild is welcoming new members.

The successful writer, for all his frustrations and hard work, exists in an exciting world, a creative world, a world whose influence on its vast audience is powerful and immediate.

Most television writers enjoy what they do. It's fun. The working professional's income is high. The lifestyle of the successful writer is interesting and exciting. He is respected and envied.

You can join this select few.

You know how to do it! If you haven't already, begin! Now! And GOOD LUCK!

Appendix A

The Redemption of Nick Lang is a treatment for a two-hour movie-of-the-week which was sold to Irwin Allen Productions and Twentieth Century-Fox for a commitment they had with NBC.

This is a good solid treatment, written visually from the viewpoint of the camera or the viewer. As you can see, every scene, every character, all the relationships, the entire plot is here.

Not all treatments are written quite as visually as this one, nor in quite as much detail. But every character and every scene is always included.

You can see how a good director and good actors can almost "shoot" this.

Remember, however, before this was written, before I even tried to write it, I did a tremendous amount of work constructing and planning—as I described in the previous pages.

The actual writing was comparatively easy, of course, but still I tried to make it clear, vivid, dramatic, and as exciting as possible to read.

As an exercise, try to write a script based upon this outline. It's not necessary to write the entire script. Using the proper format, do five or ten pages.

Treatments or outlines for episodes of series are different only in the fact that they are shorter, more than half as long, and are broken down into acts—usually four, and a teaser and/or an epilogue. (Note: The first three pages of this treatment are a facsimile of the original treatment.)

THE REDEMPTION OF NICK LANG

by

ALFRED BRENNER

NICK LANG, in U. S. Army uniform, dark, lean, handsome,
but with a bitter obsessed expression, is walking tensely
along a downtown San Francisco street toward the main bus
station. The street is lined with night clubs, strip joints,
bars, etc. Most of them are closed now. It is morning. But
there are people on the street, a few in uniform. He stays
close to the buildings, keeping in the shadows, his eyes and
every muscle jumpily alert. As he goes by an empty store front,
he notices a large town poster plastered on the glass window
along with several others. It advertises THE GAMBLER'S
SPECIAL, a three day round trip bus excursion to the gambling
and resort area of Reno, Nevada which leaves at ten thirty
five A.M. every Friday from the main terminal. Checking his
watch - it's now about nine fifty - he continues onward.
Suddenly he hears a low voice calling out to him. He glances
swiftly to the side. A girl, not unattractive, is standing
in a doorway, smiling an invitation. He ignores her, keeps
walking without breaking his stride or changing his expression, but has only gone a few steps further when he sees
something just ahead. Two MPs have stopped a GI in front of

- 2 -

a bar and are checking his I.D. His papers apparently in
order, they're nodding and letting him go now - and are coming
this way. Nick whirls around, is about to run, sees the girl,
steps quickly into the doorway, pulls her to him, plants his
mouth on hers, stifling her greeting and, holding her very
tight, spins her around so that her back is facing the doorway.
At that moment the MPs arrive. They glance in. But all they
can see in the semi-darkness of the hallway is a girl embracing someone. They can't even tell if it's a man, much
less a soldier. They shrug, grin, move on. Inside Nick waits
motionlessly, his hand on the girl's mouth, until the footsteps
of the MPs die away. Then cautiously he glances out.   They're
gone. He lets her go. She starts to fire a series of outraged questions at him - who is he? What does he want? What's
going on? Glaring at her, his eyes narrowed, he tells her in
a low hard voice she's never seen him. Does she understand?
She nods nervously. He watches her a moment longer, mutters
something that sounds like thanks, grins imperceptibly, steps
back out onto the street, continues toward the bus terminal.

     People are entering, exiting as Nick cautiously approaches.
There are more MPs. He sees the reflection of two approaching
behind him in the glass of a phone booth. On the spur of the
moment he steps inside, hunches over the mouthpiece, holding
the receiver in his ear, faking a call. The MPs pass. He
doesn't move, stays there in the same position, his face

- 3 -

hidden, but his eyes watchful, studying every face that comes
by. He is looking for someone. Suddenly he reacts as he sees,
coming around a corner, a blonde young man about his own age
(late 20's) wearing civilian clothes and carrying a brown paper
wrapped package and a newspaper. This is PETE NEVINS. Reaching the entrance, Pete glances around quickly, then enters.
Nick's eyes follow him through the large plate glass window
of the terminal as he weaves between the crowds toward the
ticket booths. Pete slips into a line behind a studious -
looking fifteen year old kid (PHILIP MAXWELL) wearing glasses
and listening to classical music on his transistor radio.
There are four or five others in the line, including a
soldier. Among the posters on the walls describing various
bus excursions, tours, etc., is the one advertising the
GAMBLER'S SPECIAL. This bus, being announced over the intercom, is now boarding. It is scheduled to depart on time at
ten thirty-five. Pete listens, checks his watch. It is a
couple of minutes after ten, still a bit over half an hour.
But he's impatient. What's holding up the line? Philip,
a gregarious inquisitive kid who notices everything, asks
Pete if he's taking the GAMBLER'S SPECIAL. Pete shakes his
head and turns away in annoyance. One thing he doesn't
need to do is get involved in some stupid conversation with
this nosy kid. But Philip persists, stating that he's going
on the excursion and it's a lot of fun. He's taken it before.
His father's a pit boss at one of the gambling casinos and
he visits him whenever he can.

THE REDEMPTION OF NICK LANG

by

ALFRED BRENNER

NICK LANG, in U.S. Army uniform, dark, lean, handsome, but with a bitter, obsessed expression, is walking tensely along a downtown San Francisco street toward the main bus station. The street is lined with night clubs, strip joints, bars, etc. Most of them are closed now. It is morning. But there are people on the street, a few in uniform. He stays close to the buildings, keeping in the shadows, his eyes and every muscle jumpily alert. As he goes by an empty store front, he notices a large town poster plastered on the glass window along with several others. It advertises THE GAMBLER'S SPE-CIAL, a three-day round-trip bus excursion to the gambling and resort area of Reno, Nevada, which leaves at ten thirty-five A.M. every Friday from the main terminal. Checking his watch—it's now about nine fifty—he con-tinues onward. Suddenly he hears a low voice calling out to him. He glances swiftly to the side. A girl, not unattractive, is standing in a doorway, smiling an invitation. He ignores her, keeps walking without breaking his stride or changing his expression, but has only gone a few steps further when he sees something just ahead. Two MPs have stopped a GI in front of a bar and are checking his I.D. His papers apparently in order, they're nodding and letting him go now—and are coming this way. Nick whirls around, is about to run, sees the girl, steps quickly into the doorway, pulls her to him, plants his mouth on hers, stifling her greeting, and, holding her very tight, spins her around so that her back is facing the doorway. At that moment the MPs arrive. They glance in. But all they can see in the semi-darkness of the hallway is a girl embracing someone. They can't even tell if it's a man, much less a soldier. They shrug, grin, move on. Inside Nick waits motionlessly, his hand on the girl's mouth, until the footsteps of the MPs die away. Then cautiously he glances out. They're gone. He lets her go. She starts to fire a series of outraged questions at him—who is he? What does he want? What's going on? Glaring at her, his eyes narrowed, he tells her in a low, hard voice she's never seen him. Does she understand? She nods nervously. He watches her a moment longer, mutters something that sounds like thanks, grins imperceptibly, steps back out onto the street, continues toward the bus terminal.

People are entering, exiting as Nick cautiously approaches. There are more MPs. He sees the reflection of two approaching behind him in the glass of a phone booth. On the spur of the moment he steps inside, hunches over the mouthpiece, holding the receiver in his ear, faking a call. The MPs pass. He doesn't move, stays there in the same position, his face hidden, but his eyes watchful, studying every face that comes by. He is looking for someone. Suddenly he reacts as he sees, coming around a corner, a blonde young man about his own age (late twenties) wearing civilian clothes and carrying a brown paper wrapped package and a newspaper. This is PETE NEVINS. Reaching the entrance, Pete glances around quickly, then enters. Nick's eyes follow him through the large plate glass window of the terminal as he weaves between the crowds toward the ticket booths. Pete slips into a line behind a studious-looking fifteen-year-old kid (PHILIP MAXWELL) wearing glasses and listening to classical music on his transistor radio. There are four or five others in the line, including a soldier. Among the posters on the walls describing various bus excursions, tours, etc., is the one advertising the GAMBLER'S SPECIAL. This bus, being announced over the intercom, is now boarding. It is scheduled to depart on time at ten thirty-five. Pete listens, checks his watch. It is a couple of minutes after ten, still a bit over half an hour. But he's impatient. What's holding up the line? Philip, a gregarious inquisitive kid who notices everything, asks Pete if he's taking the GAMBLER'S SPECIAL. Pete shakes his head and turns away in annoyance. One thing he doesn't need to do is get involved in some stupid conversation with this nosy kid. But Philip persists, stating that *he's* going on the excursion and it's a lot of fun. He's taken it before. His father's a pit boss at one of the gambling casinos and he visits him whenever he can.

Although he's only fifteen, he's a scholarship student at Cal Tech in mathematics and has figured out a system . . . Pete is not only not listening; he has just noticed something which has caused him to go rigid and begin to sweat all over. (Nick, watching from the phone booth outside, has seen the same thing and is also reacting with intense concern.) Two MPs are approaching the line, apparently heading right toward Pete.

Pete clutches his package, reaches grimly inside his jacket, stares down at his newspaper. For a split second it seems as if a violent confrontation will erupt. But the MPs go right past him (he keeps the paper in front of his face), step up to the enlisted man standing in front of Philip and ask him for his I.D. The GI, annoyed, complies, but wants to know what's going on. He's just come into town. Why all these MPs?

Those two soldiers, the kid breaks in—the ones who escaped yesterday still haven't been caught. He heard it on the news. The MPs check the I.D. grimly.

They were being taken from the stockade at the Presidio to their trial when they overpowered the guards, Philip continues. One of the guards is in the hospital.

Pete, listening behind his newspaper, scowls down at the headlines. But he's not reading anything.

Another ticket window opens. The line moves swiftly. The MPs okay the GI's I.D. and depart. Philip purchases his ticket and leaves slowly. Pete cooly edges up to the cage and, still keeping his face half-hidden behind the paper, asks for *two* tickets on the GAMBLER'S SPECIAL. The clerk informs him he's just under the wire. There are only a few seats left. Pete takes them, pays, then heads toward the Men's Room.

Nick, having been observing all this intently from inside the phone booth, is suddenly startled by a click on the glass. He turns his head sharply. A middle-aged woman is standing outside waiting impatiently to use the phone. He looks around guardedly, replaces receiver, steps out, then swiftly enters terminal and starts in the same direction as Pete.

In the Men's Room Pete has put his package down on the shelf and is working on his hair in front of a mirror when Nick enters. Before saying a word, Nick kicks open the door of every cubicle, glances inside, checks the whole place carefully to make sure they're alone. He's not happy. The area is crawling with MPs. He feels there could be problems. Pete shouldn't have shot that guard. Pete, a southern inflection to his voice, tells him to stay cool. He had to. The fact that the Army is checking GIs in every station and airport is to be expected. But it's not checking civilians. He points to his clothes and the package. He had his girl buy the duds. Not bad, eh? They're speaking in low nervous monosyllables, moving around, watching the door, the windows, listening for footsteps. Pete meanwhile hands Nick one of the tickets he just bought, glances at his watch. There isn't much time. Bus leaves in fifteen minutes. By the way, it's loaded, he grins. Their take's got to be at least twenty-five grand, maybe more.

At that moment they hear footsteps, separate. Pete exits quickly. Nick picks up the package off the shelf, enters the cubicle just as the man comes in. Inside he carefully locks the door, removes a pistol from his pocket, sets it down gently on the water cabinet, and begins to take off his uniform.

At the bus marked GAMBLER'S SPECIAL, a happy noisy crowd is boarding for a Reno gambling holiday. Quite a few passengers are inside already, moving about, finding seats, making themselves comfortable. Pete, pushing hurriedly down the aisle toward the last vacant seat at the rear, accidentally bangs into MAJOR GEORGE HAMILTON SCHUYLER III, a somewhat overweight AM Corps officer of about forty-five who has recently been assigned to oversee the PX at the Presidio. The Major, who had been reaching up above to stow a bag, is knocked off balance and practically falls into the laps of JOHN and ALINE MATTHEWS, an elderly retired couple. Furious, he swings around, begins bawling Pete out in a strident authoritarian voice, declaring that if he had a soldier like him under his command he'd have him courtmartialled. Pete, noticing in a flash a couple of MPs arriving and positioning themselves outside near the entrance, controls himself, mumbles an apology, hurries on to the empty seat at the rear he had his eye on. The Major continues to glare at him for a few moments longer as if trying to commit his face to memory for future reference. Simultaneously Philip Maxwell, seated nearby, has, along with several other passengers, turned to see what the commotion is all about. He spies Pete, recognizes him from the line, waves—but is ignored. Pete has turned as far away as possible from the side of the bus where the MPs are standing, and has buried his face in his newspaper.

Several seats ahead of Philip a young beautiful Chicano girl of about twenty, DOLORES ALVAREZ, is alone next to the window glancing outside where EDDIE SMITH, the driver, a boy scout type in his early 40's, has nodded in friendly fashion to the MPs and is now taking the suitcases and bags of ART and ELLEN O'BRIEN, a young married couple who've just arrived. The two are incessantly bickering. Art, a stockbroker, keeps insisting that Ellen has brought much too much clothing for so short a trip. Ellen answers that they're her clothes and she'll take what she wants—and would he mind turning off that football game on his transistor set? Doesn't he ever get tired of that droning? Eddie patiently stows their bags along with the others in the luggage compartment.

While this is taking place, CONRAD BERLIN, a successful tract builder in his fifties, a loud friendly salesman type who wears western type clothes as if he were a Texas rancher, enters. Coming down the aisle, he notices the empty place beside Dolores, sits down, breathing hard from the exertion, gives her a big smile, starts telling her how he rushed to get here. He didn't want to miss this bus. Couldn't afford to. Or, he guffaws, maybe the blackjack tables at Reno couldn't afford it. Say, did she see those MPs out there giving everybody the once-over? Wonder what they want? She ignores him politely, quickly turns away and, trying to keep her movements hidden, opens a small suitcase in which—Berlin notices in a flash—is a syringe kit, a skimpy rhinestone dancing costume, a makeup case, and several textbooks. She takes out one of them, a heavy tome on Constitutional Law, starts reading and making notes.

Eddie is at the front entrance of the bus now talking briefly to the MPs, checking the time and receiving last minute instructions from the dispatcher. He's ready to depart. Simultaneously a black preacher, the REV. JEFFERSON WILLIAMS, edges past them, climbs in rapidly. As the MPs glance at him, then check inside once more before departing, Nick can be seen in the background, hurrying through the station. He is now in civilian clothes.

Nick arrives, his eyes darting around jumpily, but the moment he starts up the steps, he goes rigid. Emerging from inside and coming down right toward him are the two MPs. He steps aside abruptly and turns his face away to let them pass. As they do, they stare at him for a long moment, finally continue on their way.

Without an outward flicker of emotion, Nick climbs through the entrance, stands there in the front of the bus glancing rapidly out of the window at the two disappearing MPs, then down the aisle at the passengers, finally catching sight of Pete at the rear. The eyes of the two men meet for an instant. As Nick turns, he notices that someone is in the seat he had planned to take. Frustrated, he grabs the closest empty one he can find to the driver, which is directly in front of Art and Ellen O'Brien, drops into it, and starts to relax.

Meanwhile Eddie Smith has entered. He stands for a moment counting the passengers one last time, then bends into his seat and steps on the starter. The motor roars. At that same moment there is a banging on the door. Two MPs (different ones) are standing there knocking on it with their nightsticks. They're breathing hard as if they had been running. Eddie glances at them quizzically, opens it. As the MPs enter, Nick stiffens. Pete at the rear watches intently. This bus is going to Reno, right? the MPs ask. Eddie nods.

Well, they want to go along—not all the way to Reno—but to Emigrant Gap, a little town just off Highway 80 right before the Donner Pass area. It's not out of his way. All he has to do is stop long enough to let them off. Okay? Okay—but what's up? Eddie wants to know.

A tip just came in from the police in Emigrant Gap that the two army fugitives who escaped may be in that area. Tension as the two military policemen come down the aisle looking for seats. Nick quickly turns his head away from them and begins talking to the first person he sees—Ellen O'Brien, who sits behind him near the window. As one of the MPs slips into an empty seat not far from him, he continues his conversation with intensity and animation, continuing to keep his face averted. Ellen, to spite her husband, allows herself to become interested. But not merely to spite her husband. Nick is a handsome, attractive man. Her interest grows.

There are only two other empty seats on the bus—one next to the Reverend, the other toward the rear, near Pete. The second MP decides on that one, heads toward it, passing CLARA RHINE, an uptight conservative-looking woman of 45 who glances at him nervously, and a young couple across the way with long hair and matching unisex shirts and jeans—latter-day hippie types—DIANA HARRIS and FRANK BOWERS—who are too much involved with each other to even notice. Pete swiftly thrusts a road map, which he had begun to unfold, back into his pocket, stares out of the window. Watching in the rear view mirror, Eddie waits until the MP reaches his seat, then he shifts into gear, and the bus finally takes off.

As the GAMBLER'S SPECIAL speeds along Highway 80 through Sacramento toward the foothills of the Sierras and the resort area of Reno, the passengers begin to relate to each other; and the tension builds during several short scenes: the 15-year-old Philip, having failed to catch Pete's eye, now goes back to speak to him. As he sways down the aisle past Conrad Berlin, the builder takes out a bottle and passes it to Dolores. But she, continuing to study, politely refuses. He won't take no for an answer, insists she take a nip, telling her what rare Scotch this is. Come on, don't be a stick. She's too pretty for that. He starts to nudge closer to her; but quietly, calmly, without flicking an eyelash, she stops him cold with an ego-deflating remark involving his machismo—from a woman's point of view. He strikes back with a crack that maybe she'd rather have a shot of dope. She gives him a withering glance, goes back to her book.

Philip now has reached Pete, greets him like an old friend. He did decide to come to Reno after all. Was it because of Phil's buildup? But he saw Pete buy two tickets. Who's the other one for? He is alone, isn't he?

Pete, annoyed, nervous, jumpy at the kid's intrusion—some of the nearby passengers, including the MP, are turning and glancing back at him—tries to ignore him, to shut him up. But Phil continues chattering, talking about his parents, who are divorced, and his system for beating blackjack—he's a lonely but extremely sharp kid—and has soon begun to engage several of the others in his conversation—including the MPs, drawing them out about their mission.

Pete sits there rigidly listening to every syllable. Do they know where the GIs are? he asks casually.

The MP looks at him. They think so . . .

Do they have pictures? Another passenger breaks in.

No, but the photos are on their way, the MP explains. There's been a slight bureaucratic delay. Usual army snafu. But they have names and descriptions. One, Nick Lang, is from New York City, dark, six-one, etc.; the other, Pete Nevins, is blonde, from Tennessee. They're armed, dangerous. If anyone should chance to see them . . . As he speaks, his eyes keep focusing on each of his listeners. One of them, laughing a bit nervously, says that description could fit a lot of people, including him. He's dark, six-one . . . That fellow there—indicating Pete—is blonde.

The MP stares at his questioner, then at Pete, who meets his eyes with cool innocence. Don't worry, he answers finally. They'll know the criminals when they see them. All through this Phil is listening thoughtfully.

On a transistor toward the front of the bus Art O'Brien has tuned in another football game. The Major, wanting to hear how the Rams are doing, joins him. They get into an absorbing discussion about the relative abilities of various teams and players—and are soon joined by the MP, who is also interested and wants to get a word in. Ellen, however, is upset at this, seeks to get even with her husband by continuing her conversation (relationship) with Nick. In fact she now takes the initiative, asking him questions about where he's going to stay when he gets to Reno; is he married; what's his job; etc. He improvises, but his answers are vague. His mind is on other things—specifically, the MP seated only a few spaces away who keeps glancing at him. Ellen reacts to his sudden caution by becoming more aggressive-seductive. Art notices what is going on, grows increasingly irritated, and starts making low cracks to the Major and MP directed at Nick.

Clara Rhine, embarrassed and her equilibrium upset by Diana and Frank's continual smooching and their announcement without the slightest qualms of how much fun it is living together, moves out of her seat to the one beside Reverend Williams—across from Aline and John Matthews. She feels better among her own kind of folks (which doesn't quite include the Reverend), tells the retired couple about her job—she was an executive secretary for an insurance firm, was devoted to her boss for the last twenty-five years, and practically ran everything herself because he was the president of the firm. But he suddenly died of a heart attack, after which she was eased out of her job, to which she was totally dedicated, by a younger woman. As a result, her world totally collapsed. Her job, her boss meant everything. Now it was gone. Seeking a new pattern of existence on the advice of a psychologist, she has decided to go on this vacation and lose herself in the excitement of Reno.

John and Aline invite her to their fiftieth wedding anniversary dinner which will take place in Reno on Sunday. They also invite the Reverend, who declines politely, returns to the Bible which he's trying to read, but he is having difficulty concentrating. In fact there are tears in his eyes. Aline asks him if there's something wrong. At first he doesn't want to talk about it, then he mutters brokenly that he's going to Reno to take over a congregation there—but has lost faith, and doesn't know what to do.

A sign on the highway indicates that the town of Emigrant Gap is just ahead, perhaps a mile. The MP at the rear of the bus rises, starts forward. Philip sees the MP, feels a sense of urgency, rises abruptly, stops him as he passes, asks him where he's going. The MP answers that he and his partner are about to get off. Why? Well, Philip answers, because he thinks that . . . well, maybe they shouldn't—at least not just yet. Why? the MP asks. Philip cannot quite say what he suspects. He must make sure. He continues on to the back of the bus where Pete is seated. Pete sees that there is something on the kid's mind, senses that he is up to no good—especially when he hangs around, offers him a piece of chocolate, keeps looking at him in that peculiar way. Pete refuses the chocolate, tries to slough the kid off. But the kid just stands there eating the chocolate bar and tuning the transistor. Suddenly he asks him if he comes from the south. Why? Pete wants to know. Sort of guessed it from the way he talked, Philip says. He's got a great ear—he's heavy into music. This is one of Beethoven's last quartets he's listening to now. It's really complex stuff, like calculus. Pete snorts sarcastically, tells the kid he sure has an ear all right—it really takes an ear to guess that he comes from below the Mason and Dixon line. Practically everybody he's ever met knew that five minutes after they met him from his accent.

What about Tennessee? Philip blurts out nervously.

Pete's eyes narrow. What about it? Well, Philip asks, is that where he's from? Never been there in his life, Pete answers quietly, unemotionally.

Simultaneously, at the front of the bus, which is beginning to slow down now, the first MP, who has been studying Nick suspiciously, breaks into the conversation between Ellen and him. Hasn't he seen him someplace? Nick meets his gaze unflinchingly, shakes his head. The MP continues to stare at him. Extreme tension. The bus stops. His partner nudges him. This is where they have to get off. The MP nods but still continues to stare at Nick. He's sure he's seen him before. But dammit he can't remember where.

And so the MP, still baffled by the uncertainties of his memory, finally gives up . . . A few minutes later, after a word of thanks and farewell to Eddie Smith, the two MPs leave.

The bus starts moving. The moment the kid turns and scuttles back to his seat, Pete takes out his road map, opens it, and begins to concentrate on it intently.

Back in his seat, back to his game of chess, Philip continues to glance surreptitiously over his shoulder at Pete. He is uncertain about what to do—if anything. Nevertheless his suspicions have been aroused—but the MPs have gone. Besides, what is there to do? He doesn't want to be laughed at, if he's wrong. He's always had this vivid imagination. Yet . . . Just then he notices—as some of the passengers start to move toward the center of the bus and look out of a side window to view a mountain peak in the nearby Sierras—that Pete has joined them . . . and, on the way, has "accidentally" bumped into the dark haired man who has been sitting up toward the front near the driver. The two men exchange a few surreptitious words, their lips barely moving. He keeps watching them as they return to their respective places. Philip's suspicions have been aroused further. Something definitely is afoot . . . He must do something—tell someone about what he has seen. Some authoritative figure. His eyes alight on Major Schuyler up front talking to Art O'Brien. He rises and starts forward. Pete, in the rear, notices. At once he becomes concerned. He tries to signal Nick without success. The bus is entering the Donner Pass area. Phil has reached the Major and is trying urgently to get his attention. However Schuyler is too deeply involved with Art in a discussion of various gambling systems and the stock market to listen. The kid, annoyed, grabs the Major's arm, bursts out that he's just like his father, never pays any attention. Major Schuyler stares at him. What the devil is wrong? What does he want?

At that moment Nick sees the place he's been looking out for. It is on the highway just ahead. He quickly looks back toward the rear of the bus. Pete gives him the signal.

Philip yells, "They're the escaped soldiers!"

Pete and Nick draw their guns. Pete, on his feet, points his at the passengers, announces that this is a hijack. Everyone is to remain calm; if they do no one will be hurt. Nick meanwhile has moved just behind the driver, pressed his pistol into Eddie Smith's back, and orders him to turn off the highway just ahead into that narrow side road. Eddie obeys—he is in no position not to—and most of the other passengers are immediately subdued, frightened. But not all. There are the beginnings of protest from Conrad Berlin, who must prove his manhood to Dolores, and the Major, who must maintain the image and responsibility of the uniform he's wearing. Conrad leaps out of his seat and starts back toward Pete, protesting this outrage, demanding that he put down his gun, warning that he'll never get away with it. At the same time the Major, with the reluctant Art at his heels (spurred on by Ellen), moves toward Nick. But the hijackers quickly subdue the resistance—Pete firing a shot just past Conrad's ears. Conrad ducking and leaping nervously back into his seat, the rest of the passengers cowering in their places, Nick turning and hammering the butt of his pistol down on the Major's head, dazing him . . . as the bus makes its way through the very narrow winding road up into the mountains. It is an area where once you are off the main thoroughfare you are quickly into a wild rocky wilderness. Eddie, hunched over the wheel, insists that the road is too narrow and too precarious for the bus. They won't be able to make it. Nick orders him to keep going.

Eddie drives along this very treacherous area, winding between high mountain peaks, taking one hairpin curve after another very tensely, very slowly. It is extremely dangerous. One false turn, a loose stone and they'll crash down into the rocky gorge hundreds of feet below. Every couple of minutes the passengers turn their heads away from the windows, covering their eyes, holding each other, praying. A hysterical scream from Clara as the bus climbs up this scarcely travelled road, meant for a vehicle no larger than a jeep, into the high country of the Sierras. Mists and fog are coming in, blinding the driver.

He pulls to a stop, pointing to the speedometer. They've already gone a dozen miles. How much further? Nick looks out through the window—the outer wheels are almost off the road—orders him to keep going until there's a place to turn around.

Eddie doesn't understand what the hijackers are intending to do.

Nick tells him not to worry about it. Just do as he says. As the bus starts moving again, one of the passengers, in desperation, tries to escape out of the emergency door. He is about to step off into the void and plunge to his death hundreds of feet below, when the Reverend makes a wild grab for him and saves him at the last moment. Several times the bus teeters at the edge of the road, almost slipping over. Eddie, as well as Nick and Pete, keep their eyes peeled for a place to turn. But to everyone's consternation there doesn't seem to be any. The road is too narrow, doesn't appear to widen at any spot. It is clear that the hijackers' plans have been affected. They obviously hadn't expected this either. The bus has already been travelling several hours by now and has gone about thirty-five miles—far beyond the hijackers' original intentions.

Finally, well into the wilderness of the Donner area, as heavy mists envelop the vehicle and the winds whine and the temperature is dropping . . . dropping . . . Nick spies a place where a maneuver seems possible. He orders Eddie to stop, suggests that he make the U-turn here. It's going to be tough, Eddie says, but he will try.

It is a precarious, nerve-racking operation. Once it seems surely the bus must go over. Once a big falling rock misses it by inches. But Eddie is an excellent driver and is at last able to get the big lumbering vehicle around, facing in the direction from which it just came.

At this point the two hijackers, at gunpoint, command the passengers to leave the bus, one at a time, through the rear door. Pete moves to that exit and, as each person goes out, he relieves him of his money, jewelry, etc. The people react to this in various ways—most accept the situation; a few of the bolder ones warn Pete he'll never get away with this; a couple ask if he's just going to leave them there to die in this wilderness; John and Aline Matthews would like to get to Reno in time to celebrate their anniversary. But the one who pleads the hardest is Major Schuyler. In a low, broken voice he is forced to admit that the money being taken from him is not his. Desperately he whispers to Pete that he "borrowed" it from the PX to gamble with and hopefully pay back other gambling debts. He's over his head. But he has an unbeatable system. He's worked it out carefully. If Pete takes this stake from him, he'll be destroyed. He promises Pete anything if he lets him keep the money—or at least part of it. He has influence with the top brass. He'll get Pete off with only a slight punishment. He offers him an easy job at the PX. Pete, however, shows him no mercy and relieves him of every cent.

After everyone is out, Nick climbs behind the wheel. With Pete seated beside him, he starts the motor, shifts into gear and begins to move very slowly along the difficult road back in the direction of the main highway. But almost immediately he jams on the brakes and comes to a stop. Ahead of him on the road are a group of the passengers blocking his path. Others are all around the vehicle yelling and gesticulating.

It is severely cold outside now. Winds are howling down the mountainside. Mist and fog continue to pile up. The people are shivering, blue. A few had grabbed sweaters and coats when they were forced out of the bus, but many did not. Now they appeal to the hijackers for mercy. It is clear that under these weather conditions not all of them will be able to make it back. If they're abandoned without adequate clothes, shelter or food, some of them will surely die.

Nick is a bitter, angry man who hates and resents authority (which got him into the trouble he's in), but he refuses to drive over the group blocking the road. He cannot take responsibility for letting them freeze to death. The original plan had been to take the bus no more than ten or so miles off the main road, rob the passengers, leave them there and drive it back themselves, then abandon it. By the time the stranded passengers returned and informed the authorities, the hijackers would have had plenty of time to make their getaway. But events had forced them to alter their plans. Thirty-five miles is quite different from ten or twelve miles. Nor did they expect to get so high into the mountains, where the temperature drops so low. They've got to let the people in and take them far enough back so that they can make it the rest of the way on their own. He opens the door. But as the passengers start to crowd into the entrance, they're stopped by several shots from Pete's gun. Quickly pointing his pistol at Nick, he orders him to close the door and drive on.

The bus proceeds very slowly, edging along the sharp curves in the almost blinding mists. While Nick drives, maneuvering carefully, his eyes never leaving the road, the two men argue tensely. He'll go along with robbery, Nick mutters, but this is murder. Pete tells him not to be stupid. The passengers will be rescued. Besides, that's not his concern. He's planned this whole thing very carefully, and was nice enough to let Nick come along with him. He could have got others. Now they've got to stick to their plans—or the whole operation will fail and they'll be caught. Maybe Nick doesn't mind spending the next ten years or more in a military stockade, or a state penitentiary, but not him. He's been there. Here in this critical scene between the two men we further establish their very different characters and backgrounds (Pete is a bitter, wily farm boy; Nick is a product of the slums of Manhattan) and the essentials of the back story— their meeting in the stockade, the breakout, why Nick was there in the first place and why he went along with Pete's plan (out of anger and bitterness against authority rather than specific criminal acts, out of a sense that he was wronged by a superior officer and treated unfairly). The argument becomes desperate. Pete has his finger on the trigger. Nick continues to peer intently through the windshield at the almost invisible road. Then suddenly, in an extreme effort to distract and upset Pete and make him lose his balance, he jerks the wheel back and forth, causing the bus to swerve from side to side dangerously. Pete glances around nervously. Nick, seizing the opportunity, turns, grabs Pete's wrist, tries to knock the pistol out of his hand. Pete resists. A fight develops—during which the bus continues out of control, finally crashing against a rock. Nick is knocked unconscious. As Pete lets himself out and disappears down the road, the bus, with Nick still inside it, is left hanging there at the edge of the cliff, one wheel spinning over the side.

The bus has not gone very far, perhaps a quarter of a mile. The passengers are thus able to return without too much difficulty. With Eddie Smith, Major Schuyler and Conrad Berlin in the forefront, they reach the bus and attempt to capture Nick. But he has merely been stunned. Besides, he still has his gun and is able to hold them at bay as he climbs out.

Standing on higher ground, he tensely watches Eddie try to start the vehicle with the help of several others (most of the passengers, however, are inside)—and though the front end appears to have been badly damaged in the crash, the motor is beginning to show some life . . . Encouraged, Eddie and his helpers keep working at it, until suddenly it turns over—and catches . . . Grinning, Eddie steps on the gas and the engine roars—to the cheers and relief of everybody aboard.

But as he takes his foot off the pedal, the roar continues. It is very loud, much louder than any motor. It is not the motor. It sounds like a distant express train hurtling down the mountain, coming closer and closer, right toward them. Everyone is glancing around anxiously, puzzled, apprehensive. Outside Nick looks up, immediately sees what's happening, dashes across to the bus, yelling *avalanche!*, and pounds on the windows and motions furiously for everyone to get out and down and as close to the face of the cliff as possible. The terrified passengers comply, squeezing and pushing and thrusting themselves out through the the front and rear and emergency exits—some rushing toward the cliff, some falling on their faces, others making it to the shelter of an overhang—as the rocks come howling down in an awful clamor, stones and silt dropping all around them, the road being torn away on both sides of them—and the bus itself being almost totally buried beneath the debris.

The stunned passengers gradually rise to their feet and stare helplessly in awe and terror at the scene. A number are scratched, bleeding—there are sprained elbows, twisted ankles . . . Clara's leg is embedded under a pile of rubble. She is dug out and comforted by, of all people, Frank and Diana, both of whom she finds unexpectedly tender and sympathetic.

And now the realization dawns on all of them with sickening force—they're trapped. The road behind is totally out and the road ahead for several hundred yards has been partially torn away, leaving a path just wide enough perhaps for a man to walk on (though it's difficult and perilous—there's a sheer drop over the edge into a seemingly bottomless chasm below). Besides, it's already evening. There's nothing to do but try to dig into the bus where it's warm and get some sleep.

The next morning Nick, whose warning and assistance during the avalanche undoubtedly saved quite a few lives (and who slept outside last night under an overhang), approaches the passengers and tells them that he's going to try to make it across the path ahead to the road which winds downward through the mountains (parts of which they can see curling far below) back to the main highway. Once there he'll call the authorities and tell them about the bus—and they'll be rescued. All they have to do is wait here. But most of the passengers do not believe him. How can they be sure he'll do what he says?

The same reason he didn't just run off like his partner (who has their money), he answers. Because he feels responsible for their plight. Their safe return therefore has also become his responsibility. But he doesn't want to give anyone the wrong impression. He doesn't intend to give himself up or be captured. Anyway he'll probably never see any of them again, so . . .

And off he goes, stepping on to the narrow path ahead, and beginning to make his way cautiously toward where the road begins.

The majority of the passengers, including Eddie Smith (who has assumed a leadership role), do decide to stay and wait, not because they believe or trust Nick, but because they feel they have no other safe course of action. That stretch of half-torn-out road ahead *is* precarious, and thirty-five miles is a very long trek. Besides, a number of the people are in too poor a condition even to consider it. Most stay simply because it is the prudent thing to do . . . because established authority (their driver) has advised it, and because they're confident that sooner or later they will be found and rescued.

However, despite the danger and the obvious difficulties ahead, some refuse to wait. These are: Major Schuyler (because although he supports Eddie Smith as an authority figure, he feels an urgency to get back to his base as soon as possible in order to somehow borrow and return the money he has taken—to somehow cover the missing funds before anyone finds out about them. If they have to depend on Nick to summon help, it may take forever); Philip Maxwell, Diana Harris, and Frank Bowers (because they're young and impatient and it's a challenge; besides, *someone* has to go and get help); Ellen O'Brien (to wait is a bore. She also wants to bug her husband whom she knows wants to stay); Art (because he feels he must accompany his wife, even though he's convinced this is a foolish thing to do); John and Aline Matthews (because they want to get to Reno in time to celebrate their fiftieth anniversary, because they feel strong and healthy enough to make the trek and because they'd rather be up and doing, determining their own fate rather than waiting for someone else to rescue them); Dolores (because she's got to get to a job at one of the clubs and is already late); Clara (mainly because of Mr. and Mrs. Matthews, to whom she's begun to relate and like—even though she thinks it would be wiser to stay); Conrad Berlin (because he's still trying to impress Dolores with his youthful point of view and machismo, and simply to be near her. He's convinced he can get her to like him, even though she hasn't given him the slightest encouragement); and Reverend Williams (he flips a coin. Since he's lost faith in any sign from God, he'll play it as it lays—straight luck. Heads he goes. It's heads.).

And so the members of this little group dig into the baggage compartment of the bus (through the rubble) and take the warmest clothing they've brought, some carrying blankets or suitcases (Frank and Diana take their sleeping bags and other backpacking equipment, including a rope. Dolores brings the small bag which contains her makeup case, syringe kit, and a very brief rhinestone costume. Conrad chides her about the costume. She'll sure need it on this hike. It's what she works in, she snaps. She dances in a Reno club to support her education every weekend. Topless? he cracks. Maybe *he's* ashamed of *his* body, she answers with a withering look); then they leave the rest of the passengers (a moving moment) and start back along the partially demolished stretch of road which was whole only a little while ago. One by one they make their way slowly across the tortuous path along the face of the cliff.

The group is moving very carefully in single file, keeping as close to the side of the mountain as possible. No one dares to look down. Frank is in the lead and Diana is at the rear. Ellen is behind Frank. Art is taking one fearful step at a time and complaining unhappily to his wife that they should have remained with the bus. The old couple is finding the thin air up here difficult to breathe. Once Aline almost slips dizzily to her knees, but young Philip, right behind her, holds her steady. Conrad, just to the rear of Dolores, is hugging the side of the cliff nervously, but at the same time is trying to harass her about the needle and syringe kit—doesn't she know that stuff is illegal? She could be arrested, put in jail. Why does she take that stuff? She ought to get rid of it right now. He'll do it if she won't.

Suddenly the path gives way alongside them. Everyone stops, clutches the next person for support. Only a ledge remains for them to stand on.

They dare not move. Clara, trembling, close to tears, cries out. Conrad, staring over the edge down into the vast, empty canyon below, panics, screaming and trembling as if out of his mind. Dolores tries to hold him steady—but she herself is beginning to lose her balance. Everyone is in danger because of him. A few of them are beginning to sway precariously over the edge.

Nick at this point is well ahead of the group, but not as far as might be expected. He has been delayed: as a matter of fact he has just about reached the end of the bad stretch and is trying to find a way to navigate the treacherous gap between where he is standing and the main road, when he hears the screams and shouts of panic behind him. He turns, immediately sees what is taking place. The people are caught on the very narrow ledge, in places only a foot wide. It's maybe a hundred or more yards from across the exposed catwalk to where they are trapped. Nevertheless, without thinking twice, he steps out back across the thin ledge with the wind lashing at him. Reaching Frank (who has passed his rope to the line of people standing stiffly and fearfully against the face of the cliff), he continues swiftly and surefootedly past him, past Ellen, Art—the tension is excruciating as he blindly reaches out with one foot, finds a support, then reaches with another, moving by feel, holding on with his hands to every indentation and crevice he can find—until he reaches the sobbing, shaking Conrad. He grabs him, plows a sharp uppercut to his jaw. The shock brings Conrad out of his hysteria. Then, counselling, cautioning, advising, he leads them all very slowly, step by step, back across the catwalk he just came on. Keeping themselves flat against the side of the mountain, they continue at a snail's pace, hanging onto the rope as Nick continues to guide them.

It is well into the afternoon—the sun is beginning to disappear behind the peaks, long shadows are forming, it is becoming colder and the winds are growing even more furious. They all reach what seems like the end of their ordeal only to come face to face with a wide gap between the ledge on which they're standing and the road ahead. Nick, having been here before and studied the situation, realizes at once that though he himself might find a way across, most of the people in this group will never be able to make it. However, there is an alternative—the narrow ledge has widened here. There is no straight drop over a cliff. Actually they're on the mountainside, which slants downward through rocky pathless wilderness—and far below they can see the main road snaking between the cliffs and canyons. Their only choice is to cut down across this rugged mountainside to that road—which is the one the bus originally came on and will lead them back to the main highway and "civilization."

Nick explains they will have to climb down ledge by ledge, using the rope like mountaineers. Because he feels responsible for them, as he stated previously, he will stay with them and guide them—but under no circumstances will he allow himself to be captured. Is that clear? Okay. Unfortunately they don't have the proper clothes or equipment. But they have no choice. Can the old couple make it? They nod grimly. But the pressures on them physically are fierce. Aline has twisted her elbow during the catwalk; has improvised a sling to cradle it in, while John feels his toes beginning to become very painful. Could it be the cold? Frostbite? The extremities are the first parts of the body to feel it. He mentions it to Aline but doesn't say anything to anyone else because he doesn't want to hold them up. Somehow he'll make it.

Diana and Frank, aware that the couple needs help, supply it. (We learn that they are really quite different from what they've appeared to be. Diana teaches second grade in public school and has a great rapport with her pupils, and Frank is a scientist, a biochemist at Berkeley who knows a great deal about certain aspects of medicine.)

Philip's transistor is on—there is a news break which includes something about the GAMBLER'S SPECIAL, missing since yesterday. (No one was concerned at first about the fact that it hadn't arrived in Reno on schedule because of a blizzard in the area. Many of the vehicles were hours late. Some even had to turn back or ride out the storm alongside the road. But as dawn came and the snows stopped and every transport was finally accounted for except the GAMBLER'S SPECIAL, it became clear that something serious must have happened to it. A search along the highway has been instituted but no clues have yet been found.) And of course there won't be, everyone in the group is aware. How long will it take for the Search and Rescue teams to start looking in the mountains? How long before *they* are found? Will they be found?

By now of course everyone in the little party has abandoned his extra baggage (except Frank and Diana, who've carried their sleeping bags on their backs). They are climbing downward through more difficult terrain. Ellen is keeping up with Nick, ignoring her husband, who is lagging behind, stumbling dizzily over the treacherous ground. The Major is making his way along beside Art, breathing heavily as he talks about himself and his compulsion—which he's never been able to admit before. Dolores is just to the rear of him. Now and then she glances over her shoulder at Conrad with contempt. He is moving along silently, keeping apart from the others, ashamed, unable to lift his eyes. Only the Reverend is near him, trying to comfort him.

The group has scrambled through a small boulderfield and now is carefully making its way across the smooth, slippery surface of a wide, flat expanse of rock when it suddenly comes to a crack about a dozen or so feet wide. The other side of it is on a lower level, perhaps ten feet below—like a giant step. They all stop, look around. Nick studies the situation. There's no way around it, for it extends across their path seemingly for miles. To jump or climb is impossible. Some way *must* be found however—or they'll be trapped here without food or water at the mercy of the cold (they've got to keep moving or they'll freeze)—and who knows how soon, or if ever, they'll reach the road or be rescued. In fact the last thing Nick wants is to be "rescued" under these circumstances.

He considers the problem and finally devises a solution by using the trunks of two fallen trees to create a bridge across the chasm. Even this would be too perilous except that with the help of Frank's rope a "railing" is improvised.

It is a breathtaking procedure. Clara, John and Aline Matthews almost don't make it—and Conrad, in utter fear but trying with all his effort to fight it, finally makes it across.

At length everyone is across but as they start down to the next ridge a moment later, there is a sudden siren scream of air, and a gigantic boulder comes hurtling down, bouncing right past them. Art, terrified, loses his footing, his grip on the rope and, with a yell, tumbles down the side of the mountain, disappearing from view.

Ellen, who has been inconsiderate of his welfare and feelings until this moment, abruptly goes into a panic, sobbing, screaming, staring down into the emptiness after him. She cries out that he's gone, dead, she knows it—wanting him now, guilty for the way she treated him, declaring her love for him. She shouts his name frantically down into the canyon. At first all she hears is the echo of her own voice.

Then, miraculously, another voice! They all hear it. It's Art's! He's alive, somewhere below!

Nick immediately decides to go to his rescue. But he will need someone else to assist him. Frank and several others volunteer—Major Schuyler, however, insists. Art is his friend. They are planning to see each other in the future. Art has even promised to put up some money to help him out of his fix—he's going to wire his bank back in San Francisco. Moreover, the events Schuyler has gone through so far—his face to face confrontation with implacable nature, these dangerous, awe-inspiring peaks, death on all sides—have begun to crack his protective veneer of authority and reveal the man behind the uniform. He's still a gambler, but now he wants to gamble for a higher purpose, a man's life.

Nick carefully ties one end of their rope to a tree and then the two men start to climb down the long twisting gully of crumbling stone and dirt. Among the group watching, Dolores is impressed by the cool defiance of danger exhibited by Nick. She moves toward Ellen, takes her hand comfortingly.

After a difficult search, Nick and the Major finally find Art. He is hanging from the limb of a tree, bleeding, torn—and has lost consciousness. The two men, working strenuously, climb up and carefully lift him down—only to discover he is in shock. They take off their own jackets to keep him warm, rub his limbs, his body, and do whatever else is necessary to bring him out of danger.

At last they are successful. But the exertion has caused a severe pain in Schuyler's chest. He hides it and just sits there tending to the recovering Art, while Nick calls up to the others and signals them to climb down the rope. It is impossible to get Art back up in his weakened condition—and besides, he's heard the sound of water somewhere below.

With difficulty the members of the group lower themselves. Aline Matthews almost doesn't make it because she can only use one arm. Her husband is in an even worse way because of his feet. But with help from the others, all of them reach safety.

The moment Ellen sees Art she rushes to him, swearing she loves him, and promising that she'll never act so callously toward him again.

Day is fading fast. Nick has found the stream below. The group, footsore and bone weary, follows him down and makes camp. As they do, Frank and Diana show the others how to live off the land, gathering roots and wild plants that can be eaten—berries, fruits, nuts, even certain types of insects. They build a fire, make a lean-to out of branches. Philip is their most enthusiastic assistant and pupil. (NOTE: The wilderness survival techniques will of course be accurate, informative and interesting of themselves. In the script we will go into greater detail—but not in any way to bog down the story, rather to enhance it. At stake is survival. And these are the techniques to ensure it.)

That night Nick is trying to map out their position relative to the winding road which they have lost, when Conrad comes over to him. The older man, guilty and ashamed, confesses to his fear complex, apologizing for what happened earlier today. He's not trying to make any excuses, but he suffers from acrophobia, a fear of heights.

Dolores, who is sitting nearby with her syringe kit, needle, etc., hears this with cynicism and not an ounce of sympathy. Why doesn't he simply try to give up his machismo, she suggests coldly. It's the least attractive thing about him. The least attractive thing about her is the fact that she's hooked, he answers. Sorry, she says quietly, but she's been hooked on insulin most of her life. There's no other way to beat diabetes, so far. Conrad stares at her, stunned a bit by the revelation, starts to apologize—but she rises abruptly, walks away.

Nick follows, finds her a little later. She is alone, giving herself her daily shot of insulin. He tells her he doesn't think Conrad is going to bug her anymore. It's all right, she smiles. A lot of men bug her. She's used to it. But then she corrects herself. She really isn't used to it. She resents it. She resents having to use her body to make money. She loves to dance. And she's not ashamed of her body—but she has nightmares sometimes about the faces of the men in the audience gawking at her. She's got to have the money though. She's got to get her law degree. She's going to be *somebody*.

Nick looks at her, moved by her emotion. She has touched a chord within him. She spoke his feelings exactly. Not only that, she's beautiful.

And there is no question but that she admires him for the way he's led the group, risked his life for them. But how did he get involved in hijacking in the first place? Somehow she can't see him as a thief, a lawbreaker, or an escaped criminal.

He tells her very briefly—and without trying to justify his actions, without even a trace of self-pity—that he was not sentenced to anything but was on his way to a trial. Like her, he has this rigid sense of justice which often takes the form of a distrust of people in authority. Just because a man in an officer's uniform commits what he feels to be a wrong, he will not turn his head. Well, it's always gotten him in trouble, probably always will. Maybe, he adds with a twisted grin, he should have gone to school to be a lawyer too, instead of the army.

It's not too late, she suggests.

He shrugs.

She'd like to defend him, she says. She knows people—lawyers. How about if she tries to find someone?

Give himself up? He shakes his head. No.

Holding his hand, she tells him he can't run forever. Sooner or later he'll be caught.

He shrugs. Hopefully it'll be later.

Nevertheless, though they differ, a relationship has begun between these two—doomed, tragic, and all too brief . . . but moving and real.

The night is freezing. The winds whistle harshly. It has begun to rain. John Matthews is in much pain because of his feet. Frank examines them. It's a case of severe frostbite. He must get to a doctor very soon or infection and gangrene could set in—and he could lose his legs, or even his life. Frank and Diana give the older couple their sleeping bags.

Meanwhile, Clara, having come over to Major Schuyler to tell him what a heroic thing he did today in helping rescue Art, notices that he's not acting quite right. She is telling him about her former boss, another good man whom she worked with for twenty-five years as executive secretary, when he again gets a sudden terrible constriction in the chest . . . and several other clear indications of a heart attack.

Holding him in her arms, trying to soothe him, she tells him to rest quietly. He'll be better soon.

But he knows he won't. He's had these symptoms before. He's kept it a secret because he didn't want to be retired from the army at this early age. He's a third-generation officer and has a tradition to live up to. But somehow, though he's tried to escape it by the compulsive excitement of gambling, it hasn't worked.

Clara calls to the others as he fights for breath. They come. But it's too late.

Major Schuyler dies in Clara's arms just as her boss did only a few months ago.

Following day (the third day since starting out from San Francisco) there is a pea soup fog. Moreover, the stream has swelled during the night into a much wider, rushing river. It is difficult to see anything. John Matthews, unable to walk, is being carried in an improvised stretcher, first by Frank and Nick, then by other of the men who take turns. Once, Philip, wandering blindly in the fog, thinks he is lost and panics—almost falling into the stream—but his yells bring help just in time.

Their only hope, according to Nick's calculations, is to somehow cross the bloated stream. On the other side, not far away, is the road and salvation. But the stream is too wide. In addition, there is no sun to guide them, no stars. Nor do they have a compass. Where the road is exactly, or how far away, he has no way of knowing. But the old man must be brought to a doctor. Time is of the essence.

They continue along the stream. It gradually becomes narrower. The fog is beginning to clear a bit. Dolores is beside Nick. Everyone is looking for a place to cross, when the sound of a plane is heard. It is barely visible far up in the sky, appearing and disappearing between the mountain peaks. Everyone looks up, shouts, waves his arms, tries to signal it by every means possible. As they do Nick furiously pulls out his pistol, orders them to stop. He will not be taken prisoner. All he wants is to lead them back to safety. That's his commitment. No more. If that plane sees them it will result in his capture. He will not allow it.

The others face him angrily, their eyes meeting his. Tension. Several seem ready to fight. Quickly they try to make deals with him. John Matthews' life is in balance. Rigidly, he threatens anyone who disobeys.

At this point Dolores cooly picks up a brightly colored scarf and defies him by waving it wildly up and down at the plane. Others join in. Nick lifts his pistol, aims it at Dolores. He continues to aim at her for a moment or two longer, cocking the trigger—then resignedly lowers it and replaces it in his pocket. He can't kill her, or anyone. They continue to try to contact the plane.

But ironically the aircraft doesn't see them and continues on its way.

Later, trudging along the side of the stream, they reach a place where it seems possible to cross. Nick suggests they make their attempt here. The others agree. It's very difficult, however. The water in some places is quite deep and it is moving strongly. Nick and Frank are carrying John Matthews on the stretcher, trying to hold him high enough so that he doesn't get wet. Clara, Philip, and Mrs. Matthews are holding hands. Dolores follows them. But as she reaches the middle of the stream, she lets out a scream—she's lost hold of her precious insulin kit. Conrad, pushing along just behind her, sees where it went in the deeper section, makes a dive, and comes up with the prize. But as he lifts it above his head, shouting in triumph, the rapidly rushing current suddenly sweeps him off his feet and carries him swiftly downstream—and he disappears around a bend.

Nick and Frank, with Philip and Dolores in tow, try to find him. But the stream has twisted sharply and disappeared into underbrush so thick it's impossible to get through. They have to give up.

But during the search Nick has found a kind of trail and decides to follow it. He's sure it leads to the road. But it's well into the afternoon already and they still have a long way to go, and it's very cold. He must get John Matthews to a doctor. He must get Dolores to a place where she can get her insulin or she'll go into shock. Everyone in the struggling, weary, wet group needs rest, warmth. The toll on all of them, even the younger ones, is severe. The situation seems hopeless. They keep plunging along, trying to keep from freezing, almost without any expectation of anything. Nick is becoming more and more concerned about Dolores, who is showing signs of weakness, when suddenly he sees fresh footprints on the trail.

Despair surges to hope. If someone is nearby, maybe help is also near. The group struggles harder, over the rocky rutted road, hurrying for their lives. And then, a miracle! They see something! A Sierra Club lodge up on a ridge not far from the road. There'll be warmth there, food perhaps, some means to contact civilization—a place to rest.

But as they come within hailing distance of the building, they are met by gunshots!

Nick, bending low behind the rocks along with the others, making sure they keep their heads down, can't imagine what's in the lodge or why anyone would want to shoot at them. But he's going to find out. Dolores clutches his arm, doesn't want him to go. This is no time to get killed. There's suddenly too much at stake. He looks into her eyes. He knows. But it's freezing out here. John Matthews could lose his legs if not brought to a warm place and given treatment. He's got to get him, and her, and the others to safety, no matter what happens. They're all his responsibility. He cautions the rest of them to stay under cover. Then he creeps out alone through the underbrush around to the rear of the lodge. Shots continue to ring out, bouncing off the rocks where the others are hiding.

Reaching the lodge, he lifts himself up carefully and peers through a rear window, and stares in shock at what he sees inside.

It is Pete, his back toward him, firing at the others. He is limping; seems to have hurt his leg badly. Nick takes out his pistol, starts very carefully to open the window—but as he does, Pete catches a glimpse of his reflection in the adjoining pane, whirls about, fires.

There is a shootout and final confrontation. Both men are wounded, Nick first, then Pete. As they move about, bleeding, in pain, they spit out angry, bitter words. Pete was caught by the same freezing weather, was unable to make it all the way to the main highway and was holed up here waiting for morning and warmer temperatures.

Right, Pete answers. He broke his leg when he had to leave the road which was knocked out below in several places because of the avalanche. That's why he was delayed. But he's going to make it and get across the border to Mexico with the money as he planned. And neither Nick nor those others out there are going to expel him from this place. He needs the cabin to escape the biting cold, for survival.

Sure, he understands, Nick continues. He understands everything. Pete set him up. He used Nick. He needed someone to help him hijack the bus and Nick was his pigeon. Pete cleverly used Nick's anger at authority for his own purposes. The whole thing was planned, even the getaway—Nick wasn't supposed to get a thing.

Right, Pete growls hoarsely. Except he hadn't planned to kill him. Now there's no other way.

And he starts across, squirming on his belly, toward where he thinks Nick is, fires.

As he does, Nick rolls over out of the way, fires back. The shot is fatal. Pete dies.

Then, weak and bloody, Nick steps falteringly out into the doorway and waves the others up.

Reaching the lodge, Dolores rushes up to Nick and, with Frank and Diana's help, carries him inside and begins to take care of hi⁻ wounds.

Young Philip, the ham operator, meanwhile contacts civilization on the short wave transmitter, sends out an urgent SOS . . . and learns happily that his father has been worried sick about him and has been moving heaven and earth to find him—and that the bus has just been found with all the passengers alive.

The rescue helicopter arrives. Among those who emerge from inside is Conrad. He comes up to Dolores and hands her the insulin kit which he had rescued from the stream. He had been washed up on the shore and the helicopter had picked him up on its way here.

The others are being led or carried into the helicopter by the medics.

Nick is the last one to be lifted aboard. Dolores is at his side.

Appendix B

"Courage at 3:00 A.M." was an episode I wrote for the series *Ben Casey*.

To write it I had to do a certain amount of research, as you'll see when you read it. As a matter of fact, the central concept came from a real incident about a research worker who got cancer from an open wound while working with cancer cells in the lab. From that incident I developed a character.

I had to motivate her dedication, her using of her own body as a guinea pig. I invented a husband who died in Vietnam, and a child. And then I put her in an emotional relationship with the series protagonist, the dedicated neurosurgeon, Ben Casey.

Actually, it came out rather well, I think. It was a good powerful piece the television screen and still is run periodically on small stations throughout the country. I still get royalties for it.

Although this is a first draft, there were very few changes made in it for the actual production.

The script is an example of television script format. Study it closely in conjunction with Chapter 16. Practice it by writing your own scenes in this format. Dramatize a scene from a story, or novel, or even a play, as well as your original material. When you do, use the proper format. And of course when finally you come to writing your own script, refer to this one. (Note: The first four pages of this script are a facsimile of the original draft.)

BEN CASEY

"COURAGE AT 3:00 A.M."

(01-190)

by

Alfred Brenner

Producer: Irving Elman   FIRST DRAFT

Property of:
BING CROSBY PRODUCTIONS

BEN CASEY

"COURAGE AT 3:00 A.M."

TEASER

FADE IN:

1   INT. BIO-LAB - NIGHT - FULL SHOT   1

It's in heavy shadows, except for one brightly lit working area where DR. ELIZABETH WILSON, an attractive biochemist of about thirty, is carefully and wearily
placing some test tubes in a rack. TED HOFFMAN, wearing a suit, standing beside a table, is watching her.
CAMERA NARROWS IN on them.
                        TED
                   (a bit impatient)
            But the last show's at nine...

                        LIZ
                    (calmly)
            Be a nice fellow and put your
            friend in that cage please...

Ted looks at her, then at:

2   P.O.V. SHOT - TABLE   2

It is fenced in. On it a hamster is running around.

3   BACK TO TED   3

He reaches down, picks up hamster.

                        TED
            All right, Charlie. Bedtime.

4   ANOTHER ANGLE   4

He continues to speak to hamster as he crosses toward
cages. Liz, in b.g., starts to smile.

                                        (CONTINUED)

4   CONTINUED   4

                                   TED
                               (continuing)
                        You know your mistress is not
                        doing herself any good by all
                        this work... look at that
                        pallor on her face. Notice
                        those dark shadows under her...
                                   (looks up, to
                                    Liz, as her
                                    smile widens)
                        What's the matter?

5   FAVORING LIZ   5

       watching him gaily despite her weariness.

                                   LIZ
                        That's not Charlie. That's --
                        Charlene...

                                   TED
                        Oh, excuse me, Charlene...

       He starts to unhook cage door.

                                   LIZ
                               (pointing)
                        And not that cage.   That one.

       He looks into empty cage.

                                   TED
                        You mean you're going to put
                        Charlene in here all by
                        herself?

                                   LIZ
                        She's used to it.

                                   TED
                               (puts hamster
                                in cage)
                        Are you?

6   CLOSE - LIZ   6

       presses her lips together as a wave of pain hits her.
       He starts toward her.

                                   TED
                               (continuing)
                        Something wrong?

                                                    (CONTINUED)

6   CONTINUED: 6

3

She forces a smile, shakes her head. He continues
looking at her questioningly. A beat. Then he lets
it pass.

                    TED
                 (continuing)
          You know what you need? Hot
          sun...warm beach...

                    LIZ
                 (wanly; dreamily)
          M-m-m-m...

                    TED
          Listen, I've got a week coming
          next month. I'd be glad to
          pick up an extra plane ticket
          ...Did you ever see the water
          off Ladego Beach, Jamaica...
          it's so blue and clear...

7   FAVORING LIZ   7

taking off her white jacket, looking into the reflection of her drawn face in a small mirror perched on a
shelf, she wearily pushes some strands of hair away
from her forehead.

                    TED
                 (continuing;
                  watching her)
          You haven't heard a word I
          said...

She looks across at him.

                    TED
                 (continuing;
                  unhappily)
          Tell me something, hun --
          what have these hamsters got
          that I haven't got...?

She comes close, pats his cheek, smiles wanly.

                    LIZ
          You wouldn't want what they
          have, Ted. Nobody would...

8   INCLUDING CASEY   8

entering, approaches.

                                        (CONTINUED)

BEN CASEY

"COURAGE AT 3:00 A.M."

(O1-190)

by

Alfred Brenner

TEASER

FADE IN:

1 INT. BIO-LAB–NIGHT–FULL SHOT

It's in heavy shadows, except for one brightly lit working area where
DR. ELIZABETH WILSON, an attractive biochemist of about thirty,
is carefully and wearily placing some test tubes in a rack. TED
HOFFMAN, wearing a suit, standing beside a table, is watching
her. CAMERA NARROWS IN on them.

> TED
> (a bit impatient)
> But the last show's at nine . . .

> LIZ
> (calmly)
> Be a nice fellow and put your friend in that cage please . . .

Ted looks at her, then at:

2 P.O.V. SHOT–TABLE

It is fenced in. On it a hamster is running around.

3 BACK TO TED

He reaches down, picks up hamster.

> TED
> All right, Charlie. Bedtime.

4 ANOTHER ANGLE

He continues to speak to hamster as he crosses toward cages. Liz, in b.g., starts to smile.

> TED
> (continuing)
> You know your mistress is not doing herself any good by all this work . . . look at that pallor on her face. Notice those dark shadows under her . . .
> (looks up, to Liz, as her smile widens)
> What's the matter?

5 FAVORING LIZ

watching him gaily despite her weariness.

> LIZ
> That's not Charlie. That's—Charlene . . .

> TED
> Oh, excuse me, Charlene . . .

He starts to unhook cage door.

> LIZ
> (pointing)
> And not that cage. *That* one.

He looks into empty cage.

> TED
> You mean you're going to put Charlene in here all by her-self?

> LIZ
> She's used to it.

> TED
> (puts hamster in cage)
> Are you?

6 CLOSE—LIZ

presses her lips together as a wave of pain hits her. He starts toward her.

> TED
> (continuing)
> Something wrong?

She forces a smile, shakes her head. He continues looking at her questioningly. A beat. Then he lets it pass.

> TED
> (continuing)
> You know what you need? Hot sun . . . warm beach . . .

> LIZ
> (wanly; dreamily)
> M-m-m-m . . .

> TED
> Listen, I've got a week coming next month. I'd be glad to pick up an extra plane ticket . . . Did you ever see the water off Ladego Beach, Jamaica . . . it's so blue and clear . . .

7 FAVORING LIZ

taking off her white jacket, looking into the reflection of her drawn face in a small mirror perched on a shelf, she wearily pushes some strands of hair away from her forehead.

> TED
> (continuing; watching her)
> You haven't heard a word I said . . .

She looks across at him.

> TED
> (continuing; unhappily)
> Tell me something, hun—what have these hamsters got that I haven't got . . . ?

She comes close, pats his cheek, smiles wanly.

> LIZ
> You wouldn't want what they have, Ted. Nobody would . . .

8 INCLUDING CASEY

entering, approaches.

> CASEY
> (breaking in)
> Ted . . . patient wants to see you . . . Mr. Andrews . . .
> (glancing at Liz)
> Sorry . . .

> TED
> You two know each other? Dr. Wilson . . . Dr.
> Casey . . . Ben, Liz . . .

Casey and Liz nod perfunctory greetings.

> TED
> (continuing; to Casey)
> Maggie tell you I was here?

Casey nods.

> TED
> (continuing)
> What is it with Andrews?

> CASEY
> I think he just wants to be reassured about tomorrow's
> operation . . . Talk to him.

> TED
> (nods; turns)
> You'll excuse me, Liz–? Duty calls . . .

She nods. He goes to door, looks back.

> TED
> (continuing)
> Say, why don't you take my place, Ben . . . ? You two can
> still catch the last show at the Tivoli, if you hurry . . .

He goes out. Liz hangs up her white jacket, runs a comb through her hair. Casey watches.

> CASEY
> You seemed relieved . . .

> LIZ
> Do I? Well, it's not that Ted isn't fun . . . I just wasn't up to it tonight. Big day tomorrow . . .

> CASEY
> What time do you get here in the morning?

> LIZ
> (off-hand)
> Six . . . seven . . .

> CASEY
> You leave this late every night?

> LIZ
> Not *every* night.

> CASEY
> That's a thirteen-hour day . . .

> LIZ
> Is it?

She starts toward door.

> CASEY
> What are you working on?

> LIZ
> You interested?

> CASEY
> I asked you, didn't I?

A beat as Liz looks at him; then she comes back into room, approaches an electronic microscope, takes cover off, gets a slide, places it beneath lens, and carefully focuses eyepiece. He keeps watching.

> LIZ
> (looks up)
> Come here.

He approaches. She steps aside, indicates that he look into microscope. He does.

9 INSERT—SLIDE

under microscope, showing viruses.

> LIZ'S VOICE
> See those viruses?

10 BACK TO SCENE

Casey looking into microscope. Liz watching him.

> LIZ
> They cause cancer . . .

Casey lifts his head, glances at her, reacts.

> LIZ
> (continuing)
> . . . in hamsters . . . or at least they're present when a malignancy exists.

A beat. Liz starts to remove slide from microscope. He watches her.

> CASEY
> Would you like a cup of coffee?

11 CLOSE—LIZ

Her mouth tightens in a sudden spasm of pain, slide slips from her hand.

12 INCLUDING CASEY

moving toward her quickly, grips her, concerned.

> LIZ
> (breaking away)

It's nothing—a headache . . .
(looks down at floor, kneeling; almost in tears)
. . . oh, no!

13 INCLUDING SLIDE

on floor. It is broken.

CASEY
You feel warm. You may have a fever.

LIZ
(picking up pieces)
Oh, maybe I do have a touch of something. That 24-hour
virus is going around. I'll take some antibiotics and hit the
sack.

CASEY
(studying her)
When's the last time you had a checkup?

LIZ
(rising, placing broken pieces on table)
I don't know. Listen, let's not make a federal case.

CASEY
I think we ought to take a blood count.

He reaches for her arm, starts to lead her out.

LIZ
(resisting)
Wait a minute! You're not my doctor!

CASEY
(narrowly)
What are you afraid of?

LIZ
(bursting out)
Who's afraid? I have work to do. *Leave me alone!*

She twists away, starting for the door, but suddenly halts, dizzy with pain. He rushes up to her, grabs her, holds her. She clamps her jaw tight, closing her eyes, fighting it, resisting.

> LIZ
> (continuing; muttering)
> I don't want to know what I've got! I haven't time! I have work to do!

14 CLOSE SHOT

Casey continues to hold her, his face troubled.

FADE OUT.

END OF TEASER

ACT ONE.

FADE IN:

15 INT. HOSPITAL LAB—LIZ

is sitting on a chair. A TECHNICIAN is going through the process of taking blood from her arm for a blood count. Casey is examining her, mainly feeling her arms, shoulders, lymph areas. Her attitude is still angry, resistant. The technician finishes, places a piece of cotton over the tiny cut to stop the blood, indicates that she hold it. As she does, Technician goes out with test tube. All this under OPENING TITLES. When they clear:

> LIZ
> (to Casey)
> What are you trying to do? I told you, I . . .

He is touching her face and neck area with his fingertips.

> CASEY
> Tell me, have you lost weight recently . . . ?

> LIZ
> I'm busy. I don't have time to eat. I live on black coffee . . .

                    CASEY
              How many pounds . . . ?

                    LIZ
           Oh, about fifteen . . . But—

                    CASEY
         Tired all the time, you say . . .?

                    LIZ
Well, I've been working hard. Maybe I have a touch of mo-
nonucleosis . . .

                    CASEY
    Doesn't your husband ever try to get you to rest?

                    LIZ
                 (taken aback)
           Who told you I was married?

                    CASEY
              (indicating her finger)
           That's a wedding ring, isn't it?

                    LIZ
        Oh, yes—I—my husband is dead . . .

But Casey has turned away.

16 FAVORING CASEY

as he crosses toward Technician who has entered. Technician hands
him a slip of paper, glances at him, at Liz (in b.g.) quickly, expressionlessly, exits. Casey frowns at what he sees on paper, crumbles it in
his hand.

                    CASEY
              (low, to Technician)
Would you tell Dr. Axelson I'd like to see him please, immediately.

Technician nods, exits.

17 INCLUDING LIZ

who has been watching somewhat nervously, as Casey turns back to her.

LIZ
(trying to hide her concern—flippant)
Well, Doctor . . . ? How long have I got?

CASEY
Let's get a picture of your chest now . . .

LIZ
(rising)
What is this—a complete checkup?

She follows him to door. They go out.

18 INT. CORRIDOR

as Liz and Casey cross it to X-ray room.

LIZ
My blood count was low, wasn't it?

Casey looks at her, nods imperceptibly.

CASEY
That swelling on your neck—how long have you had it?

They enter.

19 INT. X-RAY ROOM

It contains camera, equipment, etc. X-RAY TECHNICIAN approaches.

CASEY
(to technician)
Chest . . .

LIZ
(to Casey)
What's the matter with me, Ben?

> CASEY
> Would you please come back into the lab when you're fin-
> ished in here . . .

Casey exits. She looks after him.

> X-RAY TECHNICIAN
> Please step in there, Doctor, and remove all your clothing
> above your waist.

20 INT. OFFICE CONNECTED TO LAB (SHOOTING INTO IT
THROUGH DOORWAY FROM LAB)

On half-open door in close f.g., we read: "DR. IVER AXELSON,
CHIEF PATHOLOGIST." Inside office in b.g., Casey and AXELSON,
mature, grey, careful, are conferring. Axelson is glancing at the crumbled
slip containing Liz's blood count which Casey just gave him. SOUND of
door opening. Casey looks up.

> CASEY
> There she is now.

Both men start toward door.

21 INT. LAB

Liz closes the door and comes into room, making final adjustment on
blouse, as the two men approach her.

> CASEY
> (to Liz)
> I've asked Dr. Axelson to take a look at you.

> AXELSON
> (indicating a chair)
> Please sit down.

> LIZ
> (sitting down)
> You're the pathologist . . .

> AXELSON
> (nods, looks at her professionally as he speaks)
> Dr. Casey tells me you're on the staff—doing research in
> biochemistry . . .

He immediately feels her neck. Almost in the same breath, without changing his expression.

> AXELSON
> (continuing)
> . . . how long have you had this lump?

Liz glances up quickly at Casey, who has been watching expressionlessly; then to Axelson:

> LIZ
> I don't know exactly . . . a couple of months . . . But . . . .

Simultaneously Casey looks toward door, goes toward:

22 INCLUDING X-RAY TECHNICIAN

who has just entered wearing rubber gloves and apron and carrying a dripping negative. Casey meets him, takes negative.

> CASEY
> Thanks.

Casey studies negative, his frown deepening, as Technician leaves.

> CASEY
> (continuing)
> Dr. Axelson—

Axelson in b.g., looks up, sees Casey, approaches. Liz remains in chair, keeps glancing nervously at the two men as Casey shows Axelson the X-ray. He looks at it carefully a moment or two, lifts his eyes to Casey's. No words are necessary.

23 ANOTHER ANGLE

as the two men approach Liz.

> LIZ
> (a bit too brightly; to hide her anxiety)
> Well, gentlemen, you going to put the photo on the cover of Life?

CASEY
(quietly)
Dr. Axelson's going to take a biopsy, Liz. Now.

Axelson is taking hypodermic needle from sterile cabinet.

AXELSON
(quickly)
It'll only take a minute . . .

He approaches.

LIZ
Must you?

AXELSON
(injecting Novocaine)
Just want to see what the tissue looks like under a
microscope . . . to be on the safe side . . .

LIZ
"Safe?" Is there such a word?

But Axelson has left her to wash his hands, get the "biopsy set,"
consisting of tray, tool for cutting lump, bottle of formaldehyde, etc.

CASEY
(tight)
There's "intelligence" though. That's a word.

LIZ
What game are we playing, Doctor?

CASEY
(controlling his anger)
Why didn't you have that lump checked the minute you
discovered it?

LIZ
I often get swollen glands when I'm run down, or have a
cold . . .

CASEY
But this one persisted. You're a biochemist, Doctor. You
know about these things.

LIZ
"Malignancy?" That's a word too.
(in another tone)
I didn't have the time.

Axelson approaches with biopsy set on tray, places it on table, examines her neck again, preparatory to cutting into the tissue.

AXELSON
Now just relax. You won't feel a thing. And there'll hardly be
a scar.

LIZ
(with a grin)
You mean I'll still be able to make that Life cover?

Axelson picks up tool, cuts. Liz turns to Casey, pressing her lips together.

LIZ
(continuing; low, intense)
You ought to be able to understand me, Ben—we're both in
the same army—fighting the same enemy! *There isn't enough
time!*

24 CLOSE SHOT—AXELSON

He takes tissue from swollen area, places it in formaldehyde.

25 INCLUDING LIZ AND CASEY

as Axelson puts small bandage on Liz's neck.

AXELSON
(to Liz)
Not so bad, was it?

She shakes her head, smiles wanly. Axelson turns to Casey.

AXELSON
(continuing)
I'll get the results of this tomorrow morning . . .

CASEY
Can't you do a frozen section right now?

> AXELSON
> Well, sure—if you want it.

> CASEY
> I want it!

Axelson takes bottle, exits. Casey and Liz look after him.

26　ANOTHER PART OF THE LAB—AXELSON

is squinting through a microscope, focusing it. In the far b.g. we can see Casey and Liz standing, glancing in his direction. Axelson finally lifts his head, looks toward Casey who quickly starts toward him.

27　REVERSE—LIZ

Liz watches Casey and Axelson meet in b.g., near microscope, but cannot hear them confer. She nervously touches the bandage on her neck, glances at it in a mirror. Casey has turned and is coming back slowly.

28　TWO SHOT

as Casey approaches, the set frown on his face deepening.

> LIZ
> (too casually—her eyes averted)
> It's malignant, isn't it?

> CASEY
> I'll talk to you about it tomorrow.

> LIZ
> (a bit frantically)
> No need to equivocate, Doctor. I know what's going on. It's my field. Remember? Shall I tell you what my cancer cells look like? What are you so solemn about? We all owe God a life . . . or a death . . .

> CASEY
> (quietly)
> It'll take twenty-four hours for the stain to show exactly what kind of malignancy it is. At that point it will be dealt with accordingly.

(a beat)
Dr. Axelson would like to see you in his office tomorrow
night at nine.

LIZ
Will you be there?

He nods.

29 INT. AXELSON'S OFFICE

Axelson is behind his desk. Casey is standing, or straddling a chair as
Liz sits calmly in a chair listening.

AXELSON
. . . You have malignant lymphoid tumors in several areas—
in the lymph nodes of neck, arms and groin.

LIZ
Hodgkin's Disease . . .

AXELSON
(nods)
Since, as you're aware, the lymphatic system circulates fluids
throughout the body, it is very likely that the cancerous
growths will spread, unless . . .

LIZ
. . . I understand the prognosis, Doctor. Just tell me, if you
can—honestly. How long I've got: maximum. Minimum.

AXELSON
The prognosis is much better than you think, Elizabeth. High
radiation treatments with the cobalt bomb and mustard in-
jections have been producing excellent results. The percentage of remissions is rising rapidly . . .

LIZ
(smiling tightly)
Please! It's not necessary to sugar-coat the pill with me . . .

CASEY
(breaking in)
Doctor Axelson is not sugar-coating!

AXELSON
(continuing to Liz)
I must warn you, however, that you should anticipate a certain amount of pain—which may become intense. Of course, morphine and other opiates are available . . .
(picks up a piece of paper)
Now there's a bed reserved for you in . . .

LIZ
(on her feet)
A bed? Listen, Doctor, I'm not going to bed! You can't make me! I have work to do!
(then quieter, almost pleading)
Must I go to bed?

AXELSON
(reflectively)
Well, normally we'd require it—in order to keep the patient under close observation . . . But seeing that you're here in the hospital every day, I guess we can make an exception. You'd better count on losing three or four hours daily, though, in treatments and tests . . .

LIZ
Well, that'll be three or four hours less lounging on the beach.
(smiles wryly)
Okay—I'll get a lousy tan this year.

FADE OUT.

END OF ACT ONE

ACT TWO

FADE IN:

30 INT. TREATMENT ROOM—SHOT—LIZ

lying on a cot under an elaborate machine used for irradiation by means of a cobalt gun. A female technician is at the controls nearby manipulating the machine and continuously checking her patient. (The QUIET HUM of the powerful electron accelerator and the almost ballet-like movements of the technician create a kind of wordless tension.)

31 ANGLE AT DOOR

as it opens. DR. NORMAN DRYFUS, mature, head of the biology lab, starts in, halts abruptly, looks across at:

32 P.O.V.—LIZ

in machine, and technician watching, manipulating controls.

33 BACK TO DRYFUS

He looks another moment, then turns away back out.

34 INT. CORRIDOR

as Dryfus emerges from treatment room. Axelson is approaching, carrying X-ray plates.

> AXELSON
> (as they meet)
> Hello, Norman . . . come down to get your top assistant back . . . ? She's only been absent two days . . .

> DRYFUS
> She *is* coming back, Iver?

35 ANOTHER ANGLE

In b.g. Casey, Ted and Miss Wills appear from around a corner. They are deep in conversation.

> AXELSON
> (nods)
> . . . .As soon as she's finished in there with the cobalt-gun . . . within the hour.

36 FAVORING CASEY AND GROUP

as they approach.

                              CASEY
                        (to Ted and Wills)
        As a last resort, we may have to do a mesencephalic
        tractotomy . . . Meanwhile continue with the drug ther-
        apy . . .

He sees Axelson, goes over to him, Ted following, as Wills continues
down corridor o.s.

                              CASEY
                (continuing: to Axelson; breaking in)
        Iver—excuse me . . . What have you found?

                             AXELSON
        We've pinpointed the malignant lymph areas . . .

                              CASEY
                            Extensive?

                             AXELSON
        Could be worse. The X-ray photos are right here, if you care
        to . . .

He hands them to Casey.

                              CASEY
                     (glancing at the photos)
                   You've started radiation?

                             AXELSON
                            (nods)

        She's getting her second treatment right now. I plan to
        give her the highest possible dosage her body can tolerate.
        Perhaps as much as 4000 rads in the next three or four
        weeks . . .
                     (abruptly; to Casey and Ted)
        You know Dr. Dryfus in charge of the bio lab . . . ? Doctors
        Casey and Hoffman . . .

AD LIB greetings.

                              CASEY
                           (to Dryfus)
        . . . .Then Dr. Wilson—Liz—works under you?

DRYFUS

Yes, in cancer research. Virology. Ironic, isn't it . . . a brilliant girl like that . . . The shame is that before this happened, she seemed to be on the verge of
something . . . opening a door to a dark place . . . Nothing
dramatic perhaps . . . but advances in our field rarely
are . . .

CASEY

She doesn't intend to stop.

DRYFUS

Oh, you know her—well?

CASEY

No. Not well.

DRYFUS

. . .Because she usually gives people the wrong impression.
She's really warm, gentle—fun even . . . Though I suppose
since she lost her husband and baby . . .

CASEY

(breaks in)
Baby?

DRYFUS

(nods)
. . .Maybe some of her gaiety *has* seeped away . . .

CASEY

How did they die?

DRYFUS

(shakes his head)
She never talks about it.

37 INT. TREATMENT ROOM—LIZ

sitting on examining table wearing hospital gown. Wills present. Axelson has just completed examining her.

AXELSON

All right . . . you're free until tomorrow morning at eight.
You may get dressed.

She doesn't move; he continues lightly.

                    AXELSON
                   (continuing)
What's the matter—have you changed your mind about going back to the lab?

                    LIZ
          (low; as Wills moves out of hearing)
Dr. Axelson—would you do something for me? Please—

                    AXELSON
                 What is it?

                    LIZ
I'd like a piece of malignant lymph tissue—mine, I mean?

                    AXELSON
              Yours . . . ? You mean . . . ?

                    LIZ
Like that piece you took the other day for a biopsy . . . ?

                    AXELSON
              It's a bit unusual.

                    LIZ
            This isn't a usual situation.
                  (urgently)
              I need it, Iver.

                    AXELSON
                 What for?

                    LIZ
            Experimental purposes.

                    AXELSON
You're working every minute, aren't you, Liz . . .

                    LIZ
I have to. There aren't very many minutes left. Well, will
                    you?

He looks at her thoughtfully, then turns to Wills.

AXELSON
Miss Wills . . . Novocaine please . . .

Wills goes to sterile cabinet, takes needle and Novocaine from it, hands it to Axelson who approaches Liz.

38 INT. PATHOLOGY LAB—AXELSON

handing Liz a test tube. She is fully dressed now. As she takes it and turns away toward door, we see a new bandage on her arm (or neck—any visible lymph area).

39 INT. BIO LAB—LIZ

carrying test tube is crossing toward her table. The other biologists, chemists, technicians, research workers, wave to her, AD LIB words of welcome at seeing her back. Dryfus comes across to shake her hand happily. She smiles back, but a little thinly, a little perfunctorily—all her concentration is on the test tube. She continues to her table, places it in a holder, starts making a slide, as Dryfus and the others watch quizzically.

CUT TO:

40 ANOTHER ANGLE—LIZ

at her table peering into a microscope. The room is in shadows, deserted. The equipment and tables are all covered. Dryfus approaches from his desk, dressed to leave, carrying a brief case.

DRYFUS
Liz . .?

LIZ
(without looking up)
Uh-huh.

DRYFUS
Don't you think you need some rest? You just came back this week . . .

She doesn't answer.

DRYFUS
(continuing)
Do you intend to stay all night?

LIZ
(absorbed)
Good night, Norman . . .

DRYFUS
Liz . . . ?

She doesn't answer. He looks at her a moment longer, shaking his head, moves away toward:

41 ANGLE AT DOOR

Casey is standing there just inside the lab. As Dryfus approaches, Casey looks at him, then glances across toward Liz questioningly. Dryfus shakes his head, shrugs, exits. Casey now crosses toward:

42 ANGLE—LIZ

completely absorbed and happy, she continues working. Casey comes along beside her table.

CASEY
Hello . . .

LIZ
(looks up)
Oh, hi . . .

CASEY
What are you doing?

LIZ
(busily)
Making a serum . . . Would you hand me that needle please . . . ?

Casey looks around, sees it, hands it to her.

CASEY
What kind of serum?

LIZ
Human virus . .

CASEY
Human?

LIZ
(abruptly)
Come here.

She goes to microscope. He follows. She puts in a slide.

LIZ
(continuing)
Look!

He squints into a microscope.

LIZ
(continuing)
You know what you see?

CASEY
Viruses. From the malignant tissue of a hamster.

LIZ
Brilliant! Now look at this.

She changes slide. He looks.

CASEY
Same thing.

LIZ
Yes. *Except*, these viruses were found with *human* cancer
cells . . .

He lifts his eyes from microscope. stares at her.

LIZ
(continuing)
Interesting. No?

She picks up needle. pours serum into its container.

                              CASEY
                            (narrowly)
          Since when did you begin to experiment with humans?

He stares at her, his face hard.

                              CASEY
                           (continuing)
                       I asked you a question!

                               LIZ
                          (smiling at him)
          . . . One at a time. You *are* assisting me, aren't you .   . ?

He turns abruptly, gets hamster, brings it to her.

                               LIZ
                           (continuing)
                         Thank you . . .
                  (she injects it while he holds it)
                            Next . . .

                              CASEY
                          (hesitating)
              What are you so cheerful about?

                               LIZ
          Progress . . . I think I see progress.

                              CASEY
          Where did you get human cancer tissue containing live
          viruses?
                       (it suddenly hits him)
                          It's yours!

                               LIZ
                         (quietly; calmly)
          I've transformed myself into an experimental
          animal . . . It's not bad, you know . . . Almost like a general
          choosing his own battlefield . . .

Controlling himself, Casey abruptly turns, takes hamster back to
cage—gets another one, brings it to her. She gets needle ready as he
holds the hamster.

                    CASEY
              (almost off-hand)
         Say, would you like a cup of coffee?

                     LIZ
               (injects hamster)
            Have you had dinner yet?

                    CASEY
                    No . . .

                     LIZ
            (finished, looks up at him)
I haven't either. Why don't we go to my apartment . . . I
suddenly feel a great desire to cook! D'you like scallopini,
sauted in wine . . . ?

                    CASEY
                   (smiles)
Lady, you just touched a gastronomical nerve! But I buy the
groceries!

                     LIZ
                  It's a deal!

They start to shake. He realizes he has the hamster in his arms.
They both look at it and laugh.

43 INT. LIZ'S APARTMENT—LIZ

wearing an apron and looking anything but like a biochemist, bustling
about the kitchen of her small, but cheery one-room apartment—
kitchen included. She dips a large serving spoon into a pot, tastes its
contents, reacts uncertainly, turns, calls out:

                     LIZ
                  Ben . . .

She stiffens slightly at what she sees.

44 P.O.V.—CASEY

on the other side of the room, strewn with magazines and books. He is
looking at two photographs framed together—one is of a young man;
the other is of a baby. He turns.

45 INCLUDING LIZ

holding spoon out.

> LIZ
> (continuing)
> How are your taste buds?

> CASEY
> Nobody's complained yet.

He crosses to her, tastes food from spoon which she continues to hold. She looks at him as he considers with great seriousness.

> CASEY
> (continuing; finally)
> I think maybe a whiff of garlic.

> LIZ
> Done!

She adds "whiff" of garlic, offers him another spoonful.

> LIZ
> (continuing)
> Now try.

Casey tastes food from spoon as before, except this time he holds her hand to steady it. He considers for a moment.

> CASEY
> (smiling)
> Absolutely—perfect!

He is looking into her eyes; their hands are touching. A beat.

> LIZ
> (breaking the spell)
> Then let's eat!

She turns abruptly to stove, gets food, dishes it out. He opens a bottle of wine, pours. They are seated. Casey holds up his glass for a toast. She follows his example.

                          CASEY
                      Your health . . .

She tenses slightly; they click glasses, sip their wine. They start to eat.
The mood is strained.

                          CASEY
                 (continuing; trying to break it)
                You know, you're not a bad cook, Liz.

                          LIZ
               Oh, I'm great—when I'm in the mood . . .
                      (then with a sad smile)
                   At least Tom thought so . . .

                          CASEY
                          Tom?

                          LIZ
             You were looking at his picture before.

                          CASEY
                      Your husband . . .

She nods, lifts her glass.

                          LIZ
             We were just kids when we got married. I was in college. He
             was in med school. The year we got our degrees we had a
             baby—Philip . . . We were very much in love and the world
             was very beautiful . . .

46 LIZ

An excruciating wave of pain hits her. Her face contorts. She drops her
wine glass, doubles up.

47 INCLUDING CASEY

on his feet, rushing around to her.

                          CASEY
                      What is it?

> LIZ
> (in agony)
> Pain! Oh my God!

He helps her across to sofa.

> CASEY
> You have something for it?
> Pills? Opiates?

> LIZ
> (pointing)
> Over there.

He goes to shelf, finds vial, pours glass of water, brings pills. She swallows them. He holds glass as she drinks water.

48 ANOTHER ANGLE

She is lying back weakly on sofa. He is watching her intently.

> CASEY
> The pain's been increasing, hasn't it?

> LIZ
> (nods)
> . . . I'm used to it. I've been living with pain a long time.
> (smiles weakly)
> We have an intimate relationship
> . . . pain and I . . .
> (presses her knuckles into her temples)
> But this!—It's unbearable!

> CASEY
> Continue taking these pills. They'll help. If the pain gets worse, we'll increase the dosage.

> LIZ
> (the opiate has begun to work)
> I don't like to take drugs. They make me groggy—they fog up my brain . . . When I can't think, I can't work.

> CASEY
> Would you rather endure pain?

> LIZ
> (nods unflinchingly)
> If it's the only way for me to continue my work . . . But there must be another way! There must be, Ben!

> CASEY
> (firmly)
> Not for you. The only way for you is remission. Cure.

> LIZ
> (smiles at him wanly)
> You know something: for a cold, unemotional, scientific neurosurgeon, you sure can go off the deep end.

> CASEY
> You think so . . . ?

He is very close to her, looking into her eyes.

> LIZ
> I think so.

Their faces begin to weave toward each other's. He is looking deeply into her eyes.

> LIZ
> (abruptly)
> Don't! Please, Ben. Don't look at me like that! I can't allow you to.
> (she turns away)
> I can't allow any human being to come too close.

She rises nervously, moves to the table, picks up her glass of wine, sips it.

> LIZ
> (continuing; very low)
> You know something. I don't even own a dog, because I don't want the dog to mourn—

DISSOLVE TO:

49 INT. BIO LAB—DAY—FULL SHOT

Liz is rushing excitedly from her work area through an aisle of tables, past her colleagues working busily, moving around, etc., toward Dryfus' office at far end. She reaches door, pushes it open.

50 INT. DRYFUS' OFFICE

as Liz enters breathlessly. Dryfus is at his desk, studying a culture, and dictating the results of a procedure to his secretary.

>   DRYFUS
>   (dictating)
> . . . It is therefore felt that this laboratory-strengthened vari-
> ant of a naturally occurring virus—
>   (breaks off)
>   Liz! What is it?

>   LIZ
>   (grabs his arm)
>   Come with me!

She practically pulls him to the door.

51 INT. LAB–LIZ'S TABLE

as she and Dryfus reach it. She shows him the two hamsters that she had injected.

>   LIZ
>   (pointing)
> These two hamsters! Their lymph cells are cancerous! You
> know how they got it?

She grips table in pain.

>   DRYFUS
>   (in alarm)
>   What is it?

>   LIZ
>   (shakes her head)
> —From me! *They got it from me!* From injections of viruses I
> took from my own diseased tissue!

>   DRYFUS
>   Really? Are you all right?

LIZ
(pressing her teeth together against the pain)
This miserable—miserable—
(she inhales deeply)
That's how *I* got it, Norman! You know how often I've
worked with malignant strains of lymphoid tumors in these
hamsters—many times while I've had cuts on my hands. I
never thought to protect myself. But actually what it could
have amounted to was repeated inoculations! DO YOU
HEAR WHAT I'M SAYING? *It's possible to transmit certain
virus-caused cancers from animals to man, and back again!*

DRYFUS
That's very interesting—*remarkable!*

She drops into a chair. He grips her arms.

DRYFUS
(continuing)
Liz?

LIZ
(unable to stand it; pointing)
—My purse. Please!

He hands her her purse. She takes out pills, swallows two—as he
quickly gets her a cup of water.

DRYFUS
Better?

LIZ
(sipping water; bitterly)
Great! The pain'll be gone soon . . . But then I'll be too
groggy to continue.
(practically in tears)
I *must* continue . . .

She looks at him.

LIZ
(continuing)
I'm sorry, Norman . . . I have to get out of here for a while.
Please excuse me . . .

She is on her feet, hurrying toward door, as he looks after her worriedly.

52 INT. CORRIDOR—NEAR CASEY'S OFFICE

As Liz approaches, Ted comes out. They almost bump into each other.

                          LIZ
            Oh, Ted. Is Ben in there?

                          TED
No, he's operating. It's a very unusual procedure . . . a me-sencephalic tractotomy . . . There'll be a lot of residents, internes, observing . . . Want to watch?

                          LIZ
            Well . . . Okay . . .

They hurry away.

53 INT. O.R.—HIGH ANGLE SHOT

Casey and the usual operating team of assistants and nurses are at their stations. But also present in the room are a number of other men and women observing, as well as one or two medical cameramen focusing T.V. cameras on the procedure from different angles: one of them is shooting directly at Casey himself.

54 CLOSER ANGLE—CASEY AND GROUP

Casey is wearing a small visible microphone.

                          CASEY
            . . . Today we're doing a mesencephalic tractotomy—on a
            male patient 69 years of age . . .

SOUND o.s. He turns.

55 P.O.V.—TED AND LIZ

enter, wearing masks, etc., start to take their places among the ob-servers. Liz sees Casey, nods, her eyes smiling.

56 FAVORING CASEY

halts the procedure angrily.

> CASEY
> (to anyone—but everyone can hear)
> Get her out of here!

57 ANOTHER ANGLE

Miss Wills moves toward Liz. Both Ted and Liz look toward Casey, confused, quizzical. Wills hesitates.

> CASEY
> (continuing; louder)
> Now!

Liz hurries out. Ted follows.

58 INT. O.R. SCRUB ROOM

as Liz, pulling off her mask, is crossing to door, Ted enters, following.

> TED
> Liz! There's a closed-circuit TV set in the Meeting Room down the hall. You can see it from there.

Liz nods, continues out.

59 INT. MEETING ROOM

It is darkened. A number of nurses, internes, etc., are gathered around the T.V. set watching the T.V. screen on which Casey is operating. Liz enters, finds a seat.

> CASEY'S VOICE
> (on speaker)
> This man was operated on for cancer of the prostate six months ago.

60 CLOSE—CASEY (ON T.V.)

(As he speaks we INTERCUT to Liz and others in both meeting and operating rooms, as well as on T.V. monitors.)

                         CASEY
                      (continuing)
After an improvement in his condition lasting several weeks,
he began to suffer dreadful pain once more. It is not known
whether it is a "ricochet" of the cancer, or the adhesions
following his previous operation which torture him. For the
last month he has lost two pounds every week and finds relief
only in morphine and gardenal . . . We have therefore decided upon this operation to make his sufferings endurable.

61 CLOSE SHOT—LIZ

reacting, listening intently.

                       CASEY'S VOICE
                        (continuing)
What we're going to do now is open up the brain and cut the
nerves in the region where the idea of pain is localized. As a
result, the patient will still have a normal intellect, but he will
not be conscious of pain.

62 INT. O.R.—CASEY

nodding to Nurse.

                          CASEY
                       (continuing)
. . . Then it will be possible to tackle any adhesions by a
further operation, or try additional radiotherapy if the trouble is a recurrence of cancer. Without this operation, either of
these interventions would probably be beyond the patient's
strength and resistance.
                       (to Nurse)
                    Scalpel please . . .

Nurse hands Casey scalpel.

63 INT. MEETING ROOM—LIZ

watching with her whole body and all her nerves.

64 INT. O.R.—CASEY

takes scalpel and starts his incision.

65 INT. MEETING ROOM—EXTREME CLOSE-UP—LIZ

as she watches the screen, an idea takes hold of her entire being. We can see it registering on her face.

FADE OUT.

END OF ACT TWO

ACT THREE

FADE IN:

66 EXT. BEACH AREA—DAY—FULL SHOT

On this clear bright mid-summer afternoon, tanned healthy young bodies are playing on the white sand, diving into the rolling surf, sailing boats, etc.

67 SHOT—LIZ AND CASEY (MOVING SHOT)

walking slowly on the sand. Young men and women in swim suits and bikinis dash across their path from time to time laughing and screeching happily. Liz is wearing a high collared dress to cover the several scars and/or bandages on her neck. Her clothes and her pale skin and the way she moves are in sharp contrast to the natural healthiness and vigor of everything about her. Moreover she acts a bit cold and put out with Casey. He notices.

CASEY
What's the matter?

LIZ
We shouldn't have come here.

CASEY
Why not? We're only an hour from the hospital. I left word . . . Besides, you said you couldn't work anyway—

LIZ
(looking around)

It all seems to be mocking me . . . This beauty . . . Everything is so *alive,* so *healthy* . . .

                            CASEY
                           (a beat)
You're upset about what happened in the O.R. today.

                             LIZ
                  I know why you kicked me out.

                            CASEY
            There are strict rules concerning procedure.

                             LIZ
                    I wanted to see you work.

                            CASEY
I understand—but I couldn't make an exception in your case. You know that.

They spread a blanket on the sand.

                             LIZ
                    I saw the operation . . .
       (continuing quickly as he looks at her sharply)
                          on TV . . .

                            CASEY
                          (narrowly)
                           I see.

They both sit on the blanket.

                             LIZ
             And I was impressed. What's it called again?

                            CASEY
                 A mesencephalic tractotomy.

                             LIZ
Why didn't you ever suggest it for me? You're aware of how I suffer. An operation like that could free me of pain and allow me to think. Then I could give all the time I have left to my work—to the war.

(her voice dropping)
Even now I feel guilty. I feel I should be back in the lab with my hamsters.

CASEY
You have a right to some relaxation.

LIZ
That doesn't sound like Ben Casey speaking.

CASEY
(with a slight smile)
Maybe Ben Casey's beginning to mellow . . .

LIZ
Well, Elizabeth Wilson isn't! I don't have the right—to mellow, *or* relax! There's no time!

CASEY
Why are you so guilty?

LIZ
Because I have a certain skill, certain knowledge, certain training—all of which, if used to their maximum, could make some inroads . . .
(vehemently)
I feel guilty because I'm not using my abilities!

CASEY
I don't think that's the only reason, Liz. Or even the main reason.

LIZ
(shrugs)
You're a neurosurgeon, Ben—not a headshrinker! Besides, what difference does it make?

CASEY
(into her eyes)
Very little—scientifically.

LIZ
(levelly)
Okay, then—when can you operate?

He shakes his head, frowning.

> LIZ
> (continuing)
> Please . . .

> CASEY
> I can't.

> LIZ
> (cries out)
> You mean, you won't!

> CASEY
> Liz, it's a very delicate operation. It involves great risk.

> LIZ
> It worked fine today.

> CASEY
> Tomorrow may be a different story.

> LIZ
> I'm willing to take the risk!

She is on her feet, moving toward the water. He follows.

> CASEY
> (patiently; as to a child)
> Let me tell you about pain, Liz. It's important . . .

> LIZ
> Oh, come on, Ben. I'm a big girl. I've studied anatomy and physiology—I have a Ph.D. in Bacteriology. I know all about the importance of pain to animals and man . . .

> CASEY
> (intense now)
> Okay, Big Girl, then let me repeat lesson number one: pain is one of the most vital means of protection your body has. Its removal can make you extremely vulnerable to disease; it can destroy your awareness of danger. If you were in an accident and you broke your leg, you might not know it until it was too late to reset. Your hands or ears could be frozen on a very cold winter day, and gangrene could set in before you

became aware . . . or you might be coming down with the flu . . . or have an abscessed tooth, or a headache . . . minor everyday occurrences—But if you weren't warned by pain, so they could be treated in time, any of these illnesses could become serious—even fatal!

LIZ
(laughs, wryly)
You're talking as if I had 50 years to live—or even 10.

CASEY
How do you know you haven't?

LIZ
Okay—Then why did you perform that operation today? Am I different from that man—?

CASEY
(breaking in)
. . . Yes! That patient was almost seventy years old! In his case it wasn't only a question of eliminating pain to ensure a peaceful death! It was much more important. We made it possible for him to endure certain other operations which may save his life! This is a man who had been condemned to death!

LIZ
Am I not condemned to death?

CASEY
No!

LIZ
You're letting your emotions get the better of you, Ben. Shall I tell you about cancer?

CASEY
Liz, cancer is not necessarily fatal! Not the kind you have!

LIZ
You want to believe that—because of the way you feel about me . . .

CASEY
How do you know how I feel about you?

                         LIZ
Ben, let's not play games. I have feelings too . . . But—for
people like us, emotional involvements can only end up
badly!

                        CASEY
                        Why?

                         LIZ
Because they take us away from what is really important!

                        CASEY
You called us "soldiers." Is there any law against soldiers
being friends—or . . . ?

                         LIZ
No law, Ben. But it is a fact that soldiers become
casualties . . . Those who remain cannot afford sorrow . . .

                        CASEY
You're speaking about your husband, your son . . .

                         LIZ
                    (bursting out)

I'm speaking about people everywhere!
                      (intense)
Ben, you know that there may come a time when we will be
able to inoculate people against certain types of cancer—
children against leukemia. Little breakthroughs are being
made in this direction every day. I've made one or two myself. I *must* be allowed to continue! But I can't unless I'm
physically capable, unless my brain remains clear and alert!
                      (a beat)
          Unless you relieve me of this pain!

She turns, goes back to her blanket. He follows.

                         LIZ
                    (continuing)
          Let's go . . . I'm cold.

She bends to pick up blanket. He continues to study her. Finally:

CASEY
All right, Liz. I'll consider it.

LIZ
(turns quickly)
When will you know?

CASEY
(he considers, then:)
Tomorrow . . .

LIZ
(straight into his eyes)
Okay. Tomorrow.

They pick up the blanket together.

68 INT. ZORBA'S OFFICE

ZORBA is behind desk. Casey is walking back and forth with the nervous motion of a caged animal.

ZORBA
Ben, sit down—relax . . . You make me nervous . . .

CASEY
Dr. Zorba, I came here for your opinion. I've got things to do. I . . .

ZORBA
This Dr. Wilson . . . She's not just a casual acquaintance on the staff . . . Because if she was no more than that you wouldn't even consider such an operation.

CASEY
According to Norman Dryfus, she's an extremely talented biochemist doing vital work in cancer research. According to her, the pain she suffers keeps her from working—and drugs merely cloud her brain. So the effect is the same. Besides, she's the kind of person who needs to work in order to live . . . Her work is her life.

ZORBA
(smiling)
A feeling that you're familiar with yourself . . .

KNOCK on door. They look up.

69 ANOTHER ANGLE

as Axelson enters.

                    AXELSON
You wanted to see me, Dr. Zorba? Hello, Ben . . .

                    ZORBA
Iver, this Dr. Wilson . . . who you've been treating for
Hodgkin's Disease . . . What is the present prognosis?

                    AXELSON
                (shakes his head)
Well, Dr. Zorba, you're very much aware of the success we've
been having treating lymph cancer with large doses of radiation. In fact, cure is not too strong a word to use—in statistical
terms . . . But in individual cases—especially this one where
the malignancy has invaded her entire lymph system—all the
medical knowledge we have can allow us to make no more
accurate prediction than we could if we were using witch-
craft. I say, remission is possible. I say, we're
optimistic . . . *But—*

                    ZORBA
You know the patient. You know the work she's doing. You
know the pain she suffers. She has requested Casey here to
do a mesencephalic tractotomy . . .

                    AXELSON
                (to Casey; quickly)
You refused, didn't you?

                    ZORBA
                (to Axelson)
Of course. He's just checking, that's all. It's not a simple
decision. We wanted your opinion.

                    AXELSON
At this point I would advise against it—strongly.

Zorba looks at Casey who nods, turns quickly toward door.

70 INT. BIO LAB–SHOT–LIZ

at microscope, looking at a slide. Casey enters shot, stands watching
for a moment. Finally aware of another person's presence, she turns,
glances up.

                    LIZ
                 Oh, hi . . .

                   CASEY
          Hi . . . How about some lunch?

                    LIZ
               What time is it?
               (glances at clock)
            Okay. Wait till I clean up.
           (starts taking off her lab coat)
      Have you come to a decision yet? You know—

                   CASEY
                   (nods)
           I'm not going to do it, Liz.

                    LIZ
               (suddenly rigid)
         What? All right, Dr. Casey . . .

                   CASEY
       Liz, listen—I discussed it with . . .

                    LIZ
        I don't care who you discussed it with!

                   CASEY
             Liz, calm down . . .

                    LIZ
      I'm calm. I'm very calm. You better go have lunch yourself.
      That includes from now on!

As he stands there.

                    LIZ
                (continuing)
         Do I have to scream—or something?

He turns finally, shaking his head—and starts for the door.

> **LIZ**
> (continuing: shrill)
> And remember this! There are other neurosurgeons in the
> world!

As he halts, faces her at the door, deeply concerned, we

> **FADE OUT.**

> *END OF ACT THREE*

> *ACT FOUR*

FADE IN:

71 EXT. PRIVATE HOSPITAL—DAY—(STOCK)

A new modern structure with plenty of glass, etc.

72 INSERT

Engraved letters reading: "TURNER HOSPITAL AND PRIVATE
SANITARIUM".

73 INT. LOBBY

Attractive, spotless, giving the atmosphere of wealth. About nine or
ten people are sitting reading magazines, talking—waiting. Liz comes
in, crosses to pretty RECEPTIONIST at desk.

> **LIZ**
> (nervously)
> My name is Elizabeth Wilson. I have an appointment with
> Dr. Turner . . .

> **RECEPTIONIST**
> (looks in book)
> Please have a seat, Miss Wilson.

> LIZ
> But my appointment is at three o'clock. It's three now.

> RECEPTIONIST
> I'm sorry, Miss Wilson, Dr. Turner is with a patient . . . He will see you as soon as he can . . .

> LIZ
> Do you know how many times I've heard that in the last week?

> RECEPTIONIST
> I'm sorry . . .

> LIZ
> Isn't there any way to hurry it up? Really, I just don't have time to sit around in doctors' offices.

> RECEPTIONIST
> (imperturbable)
> Dr. Turner will see you as soon as he can, Miss Wilson.

74 ANOTHER ANGLE

Liz presses her lips together, turns away, finds a seat, picks up a magazine, and starts to wait.

DISSOLVE:

75 CLOSE SHOT—LIZ

in same chair, another magazine open in front of her; a pile she has looked through is beside her; her head is dropping and she is beginning to doze off. Most of the others who had been waiting are now gone.

> RECEPTIONIST'S VOICE
> Miss Wilson, please.

Liz's head jerks up. She looks around, startled.

76 P.O.V.—RECEPTIONIST

smiling at her.

                    RECEPTIONIST
                     (continuing)
                Dr. Turner will see you now.

Liz starts to rise.

77 INT. TURNER'S OFFICE–CLOSE SHOT–SEVERAL FRAMED
DIPLOMAS

from various medical schools—specifically showing an advanced degree
in neurosurgery—all made out to "Dr. Ellis Turner."

                    TURNER'S VOICE
                 (soothing and pontifical)
                I understand, Dr. Wilson . . .

78 FULL SHOT

It is a luxurious office. TURNER, behind his desk, is a handsome man
in his 50's with white hair, wearing a dark tasteful suit.

                      TURNER
              It certainly is ironic though, is it not . . .?

79 INCLUDING LIZ

sitting in a chair facing him.

                       LIZ
          No, Doctor, merely a scientific phenomenon. I am convinced
          by what happened to me that certain virus-caused tumors
          can be transmitted from mammal to mammal, including
          man. The reason I'm asking you to perform this operation is
          so that I can continue my research . . .

                      TURNER
          Of course. I can't see any reason why I should not comply
          with your—

Liz suddenly tenses against a spasm of pain.

                       LIZ
                   (between her teeth)
                      God!

TURNER
(noticing, rising)
You have pain? Bad?

LIZ
(smiles weakly)
I was going to say, "I'll live" . . . Isn't that funny?
(inhales)
It's better. . . That was a quick one. Sometimes the pain
lasts for hours . . . It's so bad I curse God for not letting me
die.

TURNER
I'll operate.

LIZ
(quickly)
Thank you, Doctor . . . When?

TURNER
(looks at his calendar)
Today's Monday. How's about Wednesday? Wednesday
morning.

LIZ
Fine.

She starts to rise.

TURNER
The nurse will give you instructions on your way out. And, if
you wish, you can let her have your check . . .

80 INT. COUNTY GENERAL—LOUNGE ADJOINING O.R.

Casey and Ted come in taking off their masks, gloves, wearily. Nurses,
others present, moving past. General chatter.

TED
. . . You got clear of that glioma beautifully, Ben . . .

CASEY
We had to go in on the tumor directly. There was no other
way.

They reach door, Ted pushes it open.

> TED
> Hear about Liz?

81 INT. CORRIDOR

as they enter, continue along.

> CASEY
> (frowns)
> No. Haven't seen her much lately . . .

> TED
> (looks at him)
> Dryfus asked me to tell you . . . He wanted to tell you him-
> self, but you've been tied up . . .

> CASEY
> Tell me what?

> TED
> About Liz.

> CASEY
> What about Liz?

> TED
> She's going to have a mesencephalic tractotomy.

> CASEY
> What? Who told you?

> TED
> I told you! Dryfus. At lunch. Liz had asked him for some
> time off—and when he asked why, she told him.

> CASEY
> When? Who's doing it?

> TED
> You know Dr. Turner?

> CASEY
> Ellis Turner? Of course. I see him at meetings all the time. He

seems a lot more interested in the stock market and land values and business deals than he is in surgery.

TED
The operation's scheduled for Wednesday—tomorrow.

CASEY
Thanks, Ted.

Furious, Casey turns and rushes out.

82 INT. TURNER'S OFFICE—CLOSE SHOT—

TURNER
What do you mean, by what right? The patient requested it.

CAMERA PULLS BACK to include Casey.

CASEY
(vehement)
Do you perform every operation your patients request? Who's the doctor—they or you?

TURNER
I am doing what Elizabeth Wilson requested because I believe it is the correct thing to do! Dr. Wilson is involved in important research relating to cancer! Unless she's freed of pain, she'll be unable to work. She has extensive lymphoid cancer.

CASEY
It's not terminal. She could live.

TURNER
She could. But I happen to believe that she has a right—knowing all the facts—to make her own decision!

CASEY
Because it's financially profitable—That's why you believe it!

TURNER
Are you implying that I am unethical, sir?

CASEY
Take it any way you want to.

> TURNER
> (on his feet)
> Dr. Casey, I will stake my reputation as a member of the medical profession, and as a man, against yours at any time! As a matter of fact, I am beginning to suspect that *your* relationship with Dr. Wilson is not all that it should be . . . Or why else would you act like this?

Casey, trembling with fury, grips the front of Turner's shirt.

> TURNER
> (continuing; with cool sarcasm)
> Hit a nerve, didn't I, Casey?
> (a beat)
> Now please take your hands off me and get out. Patients are waiting.

Casey, absolutely rigid, drops his hands, turns, and exits.

83 INT. BIO LAB—LIZ

is putting away her equipment. Dryfus is with her, watching solemnly.

> LIZ
> Don't worry—I'll be back in a week or so, Norman—I hate to give up so many days—but I have no choice. I have to gamble this time now against whatever will be left to me afterward.

84 INCLUDING CASEY

entering. He sees her, storms over, grabs her arm.

> CASEY
> (to Liz)
> I want to talk to you! Excuse me, Norman!

> LIZ
> Wait a . . .

But he is pulling her away with him to door.

85 INT. CORRIDOR—CASEY

dragging the protesting Liz across the hall, oblivious to her low angry cries (ad lib) or the surprised and humorous glances of passing nurses and doctors. He opens a door to a treatment room.

86 INT. TREATMENT ROOM

Casey looks in; no one is present. He pulls Liz in after him. She breaks away, whirls across room. They stare at each other breathlessly a moment, then:

> CASEY
> (harsh, angry)
> You're stupid! You're neurotic, pig-headed, self-destructive! Who do you think you are? The indispensable woman or something? You think if you stop looking into a microscope or shooting viruses into hamsters, all the work being done against cancer will stop—or he held up *that much?* Do you think you'll be a better woman or a more effective scientist if you let a money-hungry quack like Dr. Ellis Turner cut your brain open . . . ?

Liz turns slowly, sits down on a chair beside an examining table.

> LIZ
> (quietly)
> Let me tell you how I came to enlist in this war. My husband was killed in Vietnam. He went after completing his residency and was under fire for weeks, operating under conditions which the army calls "extremely hazardous." He was one of the doctors who never came back. We'd had three marvelous years and I thought it was impossible but I continued going to school, managing to work for my doctorate, studying, taking care of my baby . . . It was lonely and tough, but I somehow made it. The year I got my degree . . . my son got leukemia. Blood transfusions kept him alive for fourteen months. He was six years old; his body at the end was wasted away, shriveled, eaten up by something nobody on this earth could prevent. I see him now. When he died, I had nobody's shoulder to cry on. What good are tears anyway? The part of me that can cry died too. That same year I started work on cancer.
> (a beat)
> I'm in it for the duration, Ben—and the duration for me can be counted on the pages of maybe this year's calendar.

CASEY
(breaking in)
That's not true!

LIZ
(ignores this)
. . . I am walking wounded in this war and my life is drain-
ing away very fast. I can feel it going even now as I speak to
you . . .
(quietly)
I know I am not indispensable, and whatever contribution I
may make would probably be made sooner or later by someone else if I were not here . . . Nevertheless, if my work is
able to speed up victory by only a minute, it won't have been
wasted.
(firmly)
I must have that chance, Ben.
(she looks up into his eyes)
Besides, doesn't a doctor have the obligation to relieve
suffering—as well as to save lives . . .?

A long silence.

CASEY
(with great effort)
Okay, if this is the way it is—Well, there's no sense in letting
Turner botch it up . . . is there?

LIZ
No.

CASEY
Liz, I don't want to do it! Every feeling I have tells me not
to . . .
(he inhales deeply)
But if you're going to have it done anyway—

She is on her feet.

LIZ
Yes?

CASEY
(in agony)
. . . *I'll* do it . . .

LIZ
(gratefully)
Thank you, Ben.

CASEY
(bitterly)
Don't mention it.

FADE OUT.

END OF ACT FOUR

ACT FIVE

FADE IN:

87 INT. PATIENT'S ROOM

MR. ANDREWS, in his 70's, is lying in bed, a bandage around his head. Casey has just finished checking him. Behind him are Axelson, a surgeon and a nurse with a tray.

ANDREWS
. . . I tell you I feel like a new man, Dr. Casey. Since that operation, the pain is gone and I don't want to die any more . . . You know what I want to do? I want to dance. Oh, when I was a little younger, the way I used to dance! Night after night . . .

CASEY
I hope you'll be able to dance again, Mr. Andrews . . .

88 WIDER ANGLE

as he turns away to the others, the group moving away from the bed toward the door.

CASEY
(continuing; low)
In my opinion, he's strong enough now to take either radiation or surgery . . .

>AXELSON
>Good.

Casey opens door, steps out.

>AXELSON
>(continuing quickly)
>Ben . . .

He follows.

89 INT. CORRIDOR

as Axelson catches up with Casey, who hesitates.

>AXELSON
>(with meaning)
>I noticed tomorrow's O.R. schedule. You're doing another mesencephalic tractotomy.

>CASEY
>That's right.

>AXELSON
>I thought we decided . . .

>CASEY
>(impatient; bursts out)
>I changed my mind!

90 ANOTHER ANGLE

As he turns to go, Ted comes along from opposite direction.

>TED
>Ben, Zorba wants to see you in his office right away.

Casey's expression hardens. He glances angrily at Axelson, then hurries away down corridor without a word.

91 INT. CORRIDOR—DOOR OUTSIDE ZORBA'S OFFICE

Casey reaches it, knocks.

ZORBA'S VOICE
Come in.

Casey pushes door open.

92 INT. ZORBA'S OFFICE

as Casey bursts in. Zorba is behind desk studying a mimeographed sheet.

CASEY
You wanted to see me?

ZORBA
Sit down, Ben.

CASEY
I'm in a hurry. What's the problem, Dr. Zorba?

ZORBA
I noticed on this O.R. schedule for tomorrow the name of Elizabeth Wilson.

CASEY
Well?

ZORBA
Why did you change your mind, Ben?

CASEY
I reconsidered the facts.

ZORBA
Has Axelson's prognosis changed?

CASEY
No.

ZORBA
A remission is still possible, and yet you're going ahead . . . ? Knowing what it might be like for her to live for many years without the capacity for experiencing pain? Every day she'll have to examine herself for cuts and bruises. She could get a splinter in her eye and not feel it. She could . . .

CASEY
(breaking in)
If she lives . . .

ZORBA
Ben, I don't have to tell you what's happening: that the world is on the verge of a biological explosion as great—or even greater—than that of the atomic revolution of fifteen or twenty years ago. The possibility of arresting and even curing many types of cancer is almost at hand. Every day new discoveries are being made . . .

CASEY
I know all about it.

ZORBA
Dr. Wilson herself is part of that explosion. Perhaps her own research could lead to her cure.

CASEY
But she can't continue with her research because of the pain! We've gone through all that, Dr. Zorba!
(firmly)
Tomorrow morning I'm going to relieve her of the pain in accordance with her wishes.

ZORBA
But not yours . . .

CASEY
We do what we have to do, not what we want to do!

ZORBA
(quietly)
What is Elizabeth Wilson to you, Ben?

CASEY
Dr. Zorba, would you please initial that schedule?

ZORBA
I don't mean to pry, Ben. Your personal life is your own—*except* where it impinges upon your duties here, your judgment.

                              CASEY
Do you think that's the case? That my judgment is impaired?

                              ZORBA
                             (levelly)
                          I don't know. Is it?

                              CASEY
The decision I've made is based upon a recognition of all the
facts available . . .

                              ZORBA
                        (picks up schedule)
              Suppose I tell you I won't initial this . . . ?

                              CASEY
Suppose I were to tell you you better get yourself a new Chief
Resident . . . !

                              ZORBA
                    You feel this strongly . . .

                              CASEY
                          (bursting out)
I feel lousy and rotten and sick! Okay, Dr. Zorba? Now will
you initial that schedule?

Zorba looks at him for a long moment.

                              ZORBA
                         All right, Ben.

He picks up pencil, initials schedule.

93 INT. ROOM IN HOSPITAL—NIGHT

Liz is lying in bed with a thermometer in her mouth and Miss Wills
standing beside her, taking her pulse. Wills finishes with pulse, takes
thermometer out, makes notation on chart.

                              WILLS
              You had a radiation treatment today . . . ?

> LIZ
> Yes. Also nitrogen mustard gas.

> WILLS
> Was there a reaction?

> LIZ
> Slight nausea . . .

Wills crosses to side, brings wash basin on a tray, with a scissors, razor and soap to bed. She takes scissors and approaches Liz.

> LIZ
> (continuing)
> What're you doing?

> WILLS
> I have to shave your head.

> LIZ
> (reaches up, touches her hair protectively)
> Now I know what it feels like to become a nun . . .

> WILLS
> Don't worry. It'll grow back . . .

Wills starts to snip Liz's hair.

94 LIZ—IN BED

A turban around her head. Door opens. Casey enters.

> CASEY
> Everything under control?

> LIZ
> (with a tight smile)
> A-Okay.
> (a pause)
> I'm glad you came, Ben . . . I want to talk to you . . .

> CASEY
> Do you want to change your mind?

                    LIZ
              (shakes her head)
                 No. Ben—

                   CASEY
                   Yes?

                    LIZ
You know how I feel about you . . . or you should know . . .

Casey reaches for her hand.

                    LIZ
               (continuing)
   And I think I know how you feel about me . . .

95 CLOSE—CASEY

reacting, tortured, about to speak.

96 FAVORING LIZ

reaches to his lips with her finger, stopping his speech.

                    LIZ
               (continuing)
Another time, another place, another world, we might have
been a thing—a real thing together. I've dreamed of it—but
only for a moment . . . You know, when you walk around in
the shadows, you feel things more intensely, you see more
sharply . . . You hear the words that were never
said . . . and you understand . . .

97 CLOSE TWO SHOT

She smiles.

                    LIZ
               (continuing)
Let's appreciate what we had, Ben . . . and let's agree that
no matter what happens tomorrow or afterward—win, lose,
draw—we remain just friends. Love between us is foolish and
wrong.

> (a beat)
> Okay?

He doesn't answer.

> **LIZ**
> (continuing)
> If we can't, I'll go to another lab when I recover . . . and
> work there . . . and never see you again.

> **CASEY**
> However you want it, Liz. Good luck.

They are looking into each other's eyes. Their faces are weaving very
close. He abruptly kisses her cheek, rises, starts to turn.

> **LIZ**
> (continuing)
> Ben . . .

He looks back.

> **LIZ**
> (continuing)
> Good luck.

> **CASEY**
> Thanks.

He exits.

98   CLOSE UP—LIZ

her eyes are moist.

99   INT. SCRUB ROOM—DAY

Casey, Ted and an Interne are scrubbing.

> **TED**
> What approach, Ben?

> **CASEY**
> Standard craniotomy . . .

Nurse comes into door.

>   NURSE
>   All ready in here, Doctor.

>   CASEY
>   (takes a deep dreath)
>   Let's go.

Casey and the others start toward door.

100 INT. O.R.–CLOSE SHOT

Liz is on table, conscious. Casey is feeling with instrument into brain area (o.s.).

>   CASEY
>   (to Liz)
>   Can you move your left leg?

>   LIZ
>   I think so . . .

>   CASEY
>   Try . . .

He looks in direction of her legs.

101 ANOTHER ANGLE

Her left leg moves.

>   CASEY
>   (continuing: to Nurse)
>   Good—

Nurse hands him ————. He continues testing, touching.

>   CASEY
>   (continuing: to Ted)
>   We're close now. Let's stay a little on the outside to make
>   sure. Outline the borders.
>   (to Liz)
>   Can you whistle?

LIZ
Dixie?

CASEY
(wry; sharp)
No. Give me the final chorus from Beethoven's Ninth . . .

LIZ
I don't remember it.

CASEY
Where are you?

LIZ
I'm being operated on—my brain . . .

CASEY
(quickly)
Whistle!

She puckers up her lips, whistles.

LIZ
The first time a boy told me to do that he kissed me . . .

INTERNE
(to Casey)
That's a cool cat.

CASEY
(sweating, tense; barely looks at him)
This is it!
(to Ted)
Alcohol!

TED
(to Nurse)
Alcohol!

Nurse hands it to him.

CASEY
Inject neurotract!

Ted does, carefully.

CASEY
Sew up!

102 INT. LOUNGE

Casey comes out of O.R., takes a deep breath, drops into chair, presses his knuckles into his eyes. His whole frame seems to shudder with weariness and emotion.

DISSOLVE TO:

103 INT. CORRIDOR OUTSIDE TREATMENT ROOM

Door opens and we see Dr. Axelson in doorway, and in b.g. the cobalt gun. Then Liz and an Attendant holding her arm appear, approach door. Axelson stands aside, allows them to pass out into corridor. Liz is walking mechanically, holding herself very carefully.

104 ANOTHER ANGLE

Casey appears from opposite direction, halts as he sees Liz. They smile at each other like neighbors who have merely a nodding acquaintance; then Liz and Attendant continue onward down corridor o.s. Casey watches them for a moment, approaches Axelson.

CASEY
How is she doing?

AXELSON
This was her last treatment for a while. We've arrested the malignancy, at least for the moment. I think, though, we can look forward with real hope toward a complete remission—of the cancer.

105 CASEY

He nods heavily, starts walking slowly away down corridor, but hesitates after a few steps, glances back toward:

106 P.O.V.—LIZ AND ATTENDANT

at opposite end of corridor, walking slowly away. Abruptly she halts, turns, looking around for something. WHISTLES.

107 BACK TO CASEY

looking toward her, toward open door of treatment room quizzically:
then he sees something.

108 ANOTHER ANGLE

Out of the open door of the treatment room, scooting past Axelson,
comes a little dog. It runs down corridor directly up to Liz. She bends
stiffly, picks it up; then she and Attendant continue o.s.

109 CLOSE—CASEY

A fleeting smile crosses his face, at once wry and sad, as he turns and
walks slowly away in the opposite direction. CAMERA PULLS
BACK SLOWLY to see Liz and Casey far away from each other,
going further and further.

FADE OUT.

-THE END-

Appendix C

Love, Marriage and Five Thousand Dollars was written a long time ago, during the 1950s. It is one of my early scripts, originally done on an hour-long anthology series entitled *Matinee Theatre*.

Matinee Theatre should be remembered as one of the more interesting experiments in early live television because an original hour-length TV drama was presented every weekday afternoon. The sets were sketchy and unrealistic, but many of the plays were interesting. In those days the writer had to explore character, and he often dealt with the small but powerful explosions in people's lives. Melodrama was of much less importance than it is now. So were chases, physical violence, and the big climaxes you see now every night.

When you read this script, remember when it was written. It was a different world then. The relationship between men and women was not the same as it is now. The chasm between the fifties and now is wide. Thus, in many ways, this play is dated.

I am including it here, however, for several reasons. One, it's a good example of a typical drama done during that era. It's also a work that I happen to like. I particularly want you to notice the amount of dialogue in this script as compared to Appendix B. The high ratio of dialogue to action is a result of the concern with costs in the early days of television. The budgets did not allow elaborate sets, so for the most part dialogue had to carry the play.

I also want you to see how the format differs from the film format we use now. Compare it with the script in Appendix B.

This live format is still used, only now the shows are taped—videotaped. The format is used today mainly on situation comedies that are a half hour in length, or about half as long as this.

Soaps, an occasional afternoon children's special, and some nighttime specials are also videotaped. This is essentially the format that they all use. (Note: The first four pages of this script are a facsimile of the original.)

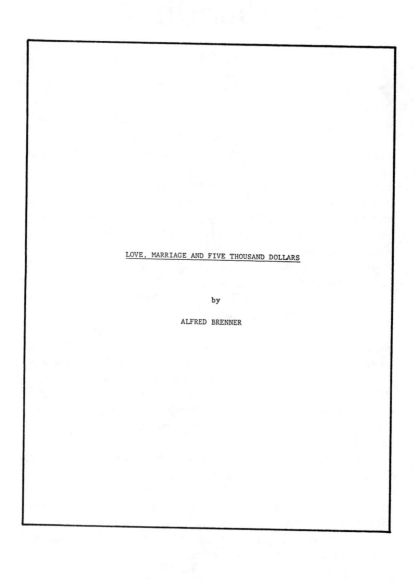

LOVE, MARRIAGE AND FIVE THOUSAND DOLLARS

by

ALFRED BRENNER

"LOVE, MARRIAGE AND FIVE THOUSAND DOLLARS"

ACT ONE

FADE IN:

A LOCAL POST OFFICE STATION IN NEW YORK
CITY. A SMALL LINE HAS FORMED AT ONE
OF THE WINDOWS OVER WHICH ARE TWO SMALL
PRINTED SIGNS. ONE READS: "STAMPS"; THE
OTHER "PACKAGES". AT THE HEAD OF THE
LINE IS A BOY, ABOUT 11 OR 12. BEHIND
THE WINDOW IS DAVE, THE POSTAL CLERK.
HE IS 35, OF AVERAGE HEIGHT, STOCKY,
WITH AN EVEN TEMPER AND A PLEASANT
DISPOSITION. AT THE MOMENT, HOWEVER,
THERE IS A PREOCCUPIED EXPRESSION ON
HIS FACE.

        BOY:

    Is the latest Commemorative
    in, Mister?

        DAVE:

    What do you want, a single
    or a plate block?

        BOY:

    A plate block... I save
    plate blocks... I got
    almost every U.S.
    Commemorative that was
    ever issued...

DAVE REACHES DOWN INTO DRAWER FOR
STAMPS AS BOY TALKS, TEARS OFF A
BLOCK OF FOUR FROM A LARGE SHEET

        BOY:

You see, my uncle gave me
his collection for my
birthday. He says it's
worth more than a hundred
dollars!

JOE, A FELLOW EMPLOYEE, APPROACHES
DAVE.

        JOE:

Checks are in...

DAVE, PREOCCUPIED, SCARCELY LOOKS AT
HIM, PLACES STAMPS ON COUNTER.

        DAVE:

TO BOY

Thirty two cents...

BOY HANDS HIM A DIME AND A QUARTER. DAVE
GIVES HIM THREE CENTS CHANGE. BOY TAKES
STAMPS, PENNIES, LEAVES.

        JOE:

Go on, Dave... Get yours...
I'll take over till you get
back...

        DAVE:

STARTS TO MOVE AWAY, HESITATES.

Did I get a call, Joe?

ACT I - 3

JOE:

Not that I know of...

DAVE STANDS THERE A MOMENT.

What's the matter?

Something wrong?

DAVE SHRUGS, SHAKES HIS HEAD, SHUFFLES
AWAY TOWARD INTERIOR OF MAIL ROOM.
MR. GORSKY, THE SUPERVISOR, STUDYING
SOME PAPERS ON A CLIP BOARD, IS COMING
SLOWLY FROM THE OPPOSITE DIRECTION. HE
GLANCES UP, SEES DAVE.

GORSKY:

Dave... Listen, got a minute:

DAVE:

Sure, Mr. Gorsky... I was just
gonna pick up my check, that's
all...

GORSKY:

I spoke to my brother about
you...

DAVE:

EAGERLY

You did? What'd he say?
I mean, does he want me
for the job?

LOVE, MARRIAGE AND FIVE THOUSAND DOLLARS

by

ALFRED BRENNER

ACT ONE

FADE IN:
A LOCAL POST OFFICE STATION IN NEW YORK CITY. A SMALL
LINE HAS FORMED AT ONE OF THE WINDOWS OVER WHICH
ARE TWO SMALL PRINTED SIGNS. ONE READS: "STAMPS"; THE
OTHER "PACKAGES." AT THE HEAD OF THE LINE IS A BOY,
ABOUT 11 OR 12. BEHIND THE WINDOW IS *DAVE*, THE POSTAL
CLERK. HE IS 35, OF AVERAGE HEIGHT, STOCKY, WITH AN
EVEN TEMPER AND A PLEASANT DISPOSITION. AT THE MO-
MENT, HOWEVER, THERE IS A PREOCCUPIED EXPRESSION ON
HIS FACE.

BOY:
Is the latest Commemorative in, Mister?

DAVE:
What do you want, a single or a plate block?

BOY:
A plate block . . . I save plate blocks . . . I got almost every U.S.
Commemorative that was ever issued . . .

DAVE REACHES DOWN INTO DRAWER FOR STAMPS AS BOY
TALKS, TEARS OFF A BLOCK OF FOUR FROM A LARGE SHEET.

BOY:

You see, my uncle gave me his collection for my birthday. He says it's worth more than a hundred dollars!

JOE, A FELLOW EMPLOYEE, APPROACHES DAVE.

JOE:
Checks are in . . .

DAVE, PREOCCUPIED, SCARCELY LOOKS AT HIM, PLACES STAMPS ON COUNTER.

DAVE:
TO BOY.
Thirty-two cents . . .

BOY HANDS HIM A DIME AND A QUARTER. DAVE GIVES HIM THREE CENTS CHANGE. BOY TAKES STAMPS, PENNIES, LEAVES.

JOE:
Go on, Dave . . . Get yours . . . I'll take over till you get back . . .

DAVE:
STARTS TO MOVE AWAY, HESITATES.
Did I get a call, Joe?

JOE:
Not that I know of . . .

DAVE STANDS THERE A MOMENT.

What's the matter? Something wrong?

DAVE SHRUGS, SHAKES HIS HEAD, SHUFFLES AWAY TOWARD INTERIOR OF MAIL ROOM. *MR. GORSKY,* THE SUPERVISOR, STUDYING SOME PAPERS ON A CLIPBOARD, IS COMING SLOWLY FROM THE OPPOSITE DIRECTION. HE GLANCES UP, SEES DAVE.

GORSKY:
Dave . . . Listen, got a minute?

DAVE:

Sure, Mr. Gorsky . . . I was just gonna pick up my check, that's all . . .

GORSKY:

I spoke to my brother about you . . .

DAVE:

EAGERLY.
   You did? What'd he say? I mean, does he want me for the job?

GORSKY:

Well, Dave, that's what I wanted to tell you. I showed him that album you made. You know, the one of Mike Caminetti's wedding that you brought into the office? He liked it a lot, Dave . . .

DAVE:
He did?

GORSKY:

If it was up to *him* you'd be in . . . But well . . . The fact is, his fiancee's father's paying for the wedding . . . It's going to be a big affair . . . At the Waldorf . . . They expect over a hundred guests . . . You see, Dave, this father-in- law is the kind of guy once he gets involved in something, he's got to run it . . . I mean, he's handling the whole thing like it was some big business enterprise . . . You know the type . . .

DAVE:
Didn't he like my work?

GORSKY:

Sure, Dave . . . He liked it . . . But when he heard you were a clerk in the Post Office, that you only took pictures in your spare time, so to speak . . . Well, he lost interest . . . He decided to get some well-known studio to handle the job . . . I built you up, Dave, but there are some people like that . . . They got money and they're willing to pay, but they want to make sure they're gonna get what they paid for . . . a real professional job . . . I mean, he figures how can you be good enough if you don't even make a living at it? Well, he has a point, Dave . . .

DAVE:
Yeah . . . I guess so. . . .

GORSKY:

You're not upset about it . . . I mean, you didn't count on it too
much . . .

DAVE:

No . . . It's nothing . . . It's nothing, honest . . .

GORSKY:

Dave, I know I'm your supervisor and I shouldn't be talking like
this . . . but I'm going to tell you something . . . You're wasting
your time here . . .
DAVE STARES AT HIM.

And it's really a shame . . . a talented guy like you . . .

DAVE:

Yeah . . . Well, I better get my check, Mr. Gorsky . . . Joe's holdin'
down the window for me and I can't take all day . . . Thanks anyway . . .

DAVE TURNS, MOVES OUT OF PICTURE. GORSKY STARES AF-
TER HIM, SHAKING HIS HEAD SLOWLY.

CUT TO:

A SMALL TABLE AT THE REAR OF THE MAILROOM ABOUT
WHICH SEVERAL WORKERS ARE GROUPED. TWO OF THEM,
TOM AND *ARNIE*, HAVE JUST BEEN PAID AND ARE STUDYING
THEIR CHECKS. A THIRD—*COSMO*—WEARING A POSTMAN'S
UNIFORM, IS PLACING SOME PACKAGES AND PERIODICALS IN
A LARGE LEATHER MAIL BAG. ED, WHO IS ACTING AS PAY-
MASTER, IS SEATED AT THE TABLE WITH A BUNCH OF CHECKS
IN HIS HANDS. BEFORE HIM IS A SHEET OF PAPER CONTAIN-
ING A LIST OF POSTAL EMPLOYEES' NAMES. *JULES* IS STAND-
ING BEFORE A SERIES OF WOODEN CUBBYHOLES BEHIND THE
TABLE SORTING THE MAIL.

TOM:

FROWNING DOWN AT HIS CHECK

What're they tryin' to do to me? I'm hardly gettin' any more this time
than I did last . . . an' I just got an increment . . .

ARNIE:

Let's see . . .
HE LOOKS AT THE SLIP ATTACHED TO TOM'S CHECK.

It shows your increase right here under "gross" . . .

DAVE APPROACHES. ED SEES HIM, FLIPS THROUGH CHECKS IN HIS HANDS, TAKES OUT ONE, HANDS IT TO HIM AS HE REACHES THE TABLE, AND AT THE SAME TIME SHOVES THE SHEET OF PAPER TOWARD HIM. DAVE SIGNS HIS NAME ON THE PAPER, GLANCES AT HIS CHECK.

Wait a minute! You're in a new tax bracket . . . That's what happened . . .

TOM:
Well, they took practically the whole raise . . .

ARNIE:
That's the way it works, ol' boy . . .

TOM:
I don't care how it works! My oldest kid's gotta have his teeth straightened . . . You know what an orthodontist costs?

DAVE:
QUIETLY.
Didn't I get a telephone call, Ed?

ED:
Not while I was aroun' . . .

JULES:
So you know how long I got till my pension, Cosmo? Sixteen years, eight months, three days . . . I figured it out this morning on the subway . . . I was in such a hurry I forgot to buy a paper . . . So I had nothing to do, so I figured out my pension . . .

COSMO:
You know what I'm gonna do when I get mine? I'm gonna buy me a little house down in Florida . . . Sarasota . . . with an orange grove in the back, an' just lay in a hammock an' let those red oranges drop in my mouth . . .

DAVE LOOKS ACROSS AT COSMO, FROWNING.

ARNIE:
I'm gonna settle in California . . . San Diego . . . I was stationed out there when I was in the army. Man, that's God's country . . .

DAVE NOW SHIFTS HIS GAZE TO ARNIE, HIS FROWN DEEPENING.

TOM:

I'd like to take a trip to some of those places they sent me when I was in the army . . . I keep promisin' to take my wife. I still haven't done it all these years. She don't believe I ever will . . . Man, I still remember how wonderful those beaches were in New Guinea and Hawaii . . . Man, that's where I'd like to live when I retire. Hawaii . . .

DAVE:

BURSTING OUT SUDDENLY, MORE IN ANGUISH THAN IN ANGER.

You guys! Is that all you got to look forward to? A pension? Is that what your life is, a nothing that doesn't even start till you're 60, when you won't have to work anymore?

THEY ALL STARE AT HIM, TAKEN ABACK BY HIS UNUSUAL OUTBURST.

COSMO:

What're you so hot about, Dave? Your life is different?

DAVE:
Yes it is!

HIS VOICE DROPPING.

Well, it's gonna be . . .

COSMO:

TAUNTING.

You gonna quit, Dave?

DAVE BITES HIS LIPS IN SILENCE.

TOM:

Well, *he* can . . . He ain't married . . . When you're married and you got kids it's different . . .

ARNIE:

I'd like to quit myself . . . My wife keeps tellin' me I ought to go to night school, get my accounting degree . . . CPAs are making big money . . . Thirty-three ain't so old, is it? I mean, to go back to school . . .?

COSMO:

Oh, Dave ain't gonna quit . . . He was just blowin' off

steam . . . Twenty years from now he'll still be here and we'll have a dinner for him and buy him a watch when they pension him off just like we did ol' man McCrary . . . Right, Dave?

DAVE, TIGHT-LIPPED, TURNS RIGIDLY, AND WALKS OUT OF PICTURE. COSMO WATCHES HIM, SHRUGS, STARTS TO PICK UP MAIL BAG.

CUT TO:

JOE AT WINDOW TAKING A PACKAGE FROM A CUSTOMER AND PLACING SOME STAMPS ON IT. DAVE APPROACHES. CUSTOMER LEAVES. THE LINE HAS GONE NOW. NO ONE IS WAITING.

JOE:
Got your check?
DAVE NODS.

You find out about that call?

DAVE:
MOVES SOME PACKAGES OFF COUNTER.
Joe, how long did you know Helen before you got married?

JOE:
How long? Oh . . . I knew her a long time . . . She's from my neighborhood, but I never had much to do with her . . . She was always younger . . . a kid . . . you know . . . But after I got out of the army I met her one night at a rock concert . . . She was all grown up . . I was only goin' with her a couple months actually when I says to myself one night: "Joe, what're you knockin' your head against a wall for? This girl is for you." So I asked her to marry me . . .
HE LOOKS AT DAVE.

Why?

DAVE:
I been goin' with Mim almost two years . . . It'll be two years next week . . . I see her practically every weekend and I guess practically everybody's got us down as a thing . . . But I don't feel right about it . . . Not that I don't like the idea. I do . . . She's a wonderful girl . . . Joe . . . I mean, if I was going to get married there's nobody I'd rather marry than Mim . . . I feel good just thinking about her . . . But what I'm trying to say is, you gotta feel you're set when you marry, that you got some kind of future . . . at least, that you're

goin' somewhere . . . Don't you? Where am I goin'? I mean, if I could make a living as a photographer . . . You know? Am I wrong, Joe?

JOE:
Well, it's what you want, I guess . . . Everybody's different . . . I been married goin' on nine years . . . I got two kids, an' some beat-up furniture, an' I'm drivin a load needs a ring job an' a new clutch, but what the hell . . . I get a check every week . . . an' I still got my G.I. insurance . . . You gotta weigh one thing against another, that's all . . .

A SILENCE. THE TWO MEN CONTINUE WORKING.

DAVE:
That call I was expecting . . . It was about a business . . . A friend of mine wants to buy a photography studio with me . . . Harry Jaffee . . . I think you seen him around . . . a little bouncy kind a guy . . .? Well, he's an accountant, an' this place he found sounds like a good deal, but there was some question about whether the owner was ready to sell . . . You see, he's going to retire but he won't sell to just anybody . . . He built the studio up himself and he has this feeling for it . . . I mean he'll only sell it to someone whose work he respects . . . Someone who can carry on where he left off. You know what I mean? Harry was supposed to find out this morning, one way or another . . . I've been expecting his call all day . .

WE BEGIN TO CLOSE SLOWLY IN ON DAVE'S FACE.

DAVE:
Well, I guess it fell through . . . Funny, I really wanted that studio . . . Started planning, dreaming . . . Even started looking in the windows of jewelry stores, pricing rings . . . You know, Joe, I'm thirty-five . . . Half my life's gone . . . I've been with the Post Office fourteen years . . . For the last ten I've been trying to get out . . . I guess I never will though . . . I guess Cosmo's right . . . I'll be here to get my pension if I live that long . . .
A PAUSE.
I'm gonna break off with Mim tonight! . . . I mean going with her the way I am is not fair to her, that's all! . . . Is it, Joe? I mean, what does she want with a guy like me anyway?

DAVE: CLOSEUP

DISSOLVE TO:

KITCHEN AND SECTION OF HALLWAY IN THE APARTMENT WHERE DAVE LIVES WITH HIS SISTER, *FLORRIE,* AND HER HUSBAND, *GEORGE.* WE COME UP ON GEORGE SOFTLY CLOS- ING A BEDROOM DOOR IN THE HALL. A BABY'S MILK BOTTLE IS IN HIS HAND. HE MOVES QUIETLY INTO KITCHEN WHERE FLORRIE IS SETTING THE TABLE FOR THREE. BOTH ARE IN THEIR LATE 20'S.

                          FLORRIE:
GLANCING UP.

                          He asleep?

                          GEORGE:
                  Went off like a doll . . .

HE SETS BOTTLE DOWN, COMES UP BEHIND HER, PLACES HIS HANDS GENTLY ON HER SHOULDERS, TURNS HER AROUND. THEY KISS LINGERINGLY. THEN, LAUGHING, SHE PUSHES HER HANDS AGAINST HIS CHEST AND TWISTS OUT OF HIS ARMS.

                          FLORRIE:
     George . . . Not now . . . Dave'll be here any minute . . .
GEORGE LOOKS AT HER, BITES HIS LIPS, BEGINS TO STRAIGHTEN SILVERWARE ON TABLE. SHE MOVES TOWARD HIM TENDERLY.
         O . . . Come on . . . The world hasn't come to an end . . .

                          GEORGE:
PETULANT.
     Listen, Florrie . . . How long is your brother going to live with us
                          anyway?

                          FLORRIE:
STIFFENING.
         I told you I don't want to talk about that anymore!

                          GEORGE:
                          Well, *I* do!
THEY GLARE AT EACH OTHER FOR A MOMENT, THEN DROP THEIR EYES. SHE GOES TO STOVE ANGRILY, LOOKS IN POTS.
     Florrie, why are you so pigheaded when it comes to him, anyway?

FLORRIE:
Why are you so selfish?

GEORGE:
COMES UP BEHIND HER.
All I want is a little privacy in my own home . . . Is that asking so much? I mean, what's so wrong if he should move out? He was only supposed to stay a few weeks after your mother died . . . It's over a year already . . .

FLORRIE:
TURNING AND FACING HIM.
George, my brother is going to stay here as long as he wants to!

GEORGE:
You gonna take him with us when we buy our house . . .?

JUST THEN THE KETTLE ON THE STOVE BEGINS TO WHISTLE, CUTTING OFF GEORGE'S WORDS.

FLORRIE:
The water's boiling . . . Make the coffee . . .
GEORGE GOES TO STOVE, TURNS OFF LIGHT UNDER KETTLE, BEGINS MAKING COFFEE. FLORRIE WATCHES HIM GUARDEDLY. SOON A TENDER EXPRESSION CREEPS INTO HER FACE. SHE COMES UP BESIDE HIM.
Look, honey, what are we fighting about anyway? Dave's going to get married one of these days . . .

GEORGE:
Yeah? When?

FLORRIE:
Well . . . one of these days . . .
THEN, WITH FEELING.
Well, why shouldn't he live here? He's no trouble . . . He does more than his share of the work . . . And you know how Stevy feels about him. Gee, the way he makes that kid laugh . . . It does my heart good to see it . . . Besides, if he moved out where would we get such a dependable baby sitter? And another thing: it should not be forgotten that my brother's contribution to this house is nothing to be sneezed at . . . We can use it . . .

GEORGE:
All right, maybe we can . . . But we can struggle along without it,

too . . . Look, I'm not an ogre. I got nothing against Dave personally. You know that. He's a sweet guy. He'd give you the shirt off his
back . . . But, well, it's no good to have a third party in the house
when you're married . . .

CUT TO:

ENTRANCE HALL OF APARTMENT, BETWEEN KITCHEN AND
LIVING ROOM. DAVE HAS JUST ENTERED. A NEWSPAPER AND
A SMALL PACKAGE ARE UNDER HIS ARM. THE DEEPENING
FROWN ON HIS FACE REVEALS THAT HE HAS OBVIOUSLY
HEARD AT LEAST THE LAST FEW SENTENCES OF THE CONVER-
SATION GOING ON IN THE KITCHEN. GEORGE'S VOICE CON-
TINUES OFF.

—If he had any backbone he'd see it and move out without being
told . . . The whole trouble is the way your mother brought him up,
waited   on   him   hand   and   foot . . . Gave   him   no
independence . . . Now you're continuing where she left off . . . I
mean, it would be good for *him* too if he'd leave . . .

DAVE PULLS FRONT DOOR CLOSED NOISILY, HIS FACE TIGHT.
GEORGE'S VOICE BREAKS OFF. A SILENCE. FLORRIE APPEARS,
SOMEWHAT NERVOUS AND EMBARRASSED.

FLORRIE:
Hi, Dave . . . You're late . . . Supper's all ready . . .

DAVE:
I'm not hungry . . .

HE TAKES OFF HIS JACKET, OPENS HIS COLLAR.

FLORRIE:
What's the matter?

DAVE:
Nothing. Is Stevy up?

FLORRIE:
George just put him in . . .

DAVE:
Here, give him this when he wakes up . . .

HE ABRUPTLY THRUSTS THE PACKAGE INTO HER HANDS. SHE
TAKES IT SILENTLY, HER LIPS TREMBLING.
> I dunno . . . I just can't resist buying things for that kid . . .

SHE IS STANDING IN FRONT OF HIM, BLOCKING HIS PATH.
> Lemme past . . .

FLORRIE:

NOT MOVING, GENTLY.
> Dave, you got to eat . . . Come on, get washed . . . We'll wait for
> you . . .

DAVE:

BURSTING OUT.
> Leave me alone, will you, Sis! I told you I'm not hungry!

HE PUSHES PAST HER, MORE ROUGHLY THAN HE HAD IN-
TENDED, TAKES A FEW STEPS TOWARD HIS ROOM, HALTS. IN
A LOW, GRUDGING VOICE.
> All right, I'll eat later . . . I got a date with Mim . . . After the movie
> I'll have a sandwich . . . Okay?

UNHAPPILY.
> If you think I wanna go out on a date tonight, you're crazy . . .

HE SHUFFLES DOWN HALLWAY PAST ENTRANCE TO KITCHEN
TOWARD THE BEDROOMS. FLORRIE STARES AFTER HIM, A
WORRIED AND GUILTY EXPRESSION ON HER FACE, LOOKS
SLOWLY DOWN AT THE PACKAGE IN HER HANDS.

DISSOLVE TO:

CLOSEUP OF PACKAGE. AS CAMERA DOLLIES BACK SLOWLY,
WE SEE THAT IT IS ON THE KITCHEN TABLE NOW AMONG THE
HALF-EMPTY POTS AND DISHES LEFT FROM DINNER WAIT-
ING TO BE WASHED. THEN WE SEE GEORGE, AND FINALLY,
FLORRIE SITTING ACROSS FROM EACH OTHER, HAVING A
FINAL CUP OF COFFEE. A MOMENT OF SILENCE.

GEORGE:
> Well, if we can't get out tonight, how about inviting somebody
> over . . .?

FLORRIE:
> Isn't it a little late to ask anyone?

GEORGE:
Oh . . . Ben and Ruth are probably home . . . We could call
them . . .
FLORRIE SIPS HER COFFEE, FROWNING, TROUBLED. GEORGE
WATCHES HER, REACHES TENDERLY FOR HER HAND.
I'm sorry about before, honey . . . I didn't realize he was . . .

BUZZER RINGS. FLORRIE IMMEDIATELY TURNS, CALLS OUT.

FLORRIE:
Come in!
WE HEAR FRONT DOOR CLOSE. FLORRIE IS ON HER FEET.
Harry . . .

WE SEE HARRY NOW COMING INTO THE KITCHEN. HE IS
SMALL, WIRY, A MASS OF ENERGY, ABOUT DAVE'S AGE. A BIG
SMILE IS ON HIS FACE.

HARRY:
Hello, you beautiful chick . . . Par'me, George . . . Your wife is
such a gorgeous creature . . . But somebody is missing from this
table . . . Don't tell me . . . Let me guess . . . Well, where is he? I
gotta see him . . .

FLORRIE:
He's in his room, Harry . . . I'll call him . . . Sit down, I'll pour you
a cup of coffee . . .

HARRY:
Well . . . Okay . . . a quick one . . .

HE SITS AT TABLE.

FLORRIE:
POURING HIM A CUP.
Say, wasn't Dave expecting a phone call from you?

HARRY:
Yeah . . . He was . . . Matter of fact, I meant to call all day . . . But
I was so tied up I just didn't have a second . . .
HE PLACES A SPOONFUL OF SUGAR IN HIS COFFEE, STIRS IT.
I got so many things on my mind . . . This morning . . . I'm at this
studio . . . You know, the one we've been negotiating for? Dave tell
you about it? You oughta see it, George! Well, I'm goin' over the
figures with Mr. Mantelli . . . He's the owner . . . He built it up

from nothin' in fifteen years . . . A man in his
60's . . . Imagine . . . So anyway here I am goin' over the books
with him when the phone starts ringing . . . All morning it keeps
ringing, one call after another, practically all for me . . . When in the
midst of everything, I pick up the receiver and who should be on the
line but my wife, her mother wants to visit us for a couple of
weeks . . . So I'm supposed to drop everything and drive to Coney
Island and bring her all the way up to the Bronx . . . Do you know
how long that takes? In traffic?

HIS VOICE ASSUMES A CONFIDENTIAL TONE.

You know, ever since I got a massage parlor for a client my wife don't
leave me alone . . .

HE SUDDENLY IS AWARE OF SOMEONE ELSE IN THE ROOM,
LOOKS UP, SEES DAVE, WHO HAS COME IN. DAVE IS WEARING
A CLEAN SHIRT AND IS TYING HIS TIE. HARRY IMMEDIATELY
JUMPS TO HIS FEET, GRABS DAVE'S HAND.

Davy!

DAVE:

I heard your voice, Harry . . . What happened to you? I was expecting your call all day . . .

HARRY:

I know . . . I'm sorry . . . I got tied up . . . I was just tellin' George
and Florrie here . .

DAVE:

What happened? Wouldn't he sell?

HARRY:

GRINNING.

Listen . . . what d'ya think I been doin' all day? Sittin' in some ball
park? The studio's practically ours!

DAVE:

STARING AT HIM.

What?

HARRY:

C'mon, grab your coat. Mr. Mantelli's waiting . . .

DAVE:

Harry, you're not kiddin' me . . . ?

HARRY:
Would I kid you, Dave? About a thing like this? Listen, I been negotiating with him since early this morning . . .

DAVE:
An' I thought . . .
HE TURNS JUBILANTLY TO FLORRIE AND GEORGE.
Man! Did you hear that, Sis? Did *you*, George? We're gonna have our own studio! . . .
THEN SUDDENLY REMEMBERING SOMETHING.
But wait a minute! I got a date with Mim . . .

HARRY:
Forget it! You'll see her later . . . This is important! Now come on. Hurry up!

DAVE:
HESITANTLY.
Well . . .
THEN DECISIVELY.
Okay, I'll get my coat!

HE STARTS QUICKLY TOWARD HIS ROOM.

DISSOLVE TO: /

SECTION OF A PHOTOGRAPHIC STUDIO. *MR. MANTELLI,* IN HIS LATE 60'S, IS ENTERING FROM OUTER OFFICE. ACTUALLY, HE IS HESITATING MOMENTARILY IN THE DOORWAY, LOOK-ING BACK OVER HIS SHOULDER.

MR. MANTELLI:
. . . Tell you the truth, it pains me in the heart to have to give this place up . . . But well, whaddya gonna do, fight with the doctor?
HE COMES INTO THE STUDIO NOW, FOLLOWED BY HARRY AND DAVE.
One thing I tell myself though, when I sell, I sell only to someone who has respect for his work; who will do only the best job alla time . . .
HE APPROACHES A LARGE PORTRAIT CAMERA.
. . . This here is my portrait camera . . . You know cameras, Mr. Edel? Look at this lens . . .
DAVE LOOKS AT IT CAREFULLY.
You know how much-a the lens is worth, by itself . . .?

PHONE RINGS IN OFFICE.
> Excuse me please. I'li be right back . . .

HE EXITS INTO OFFICE.

HARRY:
GRABS DAVE'S ARM. IN A HUSHED. EXCITED VOICE.
> Whadaya think, huh, Dave? Nice?

DAVE:
IMPRESSED.
> It's a beauty . .

WALKING AROUND, LOOKING THE STUDIO OVER.
> Boy, what I couldn't do with a place like this! Gee, he's got all the equipment in the world . . . I hardly saw it last time I was here .

STOPPING BEFORE AN ENLARGER.
> Look at this enlarger . . .

HE STUDIES IT, HANDLES IT, WORKING IT CAREFULLY UP AND DOWN.

HARRY:
And you ought to see his list of clients! With me handling the business end, and you the artistic, we can't miss, Dave . . . I'm tellin' you, for ten G's it's a steal . . .

DAVE:
Ten G's?

HARRY:
Five apiece down. I brought him down from twelve-five . . .He wants cash, but it's worth it . . . I tole him it'd take a week or two before we could make all the arrangements . . . I figure you have to give notice on your job . . . an' I've got to clear up a few things myself . . .

DAVE BITES HIS LIPS, LOOKS DOWN AT HIS FEET.
> What's the matter?

DAVE:
I was just tryin' to think, where am I gonna get five thousand dollars?

HARRY:
STARING AT HIM.
> You mean you ain't got it?

DAVE SHAKES HIS HEAD SLOWLY.
> Well, how much have you got?

DAVE:
I dunno exactly. . . . I guess there's about a thousand or so in my pension fund. . . and I got some bonds. . . I could raise fifteen hundred maybe. . . altogether. . . That's all . . .

HARRY:
What about your friends? Your family? How about George? He got any money?

DAVE:
SHAKES HIS HEAD.
Not Much. Besides, he and Florrie are tryin' to buy a house. They wanna move out on the island.

HARRY:
IN DISGUST.
Man, you're a beauty! You know how much work I put in negotiating for this place?

DAVE:
Gee, Harry, I don't know what I was thinkin'. . . It just never entered my mind about the money. . . I thought I could pay it off, I guess . . .

HARRY:
Well, you just gotta get it! We can't let this go! You don't get a deal like this every day!

DAVE:
> Well, you don't think I *want* to let it go . . .

HARRY:
LOOKING AT HIM HARD.
I don't know about you . . . It takes guts to leave a secure job and take a chance in a business . . .

DAVE:
> You think I'm scared?

HARRY:
I think if you really want this, you'll get the money. Somehow you'll get it . . .

DAVE:
Well, I'll try . . .

HE STARTS WALKING BACK AND FORTH. HALTS ABRUPTLY, LOOKS NERVOUSLY AT HIS WATCH.

My God, it's after ten . . . Mim's waiting . . . Say, Harry, could you hold Mr. Mantelli off a coupla days?

HARRY:

IN DISGUST.

Go on to Mim . . .

DAVE:
You sore?

HARRY:
Go on, will you!

DAVE STARTS TO SAY SOMETHING. CLAMPS HIS LIPS TO-GETHER. TURNS, AND LEAVES. HARRY STARES AFTER HIM. DISGUSTED. ANGRY.

DISSOLVE TO:

LIVING ROOM OF A LOWER-MIDDLE-CLASS APARTMENT IN THE BRONX. *MIM*, A NOT UNATTRACTIVE GIRL OF 30. IS STANDING AT THE IRONING BOARD IN A SLIP IRONING THE DRESS SHE IS GOING TO WEAR TONIGHT. HER FATHER, IN SHIRTSLEEVES, IS SITTING IN FRONT OF THE TV SET WATCH-ING A FIGHT. HER MOTHER IS ON THE SOFA DARNING SOCKS.

MOTHER:
So where is he?

MIM:
I guess he was delayed . . .

MOTHER:
Well, how long you gonna go on like this, Mim? What kind of a future is there with somebody like him?

MIM:
Mom, leave me alone, will you? I had a rotten day at the office . . . I'm tired . . .

MOTHER:
All right, just tell me *one* thing. Why do you keep going out with him?

MIM:
What else am I going to do on a Friday night? Watch TV?
HER FATHER GLANCES BACK AT HER DISGUSTEDLY.
Besides, I happen to like Dave . . . I think he's a sweet, generous
guy . . .
BUZZER RINGS.
Maybe that's him now . . . Let him in, Mom . . . I'll be ready in a
minute . . .
SHE TAKES DRESS FROM IRONING BOARD, HURRIES INTO
BEDROOM. MOTHER PUTS AWAY HER DARNING EQUIPMENT,
RISES; BUT BEFORE SHE HAS TAKEN A STEP, THE FRONT DOOR
OPENS AND *SHEILA*, CARRYING A SUITCASE WITH COLLEGE
PENNANTS PASTED ON IT, BURSTS IN. SHEILA IS 21, ATTRAC-
TIVE.

MOTHER:
CRYING OUT IN EXCITEMENT AND SURPRISE.
Sheila!

SHEILA:
Mom!

THEY RUSH INTO EACH OTHER'S ARMS.

MOTHER:
HOLDS HER AT ARM'S LENGTH AND LOOKS AT HER.
Sheila! Baby! How are you? But we didn't expect you till next week.
There's nothing wrong, is there?

SHEILA:
Nothing, Mom . . . I just wanted to see you all, so I bought a plane
ticket, and here I am . . .
SHE TURNS TO FATHER, WHO HAS LEFT THE TV SET AND IS
COMING TOWARD HER.
How are you, Pop?

FATHER:
Ach . . .
SHE KISSES HIM LIGHTLY.
How's college?

SHEILA:
Fine . . . Everything's fine . . . Listen, steel yourselves for a shock,
you two . . .

JUST THEN MIM, FULLY DRESSED, COMES OUT OF THE BED-
ROOM, SEES HER SISTER.

MIM:
CRYING OUT.
Sheila!

SHEILA:
TURNS.
Mim!
THEY EMBRACE. THEN, LOOKING AT HER.
Honey, what'd you do to your hair?

MIM:
Oh, I . . . Do you think it's too short?
SUDDENLY SEES SOMETHING ON SHEILA'S HAND, GRABS IT
WITH A CRY.
Say! . . . Where'd you get this?

CLOSEUP: A LARGE DIAMOND RING ON THE THIRD FINGER
OF SHEILA'S LEFT HAND.

SHEILA:
Do you like it?
SHOWING IT TO HER FAMILY PROUDLY.
I'm engaged to be married . . .

ALL THREE PRESS AROUND HER, TALKING AT ONCE, FULL OF
EXCITEMENT.

MOTHER:
KISSING HER EMOTIONALLY.
Oh, Sheila . . . Oh, Baby . . .

MIM:
Sheila! Why didn't you say something?

FATHER:
Who's the boy?

SHEILA:
Well, his name's Norman Green . . . I just met him a few weeks ago on a blind date . . . Actually it wasn't supposed to be a blind date . . . You see, the boy I was supposed to go out with, Jerry Fuller—I wrote you about him—well, he had to study for a makeup exam . . . Norman's a friend of his, so he took his place . . . He's a real high-type fella, Mom . . . He's gonna get his degree in Business Administration next June. Then he's going into business with his father . . . His father owns Jack and Jill Foundations . . . They advertise in Time magazine . . .

FATHER:
Time magazine? Is that a fact?

MOTHER:
Well, where is he? When are we going to meet him?

SHEILA:
I invited him over for Sunday . . . but I wanted to tell you myself first . . . Isn't it exciting?
MIM HAS TURNED AWAY, HER LIPS TREMBLING, FIGHTING TEARS. SHEILA SEES HER.
Mim? What's the matter?

MIM:
Nothing . . . I'm just happy for you . . . That's all . . .

SHEILA:
GOES OVER TO HER, TAKES HER HANDS.
Honey, listen . . . You'll be getting married soon yourself . . .

MOTHER:
So if she doesn't get married, is it anything to cry? You think it's so bad being an old maid, Mim? . . . I'll tell you this, you won't have the worry and the heartaches raising children and being tied down . . . and fighting with a husband . . . Mrs. Sapperstein was only telling me the other day . . .

MIM, HER BACK HEAVING, IS SOBBING NOISELESSLY.

SHEILA:
Mom! Stop it!
THEN TO MIM TENDERLY.
Mim . . . Don't think I've forgotten all you've done for me . . . I

mean, the last four years . . . I'd never've made it without your help . . . I never would've met Norman . . . Someday I'm going to pay you back . . . I swear . . .

MIM:
Oh, forget it, Sheila . . .

BUZZER SOUNDS.
That's Dave . . .
SHE RUSHES TO MIRROR, TAKES OUT HANDKERCHIEF, STARTS DRYING HER EYES.
Let him in, somebody . . .

FATHER OPENS DOOR. DAVE ENTERS.

DAVE:
Good evening, Mr. Berger . . . Mrs. Berger . . . Hi, Shirley . . . I thought you were up in Cornell . . .

SHEILA:
I just came down for the weekend . . .

DAVE:
Oh . . . I guess you're having a nice time up there, huh . . . I went to City for a year . . . but that's not the same thing . . .
HE LOOKS AROUND UNCOMFORTABLY.
You almost ready, Mim?

MIM:
One second, Dave . . .

SHE IS FIXING HER FACE. DAVE STANDS THERE. NO ONE SPEAKS.

DAVE:
Say, what's the matter? Why is everyone so quiet?

MIM:
GRABBING HER PURSE, WALKING SWIFTLY ACROSS THE ROOM.
Nothing's the matter, David . . . Nothing at all . . .
SHE TAKES HIS ARM.
Goodnight, everybody . . . Don't wait up, Mom . . .

SHE PULLS DAVE OUT THROUGH THE DOOR.

DISSOLVE TO:

SECTION OF AN ICE CREAM PARLOR NEAR A NEIGHBORHOOD
MOVIE HOUSE. JUKE BOX IS PLAYING ROCK MUSIC. WE SEE
TWO BOOTHS. IN THE FIRST BOOTH TWO TEEN-AGE COUPLES
ARE TALKING AND LAUGHING. CAMERA DOLLIES PAST IT TO
SECOND BOOTH WHERE DAVE AND MIM ARE SITTING QUI-
ETLY NIBBLING AT THEIR FOOD, PREOCCUPIED. A SILENCE.
DAVE FINALLY SPEAKS—TO MAKE CONVERSATION.

DAVE:
I didn't know Shirley changed her name . . .

MIM:
Well . . . I guess among the people she mingles with now Sheila sounds
better . . .

A PAUSE. SHE GLANCES AT HIM QUICKLY.
She's engaged to be married . . .

DAVE:
She is? That's nice . . . She's a pretty girl . . . I wish her a lot of
happiness . . . ·

MIM:
ALMOST TO HERSELF.
Sheila's ten years younger than me and she's getting married
already . . . Funny, I always thought of her as my little baby sister . . .

DAVE:
Yeah . . . kids grow up fast, before you know it . . . I got a kid
cousin . . . I remember when he was in diapers . . . Now he's married and his wife's pregnant . . .

A SILENCE. THEY PICK AT THEIR FOOD. FINALLY SHE LOOKS
AT HIM.

MIM:
WITH EFFORT.
Dave, what about us?

DAVE:
Us?
SHE NODS. HE PICKS UP A SPOON, STUDIES IT.

I was talking about that only this morning with Joe down at the place . . .
SHE KEEPS WATCHING HIS FACE.
Well, I . . . I been thinking maybe we ought to stop seeing each other . . .
THEN QUICKLY, TO SOFTEN IT.
. . . As much as we do anyway . . . The point is, it's not fair to you . . . I mean, you gotta think of getting married . . .
MIM LOOKS AT HIM, HER LIPS TREMBLING.
After all, it's practically two years we've been going together . . . Do you realize that?
SHE LOWERS HER EYES.
Well, you do wanna get married?

MIM:

ALMOST A WHISPER.

Yes . . .

DAVE:
Well, that's what I mean . . . How you gonna meet anybody if you keep hanging around with me? I mean, everybody's got us down as a thing . . . The other guys figure you're all tied up . . .

MIM:
Didn't *you* ever think of us as a thing, Dave?

DAVE:
Yeah . . . I did . . . a lot . . . But where's the percentage? What kind of a future you got with me? I'm not even set in life . . . Well, I know I'm 35 years old and maybe I should've solved the problem a long time ago . . . But, well, I didn't . . . I just never knew what I wanted to be . . . The way I used to envy the guys with definite goals in life, like Charlie Thompson, you know, who I introduced you to at Charlotte Arnheim's wedding, the accountant? And my friend Phil Stringer who went to M.I.T. . . . . He must be *really* set . . . Well, after my father died and I hadda quit City, I just drifted along and took a Civil Service Exam and got a job in the Post Office . . . And here I am . . .
AN UNCOMFORTABLE SILENCE.
I mean, if I was making a living as a photographer, Mim, it'd be different . . . Even if my salary was no more than it is now . . . At least, I could look the world in the face . . . think of a future . . .
HE LIFTS THE CUP OF COFFEE TO HIS LIPS, TAKES A SIP.
Maybe you think I haven't tried to get into the field . . .

MIM:
Well, have you?

DAVE:
You know why I was late tonight to pick you up? I went with Harry
Jaffee to look at a studio . . . with the object of buying it . . . You
oughta seen it, Mim . . . It was outta this world . . . I'd quit my job
and buy it in a minute . . . But I don't have five thousand
dollars . . . That's what my share would cost . . . Five thousand dol-
lars . . .
BURSTING OUT. IN THE MIDST OF HIS SENTENCE, THE MUSIC
GOES OFF, MAKING HIS VOICE SOUND UNNATURALLY LOUD.
How can I think of getting married when I don't even know where I
can get a lousy five thousand dollars?
HE LOOKS AROUND IN EMBARRASSMENT; THEN QUIETLY.
You finished?
SHE NODS. HE LOOKS UP, CALLS OUT:
Waiter! Check!
WAITER COMES WITH CHECK, PLACES IT ON TABLE, LEAVES.
DAVE PICKS IT UP, STARTS MOVING TO EDGE OF SEAT.
Ready, Mim?
BUT SHE HAS MADE NO EFFORT TO MOVE, IS STARING INTO
HIS EYES, HER MIND WORKING.

MIM:
Dave, wait a minute . . . I want to ask you a question . . .

DAVE:
Yeah?

MIM:
Suppose you got the five thousand dollars to buy the studio? . . .
Could we get married? I mean, then you'd be doing what you want;
you could see a future . . .Right?

DAVE:
LAUGHING.
But where would *I* get five thousand dollars?

MIM:
I asked you a question. Could we get married?

DAVE:
Well, if I had five thousand dollars . . . Sure . . .

MIM:
Okay. I'll give it to you . . .

DAVE:

STARING AT HER.

What? You're kiddin' . . .

MIM:
Don't you want it?

DAVE:
You're gonna give me five thousand dollars?

MIM:
So you can get your studio and be a photographer . . . if you want it.

DAVE:
Gee, Mim . . . I didn't know you had so much money . . .

MIM:
Do you want it?

DAVE:
Sure . . . Of course . . . but . . .

MIM:
Well then, when can we get married? Today's Friday . . . How about next week, say Thursday, at City Hall? That'll give us enough time to get our blood tests and . . .

DAVE:
Wait a minute . . .

MIM:
What's the matter? You said the only thing that was stopping you from marrying me was the fact that you weren't in your chosen field, which is photography . . . Well, now you're being offered money to buy a studio . . . Now what's the matter?

DAVE:
Well, why the big hurry, Mim?

MIM:

CRYING OUT.

Why? Because I'm 30 years old and I haven't got much time, and I
want children . . .

HER EYES ARE WET. HE IS LOOKING DOWN AT THE TABLE. AN
UNCOMFORTABLE SILENCE.
                    Dave, do you love me?

                        DAVE:
Sure . . . Sure I love you, Mim . . . But a man doesn't take on a wife
just like that . . . He . . .

                        MIM:
Take on a wife? The way you talk you'd think I'm some kind of
weight you're going to carry on your back . . .

                        DAVE:
                I didn't mean it like that . . .

                        MIM:
You're scared, you know that? What do you think marriage is, a gas
chamber? Marriage is loving somebody and making them happy and
having them near you, so that when you're in trouble or scared or just
feeling   blue,   you're   not   alone . . . It's   helping
somebody . . . It's . . .

HER EYES ARE WET. HER VOICE IS A LOW AGONIZED SCREAM.
                Dave, you gotta make up your mind! Now!

                        DAVE:
IN A TORMENT OF INDECISION.
                    Mim, I . . . I . . .

                        MIM:

DESPERATE.
        What is it? You want to just live together . . .?

                        DAVE:
QUICKLY.
                No, No, Mim! I . . . I gotta think . . .

SHE SLIDES ABRUPTLY OUT OF THE SEAT.
                    Hey, where you goin'?

                        MIM:
ON HER FEET. SCREAMING.
                        Go on! Think!

SHE RUSHES OUT. HE STARTS TO FOLLOW, BUT GETS NO FUR-
THER THAN THE EDGE OF HIS SEAT. HE WATCHES HER, UNTIL
SHE IS GONE, SHAKEN DEEPLY. THEN HE TAKES A COIN OUT
OF HIS POCKET, CAREFULLY PLACES IT ON TABLE NEAR HIS
COFFEE CUP. RISES SLOWLY.

CAMERA IS IN FOR AN EXTREME CLOSEUP.

DISSOLVE TO:

FRONT DOOR OF MIM'S APARTMENT, FROM INSIDE. IT IS IN
SHADOWS. WE HEAR KEY TURN IN LOCK. DOOR OPENS AND
MIM COMES IN CHOKED WITH SOBS. SHE LOOKS AROUND
WILDLY, THEN FLINGS HERSELF ON SOFA AND LIES THERE
FACE DOWN, HER WHOLE BODY HEAVING. A LONG SILENCE,
THEN A SOFT KNOCK ON THE DOOR. SHE DOESN'T HEAR IT.
KNOCK IS REPEATED. SHE RISES, DRIES HER EYES, STARTS
TOWARD DOOR.

                         MIM:
HER VOICE IS HUSHED.
                       Who is it?

                        DAVE:
FROM WITHOUT.
                   It's me . . . Dave . . .

                         MIM:
                     Go away . . .

                        DAVE:
                  Let me in. Please . . .

                         MIM:
                I don't want to see you . . .

                        DAVE:
Please, Mim . . . I have something to tell you . . . It's
important . . . If you don't open it I'll make a lot of noise and wake
                    up the whole house . . .

SHE STARES AT DOOR HESITANTLY, FINALLY OPENS IT. HE
ENTERS.

MIM:

BACKING AWAY.

Well . . .

DAVE:

If Thursday's still all right with you, Mim, I would like to make that
date official for our wedding . . . I mean, if you'll still have me . . .

MIM:

STARES AT HIM A MINUTE, THEN LAUGHING.
You're crazy . . . You know that . . .

THEY SLIP INTO EACH OTHER'S ARMS AND KISS. AFTER A MO-
MENT THEY SEPARATE, GAZE INTO EACH OTHER'S EYES.
BOTH ARE SMILING.

DAVE:

SUDDENLY.

Mim, is it okay if I use your phone a minute?

MIM:
Now?

SHE SHRUGS, SMILING.

Go ahead . . .

DAVE GOES TO PHONE. CAMERA STAYS ON MIM SMILING. WE
SEE DAVE IN BACKGROUND. HE IS DIALING A NUMBER.
PAUSE, THEN DAVE'S VOICE.

DAVE:

INTO PHONE.

Hello . . . Harry? Did I wake you up . . .? This is Dave . . . Wait a
minute, Harry . . . You did talk to him? What'd he say? Good!
Cause you can tell him he doesn't have to wait anymore . . . We'll
take the studio . . .   ·
WE SLOWLY CLOSE IN ON MIM'S FACE. THE SMILE SLOWLY
FADES.

Sure I got the money . . .

HE SMILES.

What'd you think, Harry? I was gonna back out? Wait a minute. I got
something else to tell you . . . I'm gonna get married . . .
HE LAUGHS.

No, I'm not drunk . . . Yeah, Mim . . . Next Thursday . . . Sure
you're invited . . .

CLOSEUP: MIM

HER HEAD HAS TURNED. SHE IS STARING ACROSS THE ROOM AT DAVE. HER EYES ARE WIDE WITH WORRY. HER LIPS ARE TREMBLING. CAMERA MOVES RIGHT INTO HER EYES.

END OF ACT ONE

ACT TWO: SYNOPSIS

Dave and Mim get married in the living room of her family's apartment. A small party ensues. While this is going on there is a scene in the bedroom between Mim and her sister, Sheila, that reveals Mim's anxiety, the cause of which she will not disclose. Mim's mother comes in asking where Dave got the money for a studio so suddenly, which adds to Mim's anxiety. In the living room Dave is talking to Mim's father and the other men about the studio that he takes for granted is his already.

The next scene takes place on the boardwalk at Atlantic City at night. The honeymooners are looking at the ocean and talking. Mim is still nervous, and becomes more so as Dave says how glad he is they got married and how scared he was about quitting his job, but now he's not scared—he knows he did the right thing. And it's all because of her. He promises to work hard to make the studio a success, and their marriage as well.

When they've returned from their honeymoon, Harry calls to tell Dave that he's arranged a meeting tomorrow at the studio with Mr. Mantelli and his lawyer. Everything's set. Bring the check. Dave asks Mim if she'll have the check ready. She tells him to hang up, and blurts out desperately that she doesn't have the money. He is stunned, outraged. Why did she lie? Did she have to get marrried that bad? he cries out. Does she know what she's done to him? He is sobbing as we fade out.

ACT THREE: SYNOPSIS

The next morning a brief, painful scene takes place between Dave and Mim in which she tries to explain, but he won't listen, won't have breakfast with her, walks out. He goes to the photography studio where Harry and Mr. Mantelli and his lawyer are waiting to close the deal. With great difficulty Dave tells them all he has no money and can't go through with the purchase of the studio. Harry is furious.

Dave then returns to his apartment, packs his clothes. The phone rings—

it's the Post Office. His paycheck is there. He shoves his suitcase back into the closet and goes to pick it up.

The fellows are glad to see him, envy the fact that he quit to start his own business. He says nothing, goes in to see Gorsky with the intention of asking for his job back. But Gorsky tells him what a wise move he made in quitting, that he's got talent, that his brother wants to see Dave about doing his wedding pictures. And somehow Dave just can't admit he wants his job back.

Dissolve to the apartment. Mim returns, sees Dave's clothes are gone, is dejected. Harry comes in asking agitatedly what happened. His reputation is involved. Is Dave crazy, walking out on such a good business venture? Mim explains that it's all her fault. Harry explodes, tells her she's done an awful thing. Meanwhile, we see Dave coming down the hall outside the apartment. He can hear voices and is about to enter, when he hears Mim speaking with deep emotion. What happened to Dave was good, she says. He wanted to quit the job. Maybe she did lie. But it was her lie that gave him the courage to quit. Now he can do what he wants. What she did was terrible, but she did it because she loved him and wanted him to fulfill himself. He can be a photographer now and she can work. They're together and they have the whole future, if he would only see it. Dave keeps listening from the hallway. As she reaches the height of her emotional speech, he walks in. Harry looks at Dave, shrugs, leaves. Dave goes to the phone. He has made a decision now. He calls Gorsky and tells him he's available to be the photographer at his brother's wedding. Then he turns to Mim, smiles tentatively, asks her what there is for supper. She begins to laugh and cry and he takes her in his arms. Both are shaking with emotion as we fade out.

Appendix D

Stringer is a good example of a presentation for a series—in this case an hour dramatic series.

It has been optioned by Metromedia, a well-known motion picture and television production company on the West Coast.

Note that this presentation introduces the series lead and his associates mainly in action.

It describes the world they live in, the kinds of melodramatic stories they will be involved in, their relationships, their backgrounds.

Reading this, a network executive can decide very quickly whether or not he wants to develop it further.

If he does, a pilot will be written, probably an hour-length film, although it could be a two-hour movie of the week.

If the pilot is shot and tested well and fits into the network schedule, it will go on the air.

But that's a lot of if's.

Presentations can be of any length and any form. Some are very long. Some are shorter than this. It depends upon the subject and the treatment.

Someday, hopefully, you might become involved in creating or writing a series, but normally this is not an area for the new writer to try his hand. (Note: The first four pages of this presentation are a facsimile of the original.)

<u>STRINGER</u>

by

Alfred Brenner

WILLIAM KAYDEN PRODUCTIONS
Metromedia Producers Corporation
5746 Sunset Boulevard
Hollywood, California 90028

"STRINGER"

You know what Paris was like during the German occupation,
how the grey uniforms of the Wehrmacht blanketed the lovely
boulevards and the music of the cafes changed to Vienna
waltzes, how the big Black Marias of the Gestapo swooped
suddenly before unsuspecting doorways, and passersby would
hurry away, their eyes averted; how the lights went down and
the pre-war gaiety turned harsh and raucous; how, nevertheless, despite all this, life did go on   men and women still
worked, business was conducted, deals were made, love affairs
took place, a bit more hectically, more intensely, more
wildly perhaps...

...But, do you know about Joe Stringer, the young American who
owned and presided over a small club in Montmartre during
those years?

Let me tell you about him.

Everybody called him by his last name. It fit him. I knew
Stringer before the war. In those days, Paris was brighter
and gayer and lovelier than any other city in Europe, and to
us one of its main attractions was his club.

STRINGER'S was the place where we always ended up, where we

-2-

met everyone, where we got the most accurate tips and heard the most interesting gossip. It had good wine, marvelous food, and the most swinging piano...

And it had Stringer.

I see him now, standing in front of the tables introducing a new singer he'd picked up somewhere - on a street corner singing for pennies, or in some Marseilles dive - giving her the kind of buildup Marlene Dietrich might envy, encouraging her softly with a gentle kiss on the cheek...or he'd be telling a joke or humming a tune, laughing at himself or grinning at Blues Oran who'd be tickling the keys of the old painted upright piano as if they had a private joke, a joke which everyone in the place somehow shared and was part of...or he'd be sitting at the table with a jockey, intensely discussing the horses and the tracks and the odds for tomorrow's races - and then when it was clear and right, he'd stand and, with a wink, announce the probable winners to his guests. They loved him and he loved them. Sometimes someone would kid him about a tie or shirt he was wearing - his suits were impeccable, tailored perfectly, his shirts were colorful, but not loud, dramatic but not theatric, his ties were in excellent taste. "You don't like it?" he'd say. "I'm sorry. I don't want to offend anyone." And he'd strip off his clothes, right down to his shorts. And then smile charmingly and graciously at the joker who was begging him to get dressed, please, he was only kidding.

-3-

Stringer was a real ham who was always on, a marvelous storyteller, but something of a con man too. Smugglers, gamblers,
jewel thieves hid out in his cellar, and he'd usually know
the moment the heat was off, when they could leave. He had
contacts with the chief of police. Sometimes the chief even
came down and joined the boys in the poker game that was
always in progress in one of the back rooms. No one will
deny that he was something of an operator who ignored the
rules most men live by. He attracted people - all kinds, all
stations, all degrees. Men and women liked to be seen in his
company. He had style.

Maybe that's what first attracted Jeanne, his lovely French
wife who married him against the wishes of her aristocratic
family (in the person of her stuffy humorless highly respectable brother, Louis Ferouc, an important political figure).
Their love affair was brief, intense, beautiful and tragic.

Whatever attracted Jeanne's love probably attracted Blues
Oran's loyalty and friendship. Blues originally came from
someplace in Algeria by ways of Tunisia, Cairo, and the South
Side of Chicago. His long, brown fingers would bring forth
music from the piano which sent chills down your spine, or
made your pulse beat faster, or he'd pick out notes of such
strange beauty you wanted to cry. Often on a quiet afternoon
before the cocktail hour, or early in the wee hours of the
morning when the night people were not yet in bed and the day

STRINGER

by

Alfred Brenner

You know what Paris was like during the German occupation, how the grey uniforms of the Wehrmacht blanketed the lovely boulevards and the music of the cafes changed to Vienna waltzes, how the big Black Marias of the Gestapo swooped suddenly before unsuspecting doorways and pas-sersby would hurry away, their eyes averted; how the lights went down and the pre-war gaiety turned harsh and raucous; how, nevertheless, despite all this, life did go on—men and women still worked, business was conducted, deals were made, love affairs took place, a bit more hectically, more intensely, more wildly, perhaps . . .

. . . But do you know about Joe Stringer, the young American who owned and presided over a small club in Montmartre during those years?

Let me tell you about him.

Everybody called him by his last name. It fit him. I knew Stringer before the war. In those days, Paris was brighter and gayer and lovelier than any other city in Europe, and to us one of its main attractions was his club.

STRINGER'S was the place where we always ended up, where we met everyone, where we got the most accurate tips and heard the most interesting gossip. It had good wine, marvelous food, and the most swinging piano . . . .

And it had Stringer.

I see him now, standing in front of the tables introducing a new singer he'd picked up somewhere—on a street corner singing for pennies, or in some Marseilles dive—giving her the kind of buildup Marlene Dietrich might envy, encouraging her softly with a gentle kiss on the cheek . . . or he'd be telling a joke or humming a tune, laughing at himself or grinning at Blues Oran, who'd be tickling the keys of the old painted upright piano as if they had a private joke, a joke which everyone in the place somehow shared and was part of . . . . or he'd be sitting at a table with a jockey, intensely discussing the horses and the tracks and the odds for tomorrow's races—and then when it was clear and right, he'd stand and, with a wink, announce the probable winners to his guests. They loved him and he loved them. Sometimes someone would kid him about a tie or shirt he was wearing—his suits were impeccable, tailored perfectly, his shirts were colorful, but not loud, dramatic but not theatric, his ties were in excellent taste. "You don't like it?" he'd say. "I'm sorry. I don't want to offend anyone." And he'd strip off his clothes, right down to his shorts. And then smile charmingly and graciously at the joker who was begging him to get dressed, please, he was only kidding.

Stringer was a real ham who was always on, a marvelous storyteller, but something of a con man too. Smugglers, gamblers, jewel thieves hid out in his cellar, and he'd usually know the moment the heat was off, when they could leave. He had contacts with the chief of police. Sometimes the chief even came down and joined the boys in the poker game that was always in progress in one of the back rooms. No one will deny that he was something of an operator who ignored the rules most men live by. He attracted people—all kinds, all stations, all degrees. Men and women liked to be seen in his company. He had style.

Maybe that's what first attracted Jeanne, his lovely French wife, who married him against the wishes of her aristocratic family (in the person of her stuffy, humorless, highly respectable brother, Louis Ferouc, an important political figure). Their love affair was brief, intense, beautiful, and tragic.

Whatever attracted Jeanne's love probably attracted Blues Oran's loyalty and friendship. Blues originally came from someplace in Algeria by way of Tunisia, Cairo, and the South Side of Chicago. His long, brown fingers would bring forth music from the piano which sent chills down your spine or made your pulse beat faster, or he'd pick out notes of such strange beauty you wanted to cry. Often on a quiet afternoon before the cocktail hour, or early in the wee hours of the morning when the night people were not yet in bed and the day people had not awakened, Blues would play for Stringer . . . . and they'd talk. And sometimes the "Countess" would join them.

The Countess was authentic. A former American beauty who had loved and married European royalty often and well, but not wisely, she was still a fascinating creature of uncertain age, with a wide acquaintance among people of all classes. She'd sit at a sort of pay desk and hatcheck counter near the entrance of the club scrutinizing everyone who entered. Not only did she have a penetrating insight into human character, but her ears were as sensitive as sonar. She heard everything and forgot nothing. She was a kind of mother figure who loved Stringer and secretly worried about him.

So in those days before the war, Stringer wheeled and dealed, he conned and he operated, he entertained and he enjoyed himself. His club was a true reflection of himself, his personal stage, a place of gaiety and relaxation, of fun and pleasure for everyone who entered.

Then the phony war became real. The Nazis broke through the Maginot Line, invaded France, and were slashing toward Paris.

The moment it became obvious to Stringer that the enemy was not going to be stopped, he closed his club, piled his wife, Jeanne, and his two loyal employees and good friends, Blues Oran and the Countess, into an old Citroen and fled south.

During the flight, a squadron of Stukas strafed the road choked with refugees. In the panic and confusion Jeanne was killed, and suddenly everything Stringer loved and valued was in ruins. All that remained were anger at those who caused this tragedy and the desire for revenge. To achieve this end, he decided to return.

Back in Paris, Stringer went to see his brother-in-law, Louis Ferouc, who had secretly been collaborating with the Nazis and who was now one of the most powerful men in France. Stringer asked for his help and protection in reopening his club. Ferouc, believing that he could make use of the young American's varied "talents" and knowing that he could crush him if he ever got out of hand, made a few phone calls, signed a few cards . . . .

Within the year Japan bombed Pearl Harbor and the U.S. entered the world conflict.

And Stringer was back in his club, but it was changed a bit now. Jeanne wasn't there anymore, and the audience was made up largely of German soldiers and French collaborationists. But Blues Oran could be heard at the piano, and the Countess had returned to her post.

Of course, there were people who didn't like what Stringer was doing—not only most members of the Resistance, but ordinary French citizens who hated the Germans. Stringer believed in nothing, they said. He was a scoundrel, a man with the morals of an alley cat.

And so it appeared; for he not only entertained the enemy, but supplied him with the finest wines, the best food, as he had done his friends in the past. These were very difficult to come by during the Occupation; however, he still knew everybody in the city and in the country, everybody that mattered. Smugglers of the past had become wealthy black marketeers now. Ordinary people had become smugglers. All kinds of deals were made in his basement and back rooms. At times the place resembled an auction, or a stock exchange—with men and women trading licenses for cars, gasoline coupons, food rations, fuel cards, permits for raw materials, soap, cigarettes, faked passports, passes through the border to the Unoccupied Zone . . . . Of course, these transactions took place quite surreptitiously; rarely were more than four or five people present at the same time.

One would have thought that the war and the occupation were quite acceptable to Stringer, part of the way things were. His main purpose in life appeared to be merely to entertain, to keep his patrons and customers happy. His jokes attacked Churchill and Hitler, Roosevelt and Stalin indiscriminately . . . and somehow he was able to get away with it—most of the time. Once, though, a German SS major, with a few too many cognacs under his belt, pulled out his pistol and aimed it at him after he made a crack pairing Churchill and Goering, calling them the two fat boys with the cigars. Stringer, faced with the threatening muzzle, seemed to turn white.

"Please put that away," he pleaded, trying to smile, but not quite succeeding. Guns made him nervous, he explained. Even unloaded pistols. Listen, would the Major like some rare champagne, out of Napoleon's personal stock? But just put that . . . thing down. The Major complied finally. But before doing so, he strode unsteadily up to Stringer, winking broadly to his comrades, and offered him the pistol. As Stringer tried to refuse, backing away, the largely German audience began to guffaw loudly. He finally was forced to take the weapon, which he held between his thumb and forefinger as if it were a contaminated rag, unable to even look at it. Suddenly it dropped and went off. At the explosion, Stringer fled to the rear. The crowd went wild. They couldn't stop laughing.

After that, the German soldiers would often place their weapons on the bar or the piano or a table near where Stringer was sitting and would howl when he moved away, enjoying their cruel joke like little boys who tie rocks to cats' tails. Stringer bore all this, as well as other outrages, with a wry smile. The Germans, for instance, discovered what a dandy he was. They resented his fine wardrobe. One evening a captain in the Luftwaffe came in with muddy boots and deliberately stepped on a pair of newly polished shoes he was wearing. Stringer, without a murmur, quietly begged the Captain's pardon and bent down and polished his boots amid the raucous guffaws of all those present.

Although the Germans never realized it, their guffaws were produced deliberately by his efforts. He was on stage and they were his audience.

He was on stage for the next four years, acting in one of the most difficult, most demanding and most dangerous roles a man was ever called on to perform.

For Stringer was one of the truly great heroes of World War II.

But he was no ordinary hero. He played a unique part . . . in the Resistance, with the Allies. Due to his position as an entertainer and his ability as an entrepreneur, with connections in every part of France and Europe— plus an apparent alliance with his powerful brother-in-law—Stringer was able to pull off some of the most wildly audacious and amazing exploits of the period.

There was the midnight, for instance, when the Countess, who often knew more about what was going on than German Intelligence, discovered that a large armored truck protected by combat-ready troops had slipped secretly through the main gates of the Bank of France . . . that the truck contained a very large stock of industrial diamonds (an essential factor in the process of manufacture, without which no belligerent could sustain its war effort for long), which the Nazis had intercepted on its way from Africa to England . . . that these industrial diamonds were being "deposited" temporarily, for transshipment to Germany within the next 48 to 72 hours . . .

How Stringer was able to round up a group of experts on such short notice and organize one of the biggest and wildest heists of all time—how he was able to get one of the great modern French painters to draw the plans, a former prefect of police to work side by side with a famous, still wanted safecracker, and how, with split-second timing and perfect precision, they were able to break into the vault and substitute zircons for the diamonds, and how the zircons crumbled in countless German factories, smashing vital machinery—is one of the most breathtakingly suspenseful and hilarious untold sagas of the entire war.

Then there was the time Stringer used his talent as an actor to play the role of a high Italian Fascist general supposedly transporting the coffin of his dead brother—who in reality was an important Italian Resistance leader rescued after being shot down on a flight from Britain—back to Italy . . . how, in order to save their lives when almost trapped, he had to act as both an undertaker and priest, officiating at a real funeral, and actually burying the coffin with the "corpse" inside . . . then how he finally had to *become* the Fascist general in reality and lead a regiment of Italian troops into a bloody skirmish, which was really a trap set up by the Resistance leader, barely escaping with his life, is another fabulous episode in his remarkable career . . . .

Once it became vital to get rid of a German general, paymaster of the Occupation Forces in Paris, who was becoming increasingly suspicious of a top Allied agent planted in his own headquarters. Blues, whose technique with a knife was on a par with his ability at the keyboard, volunteered to assassinate the general. But this was risky; besides, there would be terrible retaliation. Stringer decided on an audacious plan. He persuaded an outstanding French counterfeiter, now retired, to engrave a number of German mark notes, each of which—to the horror of the artist, who took great pride in his work—was to have a minor imperfection. The money was then run off in millions, slipped into the army payroll, and substituted for the good marks which were stolen. The soldiers sent part of their phony marks home, but when they tried to spend the rest in Paris, they were turned down by the already alerted shopkeepers. The resultant confusion, both on the German home front and in France, not only caused the immediate transfer of the general to the East and allowed the Allied agent to complete his important mission, but also filled the coffers of the Resistance with much-needed genuine German marks . . . .

One night, while working with a Resistance group to kidnap a high Gestapo officer who had just arrived from Germany, Stringer was caught. He explained to his interrogators that the men and women who were with him were really entertainers on their way to perform at a general's chateau—where the Gestapo officer was quartered, and where Stringer was actually due to perform with real entertainers later that night. How the group was taken to the general for confirmation; how Stringer was not only able—in a very suspenseful, daring, and almost disastrous but howlingly funny series of on-the-spot rehearsals and improvisations—to actually put the group "on stage," but to actually kidnap the Gestapo officer while the performance was going on . . . and elicit vital information concerning German plans to exterminate the Resistance, thereby saving countless lives—is still talked about with awe all over Paris . . . .

Because of Stringer's relationship to Jeanne, it was not easy for him to fall in love again, but when he did, it brought him face to face with one of the most terrible decisions he ever had to make . . . . The girl was a beautiful new chanteuse at his club. To his surprise and dismay, he apparently lost her to his brother-in-law and protector, the powerful Louis Ferouc. However, the Countess ferreted out the information that the girl really loved Stringer but was under orders to play up to Ferouc by a Resistance group plotting the traitor's death. Stringer, aware that his brother-in-law was more useful alive than dead, was forced into the unhappy position of having to save the collaborator's life . . . as the result of which he was branded a traitor by the girl he loved, and was marked for death by her group . . . .

These are just a few of the kinds of missions Stringer was involved in . . . .

. . . Of the kinds he *will be* involved in each week—in a TV series.

Missions—stories—which emphasize the offbeat, the unexpected, the mixture of terror and humor, the juxtaposition between a big important event and the small human and sometimes strangely ludicrous action to which it relates—which kicks it off and makes its success possible. . . . Stories of suspense tinged with carefree gaiety—gaiety under pressure, which is our hero's trademark.

Scarlet Pimpernel?

Of course. For Stringer is a modern pimpernel. . . . An American entertainer with a club in Montmartre. . . . A rogue who lives under the Nazi boot and their French puppets during the four years of the Occupation, but works for the Free World. . . . An apparent coward and buffoon who risks his life every day for a Cause. . . . Stringer. . . . A fresh and interesting new kind of hero for a TV series.

Appendix E

The following fee structures are listed in the Writers Guild of America's current contract, which expires February 28, 1985. Projections for the Writers Guild's new contract show substantially higher fees. Information on the new contract will be available in the spring of 1985 from the Writers Guild of America, West, 8955 Beverly Boulevard, Los Angeles, CA 90048; and the Writers Guild of America, East, 555 West 57th Street, New York, NY 10019.

FOR PRIME-TIME NETWORK PROGRAMS
Screenplay—theatrical motion picture: $40,000
Television
    15-minute script:
    story: $1,524; teleplay: $4,300; story and teleplay: $5,319
    30-minute script:
    story: $2,793; teleplay: $6,983; story and teleplay: $9,739
    60-minute script:
    story: $4,959; teleplay: $9,420; story and teleplay: $14,318
    90-minute script:
    story: $6,877; teleplay: $13,571; story and teleplay: $20,145
    120-minute script:
    story: $9,137; teleplay: $17,414; story and teleplay: $26,506

FOR DAYTIME SERIALS (SOAPS)

Head Writer receives:

  $4,498 for 15-minute episode

  $7,498 for each half-hour episode

  $10,872 for each 45-minute episode

  $13,870 for each hour episode

  $20,804 for each 90-minute episode

Out of the above, the Head Writer pays script fee minimums to writers on the show, whom he hires as follows:

  $444 for each 15-minute episode

  $743 for each 30-minute episode

  $1,076 for each 45-minute episode

  $1,374 for each 60-minute episode

  $2,064 for each 90-minute episode

The remainder is for the head writer's long-term projection (bible).

Long-term story minimums received by a writer other than a head writer:

  $6,432 for 3 months or less

  $9,648 for 6 months or less (but more than 3)

  $12,864 for 12 months or less (but more than 6)

Glossary

(Note: For glossary of camera directions, see Chapter 16.)

access—a term meaning that literary material, such as a script or outline, has been seen by a producer, production company, or network—a potential buyer. Proof of "previous access" must almost always be established in plagiarism suits.

action—movement of actors or cameras in a teleplay or in a dramatic production. See *dramatic action.*

adaptation—a script which is based upon another work, a book, a play, an article, etc.

advertising agency—a business that handles the advertising for any commercial company. Advertising agencies produce some soap operas on television and often advise sponsors which shows to buy into.

agent—an individual who is supposed to sell a writer's work, place a writer in the right job, and help guide his career. For this he gets 10 percent of the writer's income. He may work alone, in partnershp (as owner), or be an employee of a literary agency.

antagonist—the person or force that opposes the protagonist, or main character, in his struggle to achieve his goal.

anthology—a television series consisting of individual plays, each one unrelated to the other, without continuing characters. An anthology series may have an overall theme and/or a master/mistress of ceremonies.

arbitration—judgment of the authorship of a film or television script, usually done by the Writers Guild of America.

assignment—a job—a contract—writing for money.

basic idea—source or concept, image or character that is the springboard for a story or plot.

basic story line—the main line of development of a story or plot.

beat—pause in a speech or action.

bible—the characters, settings, and the general long-term (usually six-month) outline or projection of a soap opera. In a dramatic series, the bible usually contains the leading (continuing) characters, their backgrounds, and the general thrust of the kinds of situations in which they will become involved.

blind spot—something important that the protagonist of a drama is unaware of or fails to see in his struggle toward a goal, but which is removed in the climax.

breakdown—detailed synopsis of weekly or daily episodes of a soap opera, based upon the bible or long-term projection.

causal relationship—cause-and-effect relationship or connection. Usually refers to the relationship of scenes and characters to each other in a story or teleplay.

character—a person in a drama of film, theater, or TV.

climax—the peak of dramatic action or tension in a drama; the point where the plot is resolved, where the main character's blind spot is removed, where he makes a discovery, where the theme is revealed—the turning point. See *resolution* and *dénouement*.

collaboration—cooperation with one or several other persons in the writing of a script or the making of a television drama.

comedy—a drama of a light and humorous nature, usually provoking laughter and having a happy ending. See *sitcom*.

conflict—struggle or clash of opposing or contending characters in a teleplay.

construction—the machinery of a drama; its architecture; the arrangement of its parts or scenes into a cause-and-effect relationship or order.

continuing characters—the characters in a television series who continue from episode to episode, usually the leads.

contract—legal agreement between the television writer and the producer or production company that employs him.

credit—the name of the writer—as well as the other artists and technicians—of a television drama as shown in the titles at the beginning or end of a program.

crisis—highest dramatic point of a scene or act in a drama; the turning point of a scene or act. Sometimes used interchangeably with climax.

cutoff—decision made by producer or company or network not to take up option to have a writer write a script after he has written an outline or treatment.

daytime serial—a continuing novel-like television series without an end that portrays a group of essentially the same characters, the episodes of which are on the tube every afternoon during the week, aimed mainly at housewives. Also called *soap opera* because it used to be sponsored mainly by soap manufacturers.

deal—a contract.

dealmaker—the executive at a production company who negotiates the contract or deal.

dénouement—peak   of dramatic action and turning point of a television drama. See *climax*.

deus ex machina—a practice in classical tragedies of bringing a god onto the stage in a machine to resolve plot difficulties. More generally, a person or action artificially ،introduced in a drama to bring a poorly structured plot to a conclusion.

development—elaboration of an idea or concept by working out the characters and plot structure and sequence of a television play.

dialogue—the words the characters speak in a television play.

dialogue writer—writer employed on a daytime serial, or soap opera, to write dialogue.

director—the person who interprets the script and controls and supervises the production of a television drama or motion picture.

discovery—the revelation or unfolding of something previously unrecognized or unknown, usually by the main character in the climax of a drama.

drama—a story or narrative intended to be acted out on a stage. Television drama is a story or narrative intended to be acted out on television.

dramatic action—action in a teleplay that brings forth emotional response in an audience and/or which moves the story forward.

dramatic writing—the particular kind of writing that is intended to be acted out on stage, television, or motion pictures.

dramatist—an individual who writes dramatic stories; a playwright.

editor—person on production staff who analyzes scripts, writes or rewrites when necessary, and confers with writer at all stages of teleplay development. Usually works with the producer.

emotional line—main emotional line of development in a script, usually involving the protagonist and one or more other characters. Analogous to *story line.*

epilogue—scene at end of a teleplay after the main plot has ended whose main purpose is to tie up the loose ends of the story. See *tag.*

episode—a teleplay that is part of an episodic series.

episodic—a dramatic story which has no structural unity, whose parts don't unfold causally or inevitably toward a climax.

episodic series—a television series with continuing characters whose different adventures or stories an audience follows from week to week. Each story, adventure, episode is a self-contained unit, a complete teleplay.

exposition—technique of planting information in an audience concerning the characters and events of a teleplay which have taken place in the past, before the beginning of the drama.

false goal—the goal the protagonist in a drama is struggling to achieve that he discovers in the climax is not what he truly wants. See *blind spot.*

filmed teleplay—television drama intended for production on film.

focus—central point, point of concentration in a teleplay—usually the climax.

freelance writer—a writer not bound by a contract to any production company; one who writes and sells his scripts individually to any or all producers.

grip—a person who works in a film or TV production as a laborer moving sets, etc.

gross—the total amount of money received through the box office for a motion picture, before expenses, taxes, etc., have been deducted.

head writer—the supervising writer on a daytime serial. He develops the bible of the show, hires the dialogue writers, and is responsible for everything they write.

heavy—a villain. See *antagonist.*

hero—usually the main character, the protagonist, the person the audience roots for in a teleplay. He almost always represents the forces of "good."

hook—a striking incident or action at the opening of a teleplay, the purpose of which is to capture the attention of the audience. See *prologue; teaser*.

hyphenate—usually refers to a writer who also works as a producer, i.e., writer-producer. But it may apply to anyone in the industry who wears two hats, i.e., writer-director, producer-director, actor-writer, etc.

long form—television dramas that run two or more hours in playing time—movies-of-the-week, miniseries.

melodrama—a kind of drama, usually sensational in content, involving good and evil characters—heroes and villains—in which the hero always overcomes the villain, generally in a violent climax.

miniseries—a limited series in serial form, usually based on a book, e.g., *Masada, Roots, Scruples*.

motivation—the reasons why a character in a drama acts as he does.

narration—the events of a teleplay that are not dramatized but related by a character or a narrator.

network—a group of television stations throughout the country under one corporate and administrative control. The three commercial networks are NBC, CBS, and ABC. There is a noncommercial network, PBS. New cable networks are flourishing locally and nationally.

network executive—an individual employed by a network in an executive capacity to oversee series and/or to meet with producers and writers and help develop and buy stories and scripts.

novice—a beginner.

option—the right of a producer or company to control a "property" (script or outline, book or play) for a specific period of time for a set fee.

outline—a scene-by-scene narration of the teleplay without dialogue, written in prose, in the present tense. Same as treatment, or story.

pilot—a sample script or television drama intended to be a basis for a series.

pitch—see *spitballing*.

plagiarism—the act of stealing someone else's idea or story.

plot—a narrative of events, the emphasis falling on causality.

preparation—anticipating, making ready beforehand, motivating a scene or action in a teleplay. Showing an audience what is about to happen. See *suspense.*

presentation—a description, written in prose, usually for an intended television series.

producer—the person who plans, coordinates, and supervises all phases of a television drama from script to final film or tape.

production company—company that produces television programs.

professional writer—a writer who has sold material to radio, TV, or motion pictures and/or has received credit on the screen—or who has published a novel or had a play professionally produced on the legitimate stage.

progression—forward movement of a teleplay from scene to scene through ascending crises toward a climax.

projection room—room at studio in which television films are shown on a large screen.

projection (story)—general outline of the overall plot of a serial drama covering a specific period of time, usually six months.

prologue—the scene before the actual beginning of a television drama; the first scene of the drama; usually the teaser or hook.

protagonist—main character in a teleplay.

red herring—false clue or lead, especially in mystery shows.

registration—the act of recording an outline or script for protection against plagiarism. Similar to copyright. Writers Guild of America conducts a registration service.

release form—a form a novice must sign when submitting a script to a network or production company that frees the recipient from future legal action.

residuals—money which the writer of a television script receives each time the show is rerun in this country or abroad. The rate is determined by WGA contract with production companies and networks.

research—inquiry or investigation into factual information necessary in writing a script on any particular subject.

resolution—the turning point of a drama; the scene in which blind spot is removed from protagonist. See *climax; dénouement.*

royalties—same as residuals.

scenario—detailed synopsis of a drama. Same as treatment.

script—complete motion picture or television play.

sequence—a group of related scenes.

sitcom—*sit*uation *com*edy. Comedy series, usually a half-hour in length, with continuing characters.

soap—A soap opera. See *daytime serial.*

special—television program created for a particular occasion, using certain star performers, and having no regular weekly or monthly time-slot.

speculation—writing without a contract.

spine—the basic plot of a teleplay; its story line. The basic thrust of a character, in terms of his goal.

spitballing—relating story ideas to a producer, editor, or executive for the purpose of selling; same as pitching.

sponsor—a company that buys into or pays in part or in full—for any commercial television program, usually to advertise its products or enhance its image, and sometimes to present a political or ideological point of view.

step deal—a contract in which the writer is paid in segments, or steps, as he completes each part of the script—and in which he usually can be cut off at any stage.

step outline—a condensed treatment or outline, indicating the action to take place in each step or scene of its development.

story—a narrative of events arranged in their time sequence. Also used interchangeably with treatment or outline.

story conference—a conference between writer and others, usually the producer, but also including the editor and sometimes an executive and/or director in which an idea, story, or teleplay is discussed. Its purpose is to develop a script or to revise one already in existence.

story line—main line or thrust of development of a story or plot. See *emotional line.*.

structural unity—interconnection between all the structural elements of a television drama in terms of their causal relationships.

structure—the arrangement of the elements of a television drama.

subplot—subordinate plot. In a good teleplay the subplot relates causally to the main plot and is introduced to help move the story toward its climax.

subtext—the meaning below the actual dialogue; the implied meaning of a line, scene, or script.

surprise—a sudden shocking occurrence in a drama that takes the audience unawares; a totally unexpected action.

suspense—tension created in an audience by uncertainty of a drama's outcome, by causing it to worry about what is going to happen next. Implies giving the audience full knowledge of the situation. See *preparation.*

tag—the scene after the climax or end of a plot or story. See *epilogue.*

tape—videotape. The material (tape) on which a television program is recorded for later transmission, as contrasted with film.

teaser—the scene that comes at the opening of a teleplay, containing a striking incident or situation to capture the attention of the audience. See *hook* or *prologue.*

teleplay—a television play. A play written for television.

theme—the general meaning or idea of a play.

time lock—the setting up of a predetermined action to take place at a preset moment in a television story or play.

trades—motion picture and television trade papers, e.g., *Variety* and *Hollywood Reporter.*

unity of action—the action of a dramatic story in which all the elements are organically connected, usually by a cause-and-effect relationship.

unity of place—the place where the action of a drama takes place, which does not change—in which there is no change of location or set.

unity of time—implies that the time in which the drama actually takes place is the same as the time covered in the dramatic story. Implies no break in time, no act or scene breaks.

villain—a "bad" guy; an antagonist of the hero in a melodrama. See *heavy.*

well-made play—method of dramatic construction originated by a group of nineteenth-century French playwrights, aimed at capturing and holding a middle-class audience. Artificial and brittle, concentrating on plot machinery rather than ideas or character. Basic construction of most Broadway plays, Hollywood motion pictures and television series dramas.

writer's block—inability of writer to create or write. Usually psychological; often caused by an extremely self-critical attitude.

Writers Guild—the trade union of writers for television, motion pictures, and radio. The Writers Guild of America, East and West (WGA).

Index

Other Books of Interest

General Writing Books

Beginning Writer's Answer Book, edited by Polking and Bloss $14.95

Getting the Words Right: How to Revise, Edit and Rewrite, by Theodore A. Rees Cheney $13.95

How to Become a Bestselling Author, by Stan Corwin $14.95

How to Get Started in Writing, by Peggy Teeters $10.95

If I Can Write, You Can Write, by Charlie Shedd $12.95

International Writers' & Artists' Yearbook (paper) $11.95

Knowing Where to Look: The Ultimate Guide to Research, by Lois Horowitz $16.95

Make Every Word Count, by Gary Provost (paper) $7.95

Teach Yourself to Write, by Evelyn A. Stenbock $12.95

Treasury of Tips for Writers, edited by The American Society of Journalists & Authors (paper) $6.95

Writer's Encyclopedia, edited by Kirk Polking $19.95

Writer's Market, edited by Paula Deimling $19.95

Writer's Resource Guide, edited by Bernadine Clark $16.95

Writing for the Joy of It, by Leonard Knott $11.95

Writing From the Inside Out, by Charlotte Edwards (paper) $9.95

Magazine/News Writing

Complete Guide to Marketing Magazine Articles, by Duane Newcomb $9.95

Complete Guide to Writing Nonfiction, by the American Society of Journalists & Authors $24.95

The Craft of Interviewing, by John Brady $9.95

Magazine Writing: The Inside Angle, by Art Spikol $12.95

Magazine Writing Today, by Jerome E. Kelley $10.95

Newsthinking: The Secret of Great Newswriting, by Bob Baker $11.95

1001 Article Ideas, by Frank A. Dickson $10.95

Stalking the Feature Story, by William Ruehlmann $9.95

Write On Target, by Connie Emerson $12.95

Writing and Selling Non-Fiction, by Hayes B. Jacobs $12.95

Fiction Writing

Fiction Is Folks: How to Create Unforgettable Characters, by Robert Newton Peck $11.95

Fiction Writer's Help Book, by Maxine Rock $12.95

Fiction Writer's Market, edited by Jean Fredette $17.95

Handbook of Short Story Writing, by Dickson and Smythe (paper) $6.95

How to Write Best-Selling Fiction, by Dean R. Koontz $13.95

How to Write Short Stories that Sell, by Louise Boggess (paper) $7.95

One Way to Write Your Novel, by Dick Perry (paper) $6.95

Secrets of Successful Fiction, by Robert Newton Peck $8.95

Storycrafting, by Paul Darcy Boles $14.95

Writing Romance Fiction—For Love And Money, by Helene Schellenberg Barnhart $14.95

Writing the Novel: From Plot to Print, by Lawrence Block $10.95

Special Interest Writing Books

The Children's Picture Book: How to Write It, How to Sell It, by Ellen E. M. Roberts $17.95

Complete Book of Scriptwriting, by J. Michael Straczynski $14.95

Complete Guide to Writing Software User Manuals, by Brad McGehee (paper) $14.95

Confession Writer's Handbook, by Florence K. Palmer $9.95

The Craft of Lyric Writing, by Sheila Davis $16.95

Guide to Greeting Card Writing, edited by Larry Sandman (paper) $7.95

How to Make Money Writing . . . Fillers, by Connie Emerson $12.95

How to Write a Cookbook and Get It Published, by Sara Pitzer $15.95

How to Write a Play, by Raymond Hull $13.95

How to Write and Sell Your Personal Experiences, by Lois Duncan $10.95

How to Write and Sell (Your Sense of) Humor, by Gene Perret $12.95

How to Write "How-To" Books and Articles, by Raymond Hull (paper) $8.95

How to Write the Story of Your Life, by Frank P. Thomas $12.95

Mystery Writer's Handbook, by The Mystery Writers of America (paper) $8.95

On Being a Poet, by Judson Jerome $14.95

Poet's Handbook, by Judson Jerome $11.95

Programmer's Market, edited by Brad McGehee (paper) $16.95

Sell Copy, by Webster Kuswa $11.95

Successful Outdoor Writing, by Jack Samson $11.95

Travel Writer's Handbook, by Louise Zobel (paper) $8.95

TV Scriptwriter's Handbook, by Alfred Brenner $12.95

Writing and Selling Science Fiction, by Science Fiction Writers of America (paper) $7.95

Writing for Children & Teenagers, by Lee Wyndham $11.95

Writing for Regional Publications, by Brian Vachon $11.95

Writing for the Soaps, by Jean Rouverol $14.95

Writing to Inspire, by Gentz, Roddy, et al $14.95

The Writing Business

Complete Handbook for Freelance Writers, by Kay Cassill $14.95

Freelance Jobs for Writers, edited by Kirk Polking (paper) $7.95

How to Be a Successful Housewife/Writer, by Elaine Fantle Shimberg $10.95

How You Can Make $20,000 a Year Writing, by Nancy Hanson (paper) $6.95

Profitable Part-time/Full-time Freelancing, by Clair Rees $10.95

The Writer's Survival Guide: How to Cope with Rejection, Success and 99 Other Hang-Ups of the Writing Life, by Jean and Veryl Rosenbaum $12.95

To order directly from the publisher, include $1.50 postage and handling for 1 book and 50¢ for each additional book. Allow 30 days for delivery.

Writer's Digest Books, Department B
9933 Alliance Road, Cincinnati OH 45242

Prices subject to change without notice.